D1486154

SCHOOL OF ORIENTAL AND AFRICAN STUDIES
University of London

Please return this book on or before the last date shown

Long loans and One Week loans may be renewed up to 10 times
Short loans & CDs cannot be renewed
Fines are charged on all overdue items

Online: http://lib.soas.ac.uk/patroninfo
Phone: 020-7898 4197 (answerphone)

0 4 FEB 2010

– 8 NOV 2010

SOAS

18 0404460 5

What Women
Do in Wartime

What Women Do in Wartime

Gender and Conflict in Africa

EDITED BY

MEREDETH TURSHEN &
CLOTILDE TWAGIRAMARIYA

Zed Books Ltd

LONDON & NEW YORK

What Women Do in Wartime was first published by
Zed Books Ltd, 7 Cynthia Street, London N1 9JF, UK, and
and Room 400, 175 Fifth Avenue, New York, NY 10010, USA
in 1998

Cover designed by Andrew Corbett.
Laserset by Long House, Cumbria, UK.
Printed and bound in the United Kingdom
by Biddles Ltd, Guildford and King's Lynn

A catalogue record for this book
is available from the British Library.

ISBN 1 85649 537 X Cased
ISBN 1 85649 538 8 Limp

Contents

Acknowledgements		vii
Notes on Contributors		viii
Abbreviations		xi
Map of African civil wars		xii

X 1   Women's War Stories   1
MEREDETH TURSHEN   p.11, 12, 18.

✓ 2   South African Women Demand the Truth   27
BETH GOLDBLATT AND SHEILA MEINTJES

3   Women and Violence in KwaZulu/Natal   62
ASHNIE PADARATH

X 4   Mozambican Women Experiencing Violence   73
ALCINDA ANTÓNIO DE ABREU

5   Attack with a Friendly Weapon   85
ASMA ABDEL HALIM

6   'Favours' to Give and 'Consenting' Victims   101
The Sexual Politics of Survival in Rwanda
CLOTILDE TWAGIRAMARIYA AND MEREDETH TURSHEN

7   Women Denounce their Treatment in Chad   118
       WOMEN'S COMMISSION OF THE HUMAN RIGHTS LEAGUE OF CHAD
       & THE EDITORS

8   Hundreds of Victims Silently Grieving   129
       ASSOCIATION OF FEMALE LAWYERS OF LIBERIA (AFELL)
       & THE EDITORS

9   We Left Our Shoes Behind   138
       TECKLA SHIKOLA

10   The Militarization of Africa   150
       DANIEL VOLMAN

Bibliography   163
Index   173

Acknowledgements

Many people have helped us put this book together. Many responded to our requests for names of potential contributors and referred us to authors. We should like to thank Ibrahim Abdullah, AWEPA, the Center for Women's Global Leadership, Jacklyn Cock, Carole Collins, Imani Countess, Allen Howard, David Lord, Athanasie Mukagerasi, Jeanette Mukasafari, Sixbert Musangamfure, Paul Richards, Julius Spencer, Samuel Woods, and Alfred Zack-Williams. Others gave us invaluable information and leads on sources; we wish to thank APIC, Doug Tilton, and WOA. We also thank Bea Vidacs for her invaluable research assistance and David Lewis for his work on the map. This work could not have been carried out or brought to completion without the support of Cecile and Jerry Shore for which we are extremely grateful.

Our authors have worked with us against sometimes insurmountable odds – the very conflicts we are writing about impeded the compilation of this volume and some contributions were never received. Mail delivery to Liberia was suspended, faxes didn't go through as the city of Monrovia was without electrical power; civil war interrupted our correspondence with Sierra Leone.

Yet this book makes a case against what is sometimes called 'Afro-pessimism', the widespread Western perception that African crises defy solution. The women activists represented in these pages show that in spite of all the suffering they went through, they are still optimistic and ready to work for a lasting peace in Africa.

Notes on Contributors

Asma Abdel Halim is a Sudanese lawyer who defends human rights, women's human rights and women's legal rights. She has been active in campaigns against violence against women, and she is an advocate for the eradication of female circumcision. She is a member of the Sudan Human Rights Organization and Women in Law and Development in Africa (WiLDAF), and she is involved with Peace in the Horn of Africa, a group of American NGOs that are addressing the issue of civil war in southern Sudan and the Horn of Africa.

Alcinda António de Abreu is a Mozambican psychologist, teacher and researcher associated with the African Studies Centre at Eduardo Mondlane University and the Centre for Strategic Studies at the High Institute of International Relations. She trains cadres in development management, gender issues, and legal education. She was a Member of Parliament from 1987 to 1994. After the multiparty elections in 1994, she was nominated Minister for Social Action Coordination.

Association of Female Lawyers of Liberia (AFELL) is a non-partisan, not-for-profit, nongovernmental organization incorporated in 1994. It undertakes advocacy work for the rights of women and promotes the advancement of women, children, and indigent persons. AFELL has conducted a series of workshops to educate women on their legal and human rights and runs a legal aid clinic in Monrovia that caters to women's legal needs. AFELL's membership presently consists of professional practising female lawyers, magistrates, and judges.

Beth Goldblatt is an Attorney of the Supreme Court of South Africa. She was formerly Secretary General of the National Union of South African Students (1991) and is currently employed as a researcher in the Gender Research Project in the Centre for Applied Legal Studies, University of the Witwatersrand, where her research and teaching focus on violence against women, human rights, constitutional and family law.

Sheila Meintjes is a Lecturer in the Department of Political Studies at the University of the Witwatersrand. She was active in anti-apartheid women's organizations (United Women's Organization 1981–3; Natal Organization of Women 1984–7) and on the Research Supervisory Group of the Women's National Coalition (1992–4) as coordinator of the national research project. She teaches gender studies and is currently engaged in research on gender and citizenship and violence against women, both political and domestic.

Ashnie Padarath is the regional director of the Pietermaritzburg Black Sash, a women's human rights organization. She is actively involved in research and lobbying around violence against women and related issues. She is also involved in enabling people to understand, access, and claim their rights. She is a regular contributor to the local newspaper on issues that affect the marginalized and disadvantaged.

Teckla Shikola served in PLAN, the SWAPO guerrilla army, for eight years. This account of her experiences was recorded in an interview with the editors in June 1996. Teckla was a Hubert H. Humphrey Fellow at Rutgers University in 1995–6. She currently works in Windhoek with the Desert Research Foundation, a nongovernmental organization combating desertification.

Meredeth Turshen teaches gender and development and Third World social policy at the Edward J. Bloustein School of Planning and Public Policy, Rutgers University. She has written two books, *The Political Ecology of Disease in Tanzania* and *The Politics of Public Health* and edited two others, *Women and Health in Africa* and *Women's Lives and Public Policy: The International Experience*. She serves as Political Co-Chair of the Association of Concerned Africa Scholars and as contributing editor of the *Review of African Political Economy*.

Clotilde Twagiramariya works with the Center for Women's Global Leadership at Rutgers University. She earned a master's degree in International Development Planning and a certificate in Women's Studies at Rutgers, where she was a Hubert Humphrey Fellow (1993–4). Clotilde holds a

Licence es Lettres and a baccalaureate from the National University of Rwanda. She worked in international relations and cooperation in Rwanda for over twelve years. For ten years, she was an elected representative of the *Chambre Supérieure de Recours* a government body that heard worker complaints. She was also the family planning representative of the Ministry of Foreign Affairs and International Cooperation.

Daniel Volman received his Ph.D. degree in African history from the University of California, Los Angeles, in 1991. Since 1994 he has been director of the Africa Research Project, a research and educational centre in Washington, DC. He is a specialist on US security policy toward Africa and on African military and security issues. He is the co-editor of *International Dimensions of the Western Sahara Conflict* (Praeger, 1993) and the author of numerous articles in *The Journal of Modern African Studies, New African* and other journals and magazines.

The Women's Commission of the Human Rights League of Chad denounces cases of rape and all forms of violence against women, and particularly violence against the women of Chad. The objectives of the organization are to educate, inform and sensitize people to women's rights through seminars, talks, and conferences.

Abbreviations

AFELL	Association of Female Lawyers of Liberia
AFL	Armed Forces of Liberia
AMME	Association of Women Educators
ANC	African National Congress
ANTD	Armée nationale tchadienne en dissidence
CEA	African Studies Centre (Mozambique)
CEDAW	Convention on the Elimination of All Forms of Discrimination against Women
COSATU	Congress of South African Trade Unions
DPSC	Detainees' Parents Support Committee
ECOMOG	ECOWAS Monitoring Group
ECOWAS	Economic Community of West African States
FARF	Forces armées pour la république fédérale
FIR	Force d'intervention rapide
FNLA	National Front for the Liberation of Angola
FNTR	Front national du Tchad rénové
Frelimo	Frente de Libertaçao de Mozambique
IMF	International Monetary Fund
INPFL	Independent National Patriotic Front of Liberia
LTDH	La ligue tchadienne des droits de l'homme
MDD	Mouvement pour la démocratie et le développement
MPLA	People's Movement for the Liberation of Angola
MULEIDE	Mulher, Lei e Desenvolvimento
NGO	Nongovernmental organization
NPFL	National Patriotic Front of Liberia
NRA	National Resistance Army
NRM	National Resistance Movement
OMM	Organização da Mulher Moçambicana
PAC	Pan African Congress
PLAN	People's Liberation Army of Namibia
RENAMO	Mozambique National Resistance
RPA	Rwanda Patriotic Army
RPF	Rwanda Patiotic Front
SADF	South African Defence Force
SARA	South African Rapist Association
SASO	South African Student Organization
SPLA	Sudanese People's Liberation Army
SWAPO	South West Africa People's Organization
SWATF	South West African Territorial Force
TRC	Truth and Reconciliation Commission
UDF	United Democratic Front
ULIMO	United Liberation Movement for Democracy in Liberia
UNHCR	United Nations High Commission for Refugees
UNITA	National Union for the Total Independence of Angola
WILPF	Women's International League for Peace and Freedom

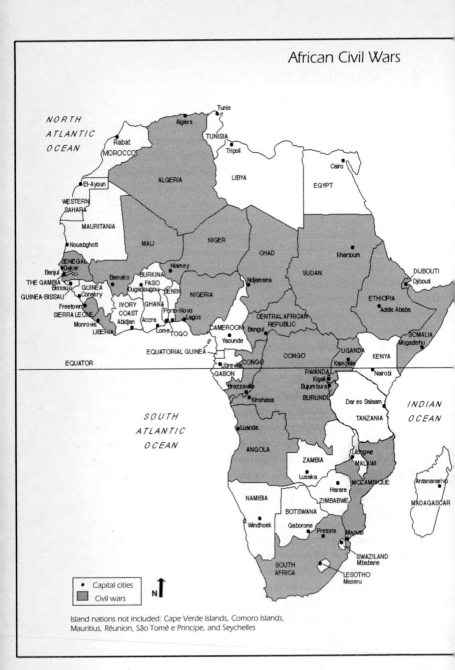

African Civil Wars

NORTH ATLANTIC OCEAN

Tunis

Algiers

TUNISIA

Rabat
MOROCCO

Tripoli

Cairo

El-Ayoun

ALGERIA

LIBYA

EGYPT

WESTERN
SAHARA

MAURITANIA

Nouakchott

MALI

NIGER

CHAD

Khartoum

SUDAN

DJIBOUTI

Djibouti

SENEGAL

Banjul Dakar

THE GAMBIA
Bissau

GUINEA-BISSAU

GUINEA
Conakry

Freetown
SIERRA LEONE

Monrovia

LIBERIA

Bamako

BURKINA
FASO
Ouagadougou

BENIN

Niamey

Ndjamena

NIGERIA

IVORY
COAST

GHANA

Porto-Novo

Abidjan Accra Lagos

Lome

TOGO

CAMEROON

Yaounde

Bangui

CENTRAL AFRICAN
REPUBLIC

ETHIOPIA

Addis Ababa

SOMALIA

Mogadishu

EQUATORIAL GUINEA

Libreville

CONGO

GABON

EQUATOR

Brazzaville

CONGO

UGANDA

Kampala

RWANDA

Kigali

Bujumbura

BURUNDI

KENYA

Nairobi

Kinshasa

Dar es Salaam

TANZANIA

INDIAN
OCEAN

SOUTH
ATLANTIC
OCEAN

Luanda

ANGOLA

ZAMBIA

Lusaka

Lilongwe

MALAWI

MOZAMBIQUE

Antananarivo

MADAGASCAR

NAMIBIA

Windhoek

BOTSWANA

Gaborone

Harare

ZIMBABWE

Pretoria

Maputo

SWAZILAND

Mbabane

SOUTH
AFRICA

LESOTHO

Maseru

• Capital cities

Civil wars

N

Island nations not included: Cape Verde Islands, Comoro Islands,
Mauritius, Réunion, São Tomé e Principe, and Seychelles

1   Women's War Stories

MEREDETH TURSHEN

I once received, as a gift, a volume of poetry by Robert Graves: *Man Does, Woman Is,* the discriminating title proclaimed. In writing of armed conflict, it is tempting to portray men as the perpetrators of war, women as benign bystanders or victims. After all, men do most of the soldiering, most women are civilians. But a more accurate, nuanced portrayal of women and conflict emerges from this book. The enduring wartime picture of 'man does, woman is' has depended on the invisibility of women's participation in the war effort, their unacknowledged, behind-the-lines contributions to the prosecution of war, and their hidden complicity in the construction of fighting forces. Once these activities are revealed, as in the work of Jacklyn Cock and Cynthia Enloe, it is no longer possible to maintain the innocence of all women.[1]

The binary stereotype of active males/passive females also breaks down as the type of war changes. Conventional wars were waged between states by national armies, but contemporary conflicts privatize violence and engage an array of state and non-state actors. As more and more civilians are drawn into conflicts, the conventional separation of male belligerents and female inhabitants no longer prevails.[2] In modern forms of war, especially civil wars and wars of liberation, women are also combatants;[3] women resist and fight back; they take sides, spy, and fight among themselves; and even when they don't see active service, they often support war efforts in multiple ways, willingly or unwillingly. For example, in the civil war of the 1980s, some Ugandan women were soldiers, integrated into the National Resistance Army (NRA) of Yoweri Museveni; others provided key intelligence information for strategic planning or supplied food.[4] Gertrude Njuba, a key mobilizer for the NRA from 1981 to 1986, established an intelligence network, recruited soldiers, and transported equipment, food, arms, and funds.[5] In short, woman also 'does', and women are deeply implicated in militarized societies.

When men alone fought in national armies, it was clear that women civilians needed protection and this was provided in various treaties adopted in the course of this bellicose century. The conventions expect battles to be fought within fixed parameters and warring armies to adhere to a set of protocols that embody international humanitarian law. However much the Hague and Geneva conventions[6] may have been ignored since their ratification, they do in principle hold governments and their leaders accountable for war crimes, and they protect civilians from a specific, though limited, list of abuses. It has been said that professional armies engaged in such battles institutionalized reciprocally recognized soldierly cultures that imposed rules of conduct enforced by systems of military justice (though admittedly some were more successful than others).[7] But it is also true that the modern military has refined and practiced the art of inflicting extensive misery and death on women, children and the elderly to an unprecedented degree – one has only to think back to the Second World War and remember the Japanese army in Asia, the Nazi death camps, the Allied bombing of German cities, and the American atom bombing of Japan.

Increasingly privatized, contemporary conflicts are fought differently from conventional wars between states. Authoritarian regimes use the tactics of 'dirty' wars that are associated with private armies, mercenaries, vigilantes, criminal gangs, paramilitary forces, death squads, and 'tribal' militias. Guerrilla insurgents and dirty warriors do not abide by international protocols for war and disrespect international laws of warfare. Armed contenders for political power hold civilians ultimately responsible for actions carried out by those who represent them (with or without their consent) – their governments, their religious and communal leaders, and their partisan fighters.[8] Guerrilla fighters attack civilians, particularly women, to an unprecedented extent.[9] Often unpaid, guerrillas depend on the local population to feed them or they take what they want, not only food but also property and sex, usually violently. Armed rebels also interfere with international relief efforts to deliver food and medicines to civilians because they regard any form of support, even humanitarian assistance, as aid to the enemy.[10] Their suspicions are often well founded: relief agencies in Ethiopia and Mozambique, for example, played a strategic military role and helped government armies to secure contested areas. Some agencies deplore the fact that their hijacked aid has merely prolonged internal struggles.[11]

The legal implications of abuses of women by non-state actors are different from those of state violators. The fact that non-state actors cannot formally subscribe to existing conventions makes this issue the leading edge of two bodies of international law – human rights and humanitarian law. International humanitarian law, which is of special value in wartime, is laid down in the 1949 Geneva Conventions and the Additional Protocols that clarify and expand the protection outlined in the conventions. Founded on the idea of respect and dignity for each person, these documents govern the treatment of all people during armed conflict and include protection for civilians. Article 3 of the Geneva Convention requires the humane treatment of persons not taking an active part in hostilities that are not of an international character, and Protocol II (1977) provides that civilian populations should be protected against the dangers of military operations and not be the object of attack. The fourth Geneva Convention, Part 1, Article 3 (reaffirmed in Protocol II), prohibits at any time and in any place whatsoever 'violence to the life, health, physical and mental well-being of persons, in particular, murder as well as cruel treatment such as torture, mutilation or … outrages upon personal dignity, in particular humiliating and degrading treatment, rape, enforced prostitution and any form of indecent assault.'[12] None of these agreements has an effective enforcement mechanism, and few African states have signed Protocol II, unwilling to be bound by restrictions over the conduct of domestic affairs.[13]

International human rights law is more applicable in peacetime. Governments are often wary of international pressure to ensure domestic enforcement of human rights conventions, which they say threatens the principle of national sovereignty, but a state's duty to protect civil and political liberties is consistent with international norms. In the absence of the rule of any type of law, however, it is difficult to imagine how violators could be brought to justice. International bodies may monitor abuses of women, but guarantees of human rights can flow only from states. In the case of the 1984 Convention Against Torture and Other Cruel, Inhuman or Degrading Treatment or Punishment, the definition entails that torture be instigated, consented or acquiesced to by a *public* official. Reflecting that reality, human rights organizations, like Amnesty International, focus on abuses by governments.[14] The question being asked now by women's rights advocates is, without an organized state body, who can the international community hold accountable for violations like the rape of women?[15]

In many contemporary conflicts, the legitimacy of the state is precisely what is contested, and not all contests end in a clear victory for one side or another. Some of the worst atrocities are committed in the vacuum left by disempowered or 'collapsed' states, as warlords rise in regions of the country to control valuable minerals and other natural resources, and to fight for territory and power: witness the situations in Chad, Liberia, and

Somalia.[16] Liberian women are acutely aware of the difference between justice in an ordered society and the lack of recourse during civil war: they knew the procedure to follow before the war – they used their legal and traditional justice systems, settling matters such as rape and seeking redress through their local magistrates and chief – but during the civil war they asked, 'Who is there to carry the matter to?'[17]

Apportioning Blame, Assigning Responsibility

It is beyond the scope of this introductory chapter to discuss the complicated and varied causes of these civil wars. But one can say generally that the policies of the international financial institutions, notably the International Monetary Fund (IMF) and the World Bank, which have weakened African states and helped to create power vacuums, have contributed to the rise of conflict. By imposing financial austerity and structural adjustment programmes that shackle the state as provider, the international financial institutions have undermined the ability of legitimate African states to govern and respond to people's needs.

This position challenges the kind of moralizing that has produced explanations of overpopulation and environmental degradation as causes of Africa's internal wars,[18] as if the policies of Western powers, the interests of transnational corporations and the demands of international financial institutions had no role in subsequent events. It has been hard to put to rest certain fallacious ideas – that violence is endemic, institutionalized, and sanctioned by culture in Africa, that African culture is essentially conflictual, that social order depends on war and internal conflict, that colonial rule suppressed these impulses, and that the withdrawal of colonial powers unleashed long-pent-up *coups*, wars, and domestic and external conflicts.[19] The Rwandan tragedy was summed up simplistically in the American media as a tribal war, majority Hutu against minority Tutsi, although the destruction of moderate Hutu was sometimes noted. This characterization fitted the media's need to simplify a complex story about a tiny nation far from the interests of the American public. It also fitted prevailing prejudices about the savagery of Africans, as in this report on Zaire: 'It can be helpful to think of central Africa today as comparable to early-modern Europe – plagued by interminable tribal and religious wars, and crowded with corrupt despots, predatory élites, and a brutalized, illiterate, superstitious peasantry, festering with disease, stagnating in poverty, *and* laden with promise.'[20] Little or nothing is said about what Western economic policies brought these countries to the brink or what arms trades and armed interventions by foreign powers flooded the continent with the means of warfare. Establishing this connection between the relatively peaceful and prosperous industrial nations and the mayhem visited on many Africans in no way exonerates the leaders of the militias and armies that have wreaked the havoc described in this volume.

The governments of industrial nations have settled on a formula of power sharing when warring factions fight to a stalemate or when one side loses significant international backing. In the settlements for Angola and Mozambique, no one is held legally accountable for past atrocities. Other countries have opted for truth commissions composed of impartial panellists and offering amnesty to all who confess their political crimes. There are compelling reasons for these commissions (see Chapter 2), not least the acknowledgement of people's suffering. This process may not satisfy everyone;[21] it may be particularly disabling to women who wish to testify but fear reprisals from their unpunished torturers and rapists living alongside them. In addition, the commissions rarely expose external interference. Few truth commissions deal with the role of international financial institutions or foreign governments in internal political violence, letting off the hook the industrial powers that funded, armed, and trained parties to the conflict.[22] A rare exception is the truth commission convened in Chad to investigate Hissène Habré's regime; its final report, released in 1992, indicts the United States for its involvement in the intelligence service responsible for the worst atrocities:

> The United States of America heads the list of countries that actively provided [the intelligence service] DDS with financial, material, and technical support. America took the DDS under its wing in the very first months of its existence. It trained it, supported it, and contributed effectively to its growth, up to the time of the dictator's fall.[23]

However different the forms and whatever the causes, war creates militarized societies, and an elaborate ideology of gender roles links masculinity to militarism.[24] Feminist analysts of the armed forces describe archetypical patriarchal institutions: the military is a male preserve, run by men and for men according to masculine ideas of male bonding, male privilege, and militarist values derived from definitions of masculinity.[25] This observation is not based on biological traits of men, nor on sociobiological attributions of behaviour, but on cultural constructions of manliness[26] and the social institutionalization of the military. Violence is the most obvious of military values, and in recent investigations of women in the military, the extent to which this violence is turned against women startles the civilian observer.[27] Some women believe that militarism intensifies women's subordination, that civil wars are men's affairs because so few women are decision makers, and that men are the ones engaged in power struggles. There is a tendency to reduce this to 'all men are guilty and all women suffer' as a result of men's military contests. It is true that some women (and men) remain nonpolitical noncombatants. In Mozambique, some civilians had difficulty distinguishing sides and did not know what the conflict was about or who the contenders were.[28] In this volume, we wish to emphasize the knowledge and active participation of women because men have so often denied women's agency in political contests. Indeed, women's usefulness as couriers in the Algerian war of liberation, for example, was predicated on the assumption that the French would not suspect women of insurgency.

The Entrenchment of Violence

Armed conflict has characterized the recent history of far too many African countries. Wars of liberation were fought by Algeria, Angola, Eritrea, Guinea Bissau, Kenya, Mozambique, Namibia, South Africa, Western Sahara and Zimbabwe. Civil wars have broken out in Algeria, Angola, Burundi, Chad, Congo (Kinshasa), Djibouti, Ethiopia, Gambia, Liberia, Mali, Mozambique, Niger, Nigeria, Rwanda, Senegal, Sierra Leone, Somalia, South Africa, Sudan, Tanzania and Uganda (see map, p. xii). In addition, as Volman notes in the final chapter of this volume, too many politically weak African governments – Algeria, Burundi, Chad, Congo (Brazzaville), Congo (Kinshasa), Ethiopia, Kenya, Nigeria, Rwanda and Sudan – stay in power by increasing militarization, by creating new state or private security forces, and by escalating the level of state-sponsored violence. This political violence forms a continuum, and it is sometimes difficult to assign the categories; for example, many of us think the struggle in Namibia was a war of liberation, but others may call it a civil war.

Many of these conflicts, and almost all of the weapons, are the legacy of colonial powers, superpower rivals, or commercial interests.[29] In addition, regional involvement in these conflicts is extensive – the spillover effect that Volman notes, of which the spread of the Liberian conflict to Sierra Leone is typical. Also salient is the deliberate fomenting of internal rebellions (for example, the involvement of Rwanda and Uganda in eastern Congo). In some cases it appears that external powers have supported internal rebellions in order to have local groups fight their international wars for them. For example, before attempting to annex Chad, Libya supported various northern Chadian rebel groups in their bid to seize power. In other cases, states wishing to avoid international censure have armed surrogates. It is interesting how few wars have been fought among African states: the conflict in Western Sahara involved Algeria, Mauritania and Morocco; and

South Africa in its destabilization campaigns attacked the neighbouring states of Angola, Lesotho and Mozambique.[30]

Since the end of the Cold War, as Volman points out, the number and type of weapons supplied to Africa have changed. There are fewer tanks, aircraft, missiles, and other expensive heavy weapons and many more land mines, cheap rifles, and machine guns. An AK-47 can cost as little as $6, as weapons are recycled from one conflict to the next.[31] And land mines, of which there are already 50 million in the ground in Africa (the most mined continent), can be bought for US$25 apiece. The consequences of this change from high to low technology are dramatic. The ready availability of light weaponry has made life more miserable for women. Although attacks 'with a friendly weapon', as Asma Abdel Halim calls it, represent the oldest and lowest form of technology, the threat of rape is magnified by firepower, and guns diminish women's ability to resist rape and survive.

The proliferation of light weapons has had another, unexpected, result: it has made children effective frontline fighters, children who are too slight to manipulate heavy and cumbersome hardware become fearsome when armed with an assault rifle. Boys and girls have been enlisted in Angola, Ethiopia, Liberia, Mozambique, Sierra Leone, Sudan and Uganda.[32] Children who returned to civilian life in Mozambique were reported to be aggressive, aloof, agitated, restless.[33] Like land mines, child soldiers continue to have an explosive effect in peacetime. Older women report that rape by young boys is especially humiliating because traditionally Africans hold elders in high respect; but this morality is breaking down under the stress of war.

Whatever the form of these almost continual struggles (and some like the wars in Chad and Sudan have been going on for thirty or more years), one result is the militarization that has permeated African societies down to levels previously unknown. Militarization in this sense 'involves mobilisation for war through the penetration of the military, its power and influence, into more and more social arenas, until the military have a primacy in state and society'.[34] Concretely, militarization means that current and former military men displace civil authorities; soldiers replace religious figures, health workers and teachers as the leaders of villages and communities.[35] In northern Namibia, the South West African white government progressively militarized the health services until, by 1986, the majority of staff were army personnel with a colonel as director of medical services.[36]

Militarization is disenfranchising; it is politically, as well as economically and physically, debilitating. In militarized societies, violence becomes a crisis of everyday life, especially when dirty war strategies are used by contenders for power.[37] A number of recent commentators are struck by the theatrical aspects of these wars.[38] State and guerrilla forces use terror, constructing absurd, horrific, and grotesque scenarios to gain or maintain control. Their targets are civilians rather than soldiers, and their hold over the population is based on fear, brutality, and murder.[39] They rape, mutilate and kill civilians, often in public as a performance that communicates dread and threatens everyone in the vicinity.[40] We, the readers of these scripts, become the ultimate spectators, and I worry about the thin line between conveying information and fostering voyeurism in this book.[41]

The entrenchment of violence creates new daily insecurities for women – constant and overwhelming fear, exposure to abuse and obscenities, and threats of rape, kidnapping or death for themselves, their children or other relatives.[42] Because of the civil nature of most of the conflicts described in this book, perpetrators are likely to be known to victims and their families and to live in close proximity;[43] killers may continue to be persons of authority in the village. Their presence is inhibiting; it deters women who are attacked from demanding prosecution of the men who raped them and compensation for abuses, and it prevents them from extending their human rights. The presence of perpetrators also discourages women, especially widows, from asserting their rights to land, the basis of life itself in agricultural societies like Rwanda where this issue is critical. And the presence of rapists and murderers hinders other women from participating in movements for democratic change.

Violence and the threat of violence against women do not end when the peace accords are signed. The violence of a regime begets a general culture of violence. In South Africa, murder, rape and assaults are now both a cultural and a statistical norm; Beth Goldblatt and Sheila Meintjes report in Chapter 2 that domestic violence and rape have escalated since 1994. Alcinda Abreu also attributes rape to the violent civil war in Mozambique (see Chapter 4). And in Uganda, two decades of civil strife resulted in increased domestic violence.[44]

The threats and insecurities are caused, not only by warring parties, but also, for women who have been raped, by neighbours and kin. In societies with strict constructions of patriarchal honour, to complain about rape is to admit to illicit sexual intercourse, an accusation frequently turned back on the woman and used to convict her of adultery or of prostitution, as Asma Abdel Halim reports for Sudan in Chapter 5. A Nigerian witness to the Biafran war (1967–70) recounts that married women who survived rape could not return to their husbands.

> These doomed women were paraded through the community, accused of infidelity, the worst of crimes. They went through a cleansing ritual, entailing sacrificing chickens and goats to appease the gods, to seek forgiveness and reacceptance into the community. I was told that even if the women's pleas were

accepted, they were nonetheless stigmatized for the rest of their lives, and their children and children's children were stained by it.[45]

With the entrenchment of political violence, women also confront issues of identity that assume new significance in these unconventional wars. Ethnic, religious or social identity, often ingrained under colonial rule, is made to seem the very basis of the internal dispute; often the purpose is to obscure the leadership's power struggles, as is made clear in the chapters on Rwanda and KwaZulu/Natal. The media usually describe the conflicts as 'tribal', implying a basis in uncontrollable, ancient rivalries.[46] Armies, themselves riven by factionalism, deliberately build upon divisive tendencies in communities to prevent the formation of resistance groups: witness Siad Barré's manipulation of the Somali clan system.[47] A comparative analysis of political violence in Mozambique and Sri Lanka goes much further than this, finding that dirty wars maim cultures, jar their very foundations, destroy crucial frameworks of knowledge and people's sense of reality, ruin social institutions as well as infrastructure, and jeopardize identities based on place and community.[48]

Under the pressure of civil conflict, once-integrated communities may fracture along lines of racial, ethnic or religious identity or party affiliation, which may be real, imagined, or instantly created distinctions.[49] If language betrays identity, it may be suppressed and disrupt the culture profoundly; women, who are generally not as well educated as men, are less likely to speak a second language and will be more marginalized. Identity-based wars raise the problem of long-cherished beliefs about women's roles in maintaining cultural rituals in the home and in socializing their children in the family's cultural affinity. Wars that manipulate identity make the task of assuring cultural continuity, of handing on a sense of communal identity to future generations, more difficult for women and challenge the foundations of their place in society. In Rwanda and elsewhere, women in intermarried couples were immediately suspect as a fifth column.[50] Inter-communal relations, which were maintained by women and which are the hope of reconciliation after hostilities cease, must be sacrificed by women who are open to charges of fraternization with the enemy or, worse, spying and collaboration.

In this setting, gender is not an obvious basis for solidarity, especially in already divided societies. Women may split with each other over many things, like men (married women feeling threatened by widows) and humanitarian aid (who qualifies for it and who doesn't); and women who are in human rights groups may distrust those who are not.[51] In Rwanda, where levels of distrust were always very high in the civilian population, the war brought out the worst in many people and a sense of neighbourliness was lost. There is no commiserating outside of kinship networks over the losses of the civil war. Women may feel too poor to entertain one another, or too angry to trust people.[52] Yet groups like the Black Sash in South Africa and Women in Black in Israel and Yugoslavia have emerged to challenge politically manipulated divisions. One of the remarkable consistencies in the contributions to this volume is the rejection of these divisions and the call for solidarity among women.

Gendered Violence

As Goldblatt and Meintjes point out in their chapter (which includes a discussion of the historical background to the civil war), women also perpetrated violence. As officers of the South African state, as warders of prisons, women practised institutionalized violence, inflicting torture on imprisoned women, even pumping water into women's fallopian tubes and administering electric shocks to women's nipples. Goldblatt and Meintjes mention that women organized prostitution in men's single-sex hostels and note that African women caught up in township violence between rival political parties were central to the necklacing of informers (in which a burning car tyre was thrown around the throat of the victim). Clearly, they say, we do not understand why women sometimes collude in their own oppression and are even complicit in the oppression of other women, beyond the fact that many are politically or economically unable to resist. The fear and uncertainty of civil war have an impact on family life, forcing some women to act even against members of their own family, as described in the chapter on Rwanda. Some, of course, were tricked or threatened into such behaviour, sometimes by the state itself. That women are capable of perpetrating violence, Goldblatt and Meintjes conclude, enables us to see that women's views are not monolithic and that women do not bear essential qualities such as kindness and compassion: 'women, like men, are divided by race, class, and ideology'. Many South African women supported apartheid, firmly convinced that racism and violence were necessary to ensure order and to maintain a particular way of life.[53]

When considering gendered forms of violence, rape is the most common and usually the first to be analysed. It is one in which men assert their power over women and groups of men assert their power over other groups by overpowering 'their' women. (Yes, men are also sexually assaulted. When men rape other men, they conquer them by emasculating them, making them impotent, turning them into 'women'.[54]) Feminists brought the use of rape as a strategy of war to international attention during the Yugoslav civil war in which, it is estimated, between 20,000 and 50,000 women were raped.[55] Five times that number of women were raped in the Rwandan civil war.[56] In Africa the strategy of raping or forcibly abducting women was also used systematically in Mozambique, Uganda, and Zimbabwe.[57]

Until recently, women enjoyed few international protections against rape. Conventions, like the 1979 Convention on the Elimination of All Forms of Discrimination Against Women (CEDAW) which protects women on a basis of equality with men, fail to address gendered violence and gender-related harms such as military sexual slavery and forced prostitution, abuses for which a male parallel typically does not exist.[58] To correct this oversight, the UN General Assembly adopted the Declaration on the Elimination of Violence Against Women in 1994, which includes recommendations that pertain to women in situations of armed conflict. Unfortunately, the UN has no mechanisms to enforce such declarations. The authors of this book support the demand for recognition of rape in war as a crime against women. They condemn rape, especially in conflict situations, for its immediate effect on women's physical and mental health (injury, shock, paralysing fear, sexually transmitted infections including HIV/AIDS, and pregnancy) and because of the many after-effects on women's lives and on the community as a whole. If society were able to read and hear their stories, if there were a national repository of oral and written testimony, would women be better able to generalize their personal suffering and move beyond victimization? This book is a contribution to such an archive.

Feminists searching for explanations of rape have advanced our understanding by looking at men's motives. They have identified numerous types of rape, examples of which can be found in all of the chapters of this book. Rape is committed to boost the soldiers' morale; to feed soldiers' hatred of the enemy, their sense of superiority, and to keep them fighting; rape is one kind of war booty; women are raped because war intensifies men's sense of entitlement, superiority, avidity, and social licence to rape; rape is a weapon of war used to spread political terror; rape can destabilize a society and break its resistance; rape is a form of torture; gang rapes in public terrorize and humiliate women; rape is used to terrorize and silence women and force them to flee homes, families and communities; rape targets women because they keep the civilian population functioning and are essential to its social and physical continuity; rape is used in ethnic cleansing, it is designed to drive women from their homes or destroy their possibility of reproduction within or 'for' their community; genocidal rape treats women as 'reproductive vessels', to make them bear babies of the rapists' nationality, ethnicity, race or religion; and genocidal rape aggravates women's terror and future stigma, producing a class of outcast mothers and children – this is rape committed with consciousness of how unacceptable a raped woman is to the patriarchal community and to herself.[59] This list combines individual and group motives with obedience to military command; in doing so, it gives a political context to violence against women, and it is this political context that needs to be incorporated in the social response to rape.

There are four general explanations of men's motivations for rape: militarism, lack of restraint (either innate or licensed), a biosocial association between sex and violence, and the observation that violence and sexuality are contingent and incremental, which would account for 'escalation to total terrorization, as sexual penetration by itself proves increasingly inadequate in a situation of escalating indiscriminate violence for its own sake'.[60] Several of these categories suggest that rape is also about sex, contrary to some feminist analyses.[61] Physiologically, rape cannot be performed without arousal of the male organ; the question is, what accounts for this coincidence of sex and violence on a mass scale? From a man's standpoint, motivation may be relevant, as in the guerrilla practice of kidnapping women and 'marrying' them to their captors. But is men's motivation relevant from a woman's standpoint? One commentator sees a parallel construction of 'our inviolate women' and 'their to-be-violated women' in conventional armed services.[62] This construction may exist, but military discipline determines whether it is acted upon. The issue is how rape is institutionalized as a military strategy. In any event, more rapes are committed by men in irregular armies[63] in situations where the distinctions between combatants and inhabitants are blurred, where women are also combatants, and where their noncombatant sisters are less easily distinguished from them as a group off limits.

Legal definitions of rape vary widely, not only from one country to another, but also from one context to another. Rule 96 of the rules, procedures, and evidence for the International Criminal Tribunal in the former Yugoslavia defines rape in terms of the force applied by the defendant rather than the resistance offered by the victim; it requires no corroboration, and the victim's sexual history is inadmissible.[64] In the new coeducational armies in the United States, a different standard is observed. The US military uses a strict definition that says sex between people of unequal rank cannot be consensual, given the unequal power relations between them. This rule, if enforced, could protect the majority of women in uniform.[65]

In Chapter 9 on Namibia, Teckla Shikola says that commanding officers in the SWAPO guerrilla army singled out young recruits for sex. Though she recognizes that the young women were 'scared of saying no', she is unwilling to call these acts rape. She says no accusation of rape was lodged in these instances, although 'maybe women didn't come forward because they felt ashamed about reporting to people what had happened'. Shikola's reluctance to call this rape may seem puzzling to women who have been following the rape trials of drill sergeants in the US Army.[66] Goldblatt and Meintjes also discuss sexual abuse or rape in the ANC (African National Congress) camps. They quote their interview with Thenjiwe Mtintso, a commander in Umkhonto we Sizwe (MK, the armed wing of the ANC), who ascribes the abuse to a few individuals and blames it on a combination of factors – their warped psychology, the challenge of women's success to male identity, and the bleakness and frustration of camp life. Goldblatt and Meintjes prefer to look for explanations in the way society condones, and even supports, discrimination and disadvantage of women. Issues of sexual abuse, they note, are often censored; for example, both the South African government – in regard to experiences in the ANC – and the Namibian government – with reference to SWAPO torture of supposed 'informers' during the liberation struggle – have attacked those who raise the issues as divisive and disloyal opponents.

Shikola's observation about fraternization in the SWAPO guerrilla army suggests some difficulty about drawing the line between forcible and consensual sex. Not all SWAPO women resisted men's advances, she says; some sought pregnancy as a way to avoid frontline duty. Her comments on the fragility of intimate relationships during war are also pertinent here; she speaks of the impermanence of connections and the burden of knowing that one could die at any moment and never see each other again. People's perceptions of what is morally acceptable seem to shift in the midst of war and continuous violence. I found this passage in the autobiography of an American nurse who served in Vietnam during the war, written about a romance in Japan:

> [Tom] is a war zone pilot ... he is married and has two little girls, something I brush aside although I can't forget. I wish I could. We know that our relationship will end when he goes back to Vietnam and that he will return to his wife and children when his tour ends. I choose to have and lose true love rather than risk never having any at all. It is my first season of love, so long awaited.
>
> ...
>
> Two weeks later his crew chief writes. Nine days after returning to duty, their chopper ran into enemy fire in what was supposedly a cleared area. Tom got zapped.[67]

The chapter on Rwanda also examines those grey areas in which it is not clear whether women are coerced or consenting. Again, the issue is defined by one's standpoint: women may feel raped when they are coerced or have no choice but to submit if they are to survive, while society may brand even victims of forcible rape, including very young children, as collaborators, adulterers, provocative, or worse. How society responds conditions a woman's experience of rape. In this sense the rape experience is socially constructed. In societies where women cannot talk about their ordeal for fear of being stigmatized by the community, the sexual trauma is often compounded by feelings of humiliation, shame, and guilt.[68] On the other hand, if abortion is socially acceptable and available on demand, if abortion facilities are accessible and affordable, if medical staff are sensitive, if the police response is sympathetic, then the psycho-social impact of rape can be mitigated.[69]

Displacement and Dislocation

The number of people uprooted in Africa's civil wars is staggering: half the population of Liberia, half of Rwanda, five million Mozambicans, over five million Sudanese, three million Somalis, one and a half million Ethiopians and Eritreans, over one million Angolans, half a million Sierra Leoneans, three million forced relocations in South Africa and more than a million people forced to flee their homes in KwaZulu – and significant numbers in Burundi, Chad, Congo (Kinshasa), Kenya, Mali, Mauritania, Senegal, Uganda, and Western Sahara.[70] The physical, psychological, social, and economic effects of the violence from which people flee spill over into the refugee experience.[71]

Women refugees are particularly vulnerable to rape during flight from home, at borders, and in camps. Hundreds of thousands of Somali women crossed into Kenya from 1991 to 1993 to escape political violence and rape, only to face rape in the camps in which they sought shelter.[72]

> Somali women as old as fifty years of age and girls as young as four have been subjected to violence and sexual assault. Most of the women whose cases we investigated were gang-raped at gunpoint, some by as many as seven men at a time. Frequently, the agony was repeated; some women were raped twice or three times in the camps. In the vast majority of cases, female rape survivors were also robbed, severely beaten, knifed or shot. Those who had been circumcised often had their vaginal openings torn or cut by their attackers. Many we interviewed were suffering ongoing medical problems.[73]

A refugee woman escaping from the Mengistu government in Ethiopia was stopped by two men. She was five months pregnant. Describing the incident she said, 'One pulled me aside and said "No safe passage before sex!"... He forced me down, kicked me in the stomach and raped me in front of my children.'[74]

Many women arrive in camps traumatized by rape and by atrocities they have been forced to witness. A relief worker, Rachel Nsimbii, at a transit camp for Mozambican refugees in South Africa, recounted the ordeal of one woman who said she was gang-raped by RENAMO rebels in front of her husband and then forced to kill him.[75] Adosinda Langa, a 26-year-old woman who walks with the aid of crutches, said that the man she paid to guide her across the border held her captive in his house for a year and forced her into concubinage. 'I had to do everything, the cleaning, the cooking. He was a bad man. He promised me everything and gave me nothing.'[76]

Before feminists called attention to the plight of women in refugee camps, the gender of refugee populations was ignored and the special needs of women received little attention beyond, perhaps, the supply of sanitary pads. Now there are guidelines on the prevention of sexual violence against refugees.[77] But the oft-quoted figure that 80 per cent of refugees are women and children is misleading; women and children under 15 years of age are only slightly over-represented in refugee populations since they account for over 72 per cent of most African populations in population censuses.[78] In other words, the demographic profile of refugees is little different from that of civilians.

Flight is one among several strategies adopted in wartime. Families rush their young daughters into marriage in an effort to protect them from rape and abduction. In Somalia, girls were married off early for their own security or to establish alliances with local militia to safeguard their families.[79] A Nigerian woman who was twelve years old at the time of the Biafran war remembers that rape was considered a fate worse than death: 'for us and families like ours whose teenage daughters were unmarried and in hiding, it was probably the single worst worry we had'.[80] Following an ambush by enemy soldiers who burnt down the hut they had constructed deep in the interior after running from their home in Nsukka, the family decided not to risk another episode from which they might not be so lucky to escape.

> Mama decided then and there that she had to save my sisters, before the unthinkable had happened. Her first step was to keep them permanently hidden in the bushes; they could no longer come 'home'.... Mama worked furiously, passing messages to relatives and friends throughout the region, letting it be known that her daughters were on the market for husbands. The urgency in her tone signaled that she was willing to settle for lesser suitors for my sisters; there was no time to be selective.[81]

But for some women, the military represent security: during Uganda's civil war, the National Resistance Movement (NRM) oversaw the destruction of the Teso economy; women fled villages to seek security next to armed military camps.[82]

Widowhood and Isolation

In many African countries, up to 5 per cent of women aged 25 to 44 are widows, 20 to 25 per cent of women aged 45 to 59 are widowed, and over 50 per cent of women over 60 years of age.[83] That was before the recent upsurge in civil conflict, which has killed many more men. There is talk now of the increase of women-headed households in Africa but little connection to war as a cause.[84] War creates widows. In Rwanda, it turned independent women into charity cases; women who before the war had access to land through their husbands are now destitute and dependent on relatives or social workers. War widows who were raped are stigmatized and find it hard to remarry; widowed rape victims with children are ostracized.[85] The psychological toll is heavy; social workers in Rwanda say that women suffer from extreme depression, nightmares, and in some cases violent fantasies against the babies.[86] In polygamous societies, the physical and financial insecurities of war may drive many women into subservient positions as third or fourth wives;[87] for women who have fought against polygamy, this is a retreat. But some see it as preferable to dependence on grudging relatives or to prostitution.

Shikola found that ongoing relationships were not possible in the SWAPO guerrilla army. Her account of the brittle bonds between couples on active service suggests that army wives are easily abandoned in wartime. She says that few soldiers were permitted to travel to base camps to see their children, so it was rare for a father to know them. Many of these women, whether widowed or abandoned, became single heads of household after the war.

War increases the isolation of many women, not only widows. Where violence is entrenched, insecurity confines women to their homes, and refugees who flee rural areas for the security of cities may find themselves imprisoned in the new urban environment. Sudanese women uprooted from the south who seek refuge in Khartoum find painful the change of environment from life in the open to life behind four walls.[88] Because war increases poverty for many women, it can also bring about the loss of social life, as when women can no longer afford to reciprocate invitations with customary hospitality. That everyone is in the same boat ought to mitigate the isolating experiences of the loss and grief that are endemic to war, but pain destroys language and for some women there is no solidarity, no sharing of misfortunes. In the type of war in which enemies are clearly delineated and geographically separated, a collective attitude of 'us against them' may result in solidarity among women. But in civil wars the old distinctions are blurred or destroyed.[89]

Health and Political Violence

The stress of political violence described in this book leads to health problems, both mental and physical: not just disease and injury, but also diffuse malaise – nervousness, vague bodily pains, weakness, and fatigue. Medical services can treat physical ills, war-related injuries, and the ghastly effects of land mine explosions. Rehabilitation services can fit the limbless with prostheses, bring victims of torture back to the community. Public health workers can stop the epidemics associated with massive population movements, like cholera outbreaks in refugee camps, and can help restore sanitation and safe water supplies. The restoration project is enormous, not least because in these civil wars health services and health care workers are targeted for destruction. In Mozambique, for example, a third of the rural health network was demolished or forced to close. The reconstruction project is too large for charities to handle, it must be undertaken by governments. But in this era of austerity, privatization and structural adjustment programmes, the IMF is denying Mozambique and other governments aid for social spending.[90] The IMF's spending caps prevented Mozambique from taking up World Bank loans for health care and roads, and Nordic help for schools in 1996.[91] Between 1994 and 1996, Mozambique was obliged to cut aid spending for war-damage repair by US$170 million a year. The Fund's policy is so controversial that donors issued an unprecedented public statement criticizing the IMF, which finally has relented somewhat.[92]

The new conditions of ill-health and dis-ease have no medical terms. Abreu talks about the consequences of a culture of violence in Mozambique and South Africa. A Mozambican traditional healer noted:

> Some of these kids have wounds because they have seen things they shouldn't see, that no child should have to see – like their parents being killed. They change their behavior. This is not like being mad. That we can treat. No, this is from what they have seen – it is a social problem, a behavioral problem, not a mental problem. They beat each other, they are disrespectful, they tell harsh jokes and are delinquent. You can see it in their behavior toward each other: more violence, more harshness, less respect – more breaking down of tradition. There is no medicine for this.[93]

The feelings that women describe in response to their trauma – the fear, pain, grief, guilt, anxiety, revulsion, hatred, loss of dignity, and sadness – are associated with the breakdown of social life, the loss of language and cultural meanings, the disruption of experience, of family and community. These conditions cannot be treated by existing medical, rehabilitation or public health services. For one thing, we know too little about them and almost nothing about how to treat them in non-Western cultural contexts. A major volume on world mental health notes that few studies of mental health consequences of civil violence have been undertaken outside of Northern Ireland![94] Clearly the work being done in Mozambique, described in Chapter 4, is ground-breaking. We lack a conceptual framework to understand what happens to families and communities in places like Liberia and Somalia where the state ceased to exist. There is remarkably little literature on social and psychological aspects of violence in situations of prolonged civil unrest.

Women's sense of responsibility and guilt for the trauma they have suffered seem to be heightened, rather than dispelled, when the sequelae of violence are treated on an individual basis. Violence needs to be addressed at a collective level, and the social forces that contribute to and legitimate such violence must be dealt with.[95] If violence is political, if the context of the violence is a civil war, even when the violence has been called 'random' or 'meaningless', the health care must also be a political act integral to a social context.[96] Not only psychiatric symptoms but also social and moral harms must be attended to. The most helpful rehabilitation services are those that reintegrate members of a community in meaningful, durable and politically valued ways.[97]

For victims of torture, there is more hope, as centres open in Africa and as nongovernmental organizations assist projects in Eritrea, Ghana, Guinea, Mali, Rwanda, Sierra Leone and South Africa.[98] But the specifics of gendered methods of torture are only beginning to surface because women are ashamed to speak of their experiences. The painful and moving interviews with torture victims recorded by Goldblatt and Meintjes make clear that there is no division between physical and psychological methods of torture; the torturers play upon women's fears for the well-being of family members as well as applying brutality aimed at their sexuality for the purpose of destroying their basic humanity. 'Although the physical symptoms of torture tend to lessen over time, psychological, behavioural, and social problems often persist for years. ... For women in particular, rape and sexual abuse suffered during detention often affect their sexual and emotional well-being for years after the abuse.'[99]

The study of world mental health asks a series of questions that reveal our abysmal ignorance.

What are the lingering effects of large-scale conflicts on the sensibilities, mores, and ways of life of a society or nation? What are the lasting behavioural consequences resulting from cultures of violence in places like Mozambique and South Africa? To what extent does domestic and street violence result from prolonged repression and conflict? What happens to the soldiers, the torturers, and the violent when they return to community life? What kinds of psychological and social difficulties do they encounter in civilian life? What happens to communities or societies after the fighting dies down?[100]

The Scope of The Damage And Its Costs

Millions of deaths have occurred since 1980 as a direct or indirect consequence of war: more than a million in Sudan, perhaps the same high toll in Ethiopia, Mozambique and Rwanda. AIDS is uncontainable during conflicts like the Rwandan civil war when rape, coerced sex and forced prostitution are common; in this context, advice to use condoms or 'just say no' appears ludicrous. There are some nine to twelve million refugees and internally displaced persons in Africa. In Chapter 5, Asma Abdel Halim describes one to two million southern Sudanese living in appalling slums around Khartoum. In refugee camps, education and health programmes have deteriorated sharply under the burden of numbers. In war zones, child mortality has soared, health systems and health standards have decayed, and education has largely come to a halt. Many African families fleeing war have been broken up, and many traumatized, orphaned children have witnessed the violent deaths of their parents.[101] Women and children have been abducted or enslaved in Sudan and elsewhere. These wars are also economically paralysing: they disrupt regional transportation networks, interfere with farming, food production, marketing and trading, and they deter national and international investors and donors.

In Africa, military spending contributes to budget and foreign exchange imbalances and the squeezing of investment and social welfare. Although governments are spending less money on expensive heavy weapons, the withdrawal of American, European and Soviet patronage (low-interest loans or grants to buy weaponry, but also direct intervention) means that African governments must rely on their own armed forces to maintain control. Thus levels of militarization may be rising, not declining, and the light weapons governments can afford may be matched by those acquired by the non-state forces they face.

The amount of money needed to reconstruct war-torn countries is enormous. The United States spent approximately $700 million in Rwanda in the 18 months following the genocidal violence in 1994, roughly the same amount as was spent in 1994 in total bilateral development assistance in sub-Saharan Africa.[102]

New Roles for Women

Working on this book of war horrors, I was tempted to conclude that all wars are damnation and all warriors depraved. I searched desperately for something positive to take away. And then I found it in the meaning of social upheaval. War also destroys the patriarchal strictures of society that confine and degrade women. In the very breakdown of morals, traditions, customs, and community, war also opens up and creates new beginnings. During the break-up of the former Yugoslavia, women disappeared from the public sphere, not only in the immediate war areas.[103] But elsewhere, paradoxically, war has opened up new spaces for women. The conflict in Chad, for example, has provided opportunities for positive change in social relationships including gender relations. When men are away fighting, or have been killed in action, women may grieve or suffer loss, but they also step into functions from which they were previously barred. In Rwanda, women rarely owned land in the past and had almost no control over the products of their own agricultural labour, but after the genocidal conflict of 1994 they accounted for as much as 80 per cent of the population in certain areas, and restrictions on women's ownership and activities were no longer appropriate.[104] In Mozambique, the war and the economic crisis that followed it forced significant changes in gender relations: the increasing economic role of women has stepped up their power within the home because they now control money. According to Terezinha da Silva, a researcher at the African Studies Centre at Eduardo Mondlane University, 'Men admit there is a real change in gender division of labour: they tell me there are no longer "men's" jobs and "women's" jobs.'[105] War and displacement in the Sudan have changed women's status from housewives to breadwinners. Halim reports that women have vowed never to give up this change and never to revert to the status of being owned or inherited or of being revered only as mothers and wives without having any property or freedom of movement. And Sudanese women are prepared to fight to keep these gains.

Historical data suggest that women have sometimes been given education or political rights precisely because of struggles to gain national independence or to establish a homogeneous national identity. Even more paradoxically, they have sometimes been able to achieve status as political subjects by acting within and then gradually moving beyond the narrow confines of the role ascribed to them as custodians of national traditions or embodiments of traditional codes of conduct.[106]

Whether these changes are temporary or permanent remains to be seen. Although the historical record in Algeria, Eritrea, and Zimbabwe is not good, Ugandan women's active participation in the NRA appears to have broken many barriers and changed men's attitudes. 'During those years in the bush, from 1981–1986, gender questions began to be consciously addressed by the NRA/NRM. The words and actions of the leadership of the NRA/NRM continue to reflect a consciousness of gender-based inequality and a determination to alter it.'[107] The Museveni government established resistance committees with a mandatory position for women, created the Women's Desk within the NRM Secretariat and then upgraded it to the Directorate for Women's Affairs, and initiated the Ministry for Women in Development.[108] In 1987, the National Organization of Trade Unions recognized the women's wing, and by 1989, ten of the fifteen member unions had women's wings. Numerous autonomous women's organizations emerged during the 1980s, many receiving foreign funding, to address issues of income generation, orphaned children and AIDS. This positive evidence of permanent changes is highly encouraging.

But what a price to pay for the freedom, equality, and dignity with which all human beings are supposedly endowed at birth! Let me end, then, with the words of the Hague Appeal for Peace 1999: 'As civilization has largely left behind slavery, colonialism and apartheid, let the 21st century be the first century without war.'

Notes

1 Cock 1991; Enloe 1983. Enloe and Cock are both interesting about the length to which the military will go to insist on the femininity of women in order to complement its self image of masculinity.

2 Nordstrom (1992:271) notes this shift to the increasing slaughter of civilians: in the First World War over 80 per cent of casualties were soldiers; in the Second World War half of all casualties were military, half civilian; today nearly 90 per cent of all war-related deaths are civilian. Of course technology has progressed in parallel: the development of anti-personnel bullets and bombs, the setting of land mines, etc.

3 It is also true that during the Second World War women were members of the French resistance, served as Yugoslav partisans, etc.

4 Boyd 1989.

5 *Ibid*.

6 The Hague Convention of 1907; the Geneva Convention on the Protection of Civilians of 1949.

7 Littlewood 1997:11.

8 Colson 1992:282.

9 Littlewood 1997:10. Violators also go unpunished when successor governments do not pursue military and government leaders, or when governments grant

amnesty for human rights abuses committed under their supervision (Etienne 1995:141).

10 Copson 1990:2.

11 De Waal and Duffield (1992:393) state that relief centres were often the site of food aid diversion to militia forces, and they estimate that relief agencies in Ethiopia and Mozambique may have provided a 10 per cent contribution to rural people's survival, but abetted the destruction of much of the other 90 per cent.

12 Three other conventions are relevant. The African Charter on Human and Peoples' Rights which prohibits 'all forms of exploitation and degradation of man particularly … torture, cruel, inhuman or degrading punishment or treatment'. Article 4 states that 'Human beings are inviolable. Every human being shall be entitled to respect for his life and the integrity of his person. No one may be arbitrarily deprived of this right.' The Convention on the Elimination of all Forms of Discrimination against Women (CEDAW) reaffirms women's rights and freedoms which include the right to life, the right not to be subject to cruel, inhuman or degrading treatment or punishment, and the right to equal protection of humanitarian norms in times of international or internal armed conflict. Gender-based violence that impairs or nullifies the enjoyment by women of human rights and fundamental freedoms under general international law or under specific conventions is discrimination within the meaning of CEDAW's Article 1. The Convention on the Rights of the Child (Article 38) requires states to ensure children under the age of 15 years do not take a direct part in hostilities and to refrain from recruiting children into their armed forces.

13 Copson 1990:4.

14 Bonner 1995.

15 Etienne 1995:158.

16 Demobilized Liberian militia members concluded that the conflict had made their leaders rich from trafficking in gold, diamonds, and timber, but left the fighters themselves as poor as ever, with families shattered (French 1997).

17 Swiss 1992:5.

18 See Kaplan 1994 for an exposition of the neo-Malthusian analysis of the causes of war in Africa and see Richards 1996 for a critique of this analysis in the context of Sierra Leone's civil war.

19 Adda Bozeman, quoted in Smaldone 1990:5.

20 Gourevitch 1997a.

21 For example, the human rights office of the Roman Catholic Church in Guatemala is undertaking its own effort to document politically related massacres, kidnappings, and torture because it is alarmed by an amnesty law they regard as a whitewash and sceptical of a new official commission to investigate the 36-year civil war (Rohter 1997).

22 Nor is private aid considered: see, for example, Austin and Minter 1994 on American private aid to RENAMO.

23 Quoted in Hayner 1994:638.

24 Cock 1989a:55. Militarism is defined as the pervasiveness of symbols, values, and discourses that validate military power and preparation for war (Luckham 1994:24).

25 Enloe 1983; Francke 1997.

26 See, for example, the analysis of Connell 1985.

27 See, for example, Francke 1997; Rayner 1997.

28 Nordstrom 1992:265.

29 For example, on the role of the Shell Oil Company in the struggle between the Ogoni minority and the Nigerian government, see Osaghae 1995 and Damu and Bacon 1996.

30 This trend is found worldwide, see Nietschmann 1987. The Tanzanian invasion of Uganda in 1979 to depose Idi Amin was an exception to the common use of mediators to resolve African conflicts (Tarr 1993).

31 After the multiparty elections in Mozambique in 1994, AK-47s formerly used in Mozambique's civil war could be bought for US$6 along the border between Mozambique and Zimbabwe; these weapons have sustained the fighting in KwaZulu/Natal (Daley 1997).

32 UNICEF 1996:14–18.

33 Desjarlais *et al.* 1995:125.

34 Cock 1989a. Luckham (1994:24) gives a more extensive definition: militarization is an inherently international process that dynamically links the accumulation of wealth and hegemonic projects to military coups and regimes, authoritarian government, the dominance of patriarchy, powerful military and repressive state apparatuses, war and armed conflict, rising military spending and arms imports, and external military intervention.

35 Zur 1993:28.

36 Cleaver and Wallace 1990:50.

37 Nordstrom 1992:261.

38 Nordstrom 1992; Richards 1996.

39 Nordstrom 1992:261.

40 *Ibid.*:263.

41 Niarchos (1995:654) maintains that it is a disservice to the victims to censor or suppress detailed testimony when the purpose is to establish truth, and that a feminist approach requires 'an exposition of the facts, in all their horrifying and indelicate detail. Only in this way can the full extent of female suffering be conveyed to a male-dominated legal culture.' In editing this book, we felt it was imperative to move these voices from private monologue to public accusation.

42 Zur 1993:28.

43 A particularly vicious version of this was practised in Mozambique by RENAMO which sent children to kill and pillage in their own villages in an attempt to secure their loyalty and demoralize civilians. Reynaldo Mucavel, who worked for the US nongovernmental organization Save the Children, interviewed one child 'who was asked to shoot his mother and father and then cut their necks like he was cutting an onion. He did it. He was 8 years old.' (Quoted in Keller 1994.)

44 Boyd 1989.

45 Ugwu-Oju 1995:192.

46 Hayner 1994:654.

47 Luckham 1994:23.

48 Nordstrom 1992:267–9.

49 Gourevitch 1997; Ranger 1992.

50 An expression coined during the Spanish Civil War, a fifth column is a group of secret sympathizers or supporters of an enemy who engage in espionage, sabotage, and other subversive activities within the defence lines or borders of a nation. A suspect woman is lyrically portrayed by Nuruddin Farah, the Somali writer, in his novel *Maps*.

51 Zur 1993:29.

52 This was true in Afghanistan after the 14-year civil war (McLachlan 1993).

53 Cock 1991.

54 The Zagreb Medical Centre for Human Rights estimates that 4,000 male Croatian prisoners were sexually tortured in Serb detention camps: 11 per cent were fully or partially castrated (sometimes by women) and 20 per cent were forced to fellate fellow prisoners; and in another report, rebellious Iraqi officers were made to rape each other before execution by slow mutilation (Littlewood 1997:9) .

55 Valentich 1994.

56 Human Rights Watch 1996.

57 El-Bushra and Mukarubuga 1995:17.

58 Etienne 1995:147.

59 Copelon 1995:204.

60 Littlewood 1997:13.

61 Seifert 1996:36; for a review of theoretical perspectives on rape, see Valentich 1994.

62 Littlewood 1997.

63 Brunet and Rousseau 1996.

64 Niarchos 1995:686. The full text reads: 'In cases of sexual assault: (i) no corroboration of the victim's testimony shall be required; (ii) consent shall not be allowed as a defence if the victim (a) has been subjected to or threatened with or has had reason to fear violence, duress, detention or psychological oppression, or (b) reasonably believed that if the victim did not submit, another might be so subjected, threatened or put in fear; (iii) before evidence of the victim's consent is admitted, the accused shall satisfy the Trial Chamber *in camera* that the evidence is relevant and credible; (iv) prior sexual conduct of the victim shall not be admitted in evidence.'

65 It also can lead to absurd situations as when applied in the cases of First Lieutenant Kelly Flynn, the female pilot discharged from the US Air Force for an adulterous affair, and Second Lieutenant William Kite charged with two counts of fraternization and two counts of making a false official statement for dating and then marrying a female airman, also in the Air Force (Sciolino 1997).

66 See coverage in the *New York Times*, e.g. 15, 16, and 25 April 1997.

67 Smith 1992:36.
68 Desjarlais *et al.* 1995:124.
69 For example, women's police stations in Brazil and rape response training of municipal police forces in the United States.
70 Figures from US Committee for Refugees, Washington, DC.
71 Desjarlais *et al.* 1995:140.
72 Human Rights Watch Women's Rights Project 1995:120.
73 *Ibid.*:121.
74 Moorehead 1995.
75 Wren 1990.
76 *Ibid.*
77 UNHCR 1995.
78 United Nations 1990.
79 Littlewood 1997:10.
80 Ugwu-Oju 1995:194.
81 Ugwu-Oju 1995:195.
82 Joan Vincent (personal communication 2 April 1993).
83 Overall, about 12 per cent of north American and west European women and 9 per cent of African women above age 15 are widows; what is striking is that African women are widowed at much younger ages (United Nations 1995: 10–11).
84 In the United Nations document produced for the Fourth International Conference on Women in Beijing, *The World's Women 1995: Trends and Statistics,* a section devoted to women-headed households notes an increase and the importance of widowhood as a cause, but it makes no mention of war as a cause of widowhood.
85 McKinley 1996a.
86 *Ibid.*
87 El-Bushra and Mukarubuga 1995:19.
88 Malou 1997.
89 Witness this account of civil war in Guatemala: 'army irregulars, the local "voluntary" civil patrols, a coerced and unpaid service … organised under local chiefs, installed in all villages in 1982, served as the army's eyes and ears, though ostensibly they were set up to eradicate "subversives" and "bandits" in the local area. After carrying out a massacre they silenced villagers by threatening them that if they spoke about what had happened they would suffer further violence. Their activities effectively destroyed all social relationships, networks, and solidarity among civilian populations.' (Zur l993).
90 Hanlon 1991.
91 *The Economist*, 28 June 1997:44.
92 *Ibid.*
93 Nordstrom 1992:270.
94 Desjarlais *et al.* 1995:121.
95 *Ibid.*:127.

96 *Ibid.*:130.

97 *Ibid.*:131.

98 The African Centre for Research and Diffusion of Information on Torture and Human Rights in Africa and the African Centre for the Rehabilitation of Victims of Torture and Repression are projects of the African Commission of Health and Human Rights Promoters (Samoura 1996). In addition, there is a Trauma Centre for Victims of Violence and Torture in Cape Town.

99 Desjarlais *et al.* 1995:124.

100 *Ibid.*:133.

101 Copson 1990:1.

102 American Assembly 1997:13.

103 Seifert 1996:41.

104 El-Bushra and Mukarubuga 1995:18–20.

105 Quoted in Hanlon 1991:72.

106 Einhorn 1996:2.

107 Boyd 1989.

108 *Ibid.*

2 South African Women Demand the Truth

BETH GOLDBLATT & SHEILA MEINTJES

Editors' Introduction

Truth commissions are bodies set up by the United Nations, governments, or nongovernmental organizations to investigate a past history of violations of human rights by the military, other government forces, or armed opposition groups.[1] Most truth commissions are created at a point of political transition to demonstrate a break with the past, promote national reconciliation or establish the legitimacy of a new government. Truth commissions are vested with authority to access even sensitive information, but not to prosecute violators.

Thirteen countries have convened 16 truth commissions to date.[2] Nine of these commissions have been held in Africa; Uganda held the very first one in 1971 (and another in 1986). The African National Congress (ANC) sponsored South Africa 's first in 1992 (the Skweyiya Commission) and its second in 1993 (the Motsuenyane Commission).[3] The third was created by the Promotion of National Unity and Reconciliation Act in 1995.[4] Despite a quarter of a century of experience, including several very successful commissions in Latin America, the idea of truth telling and amnesty rather than tribunals and convictions is still controversial. Many people hold – including some South Africans such as the relatives of Steve Biko, the leader of the Black Consciousness Movement who died in detention in 1977 – that there is a legal obligation to punish past crimes.[5] War crimes tribunals, beginning with the German and Japanese military trials after the Second World War and more recently the UN-sponsored tribunals for the former Yugoslavia and Rwanda, were set up to try individuals charged with human rights crimes.

Successful truth commissions accomplish something quite different. They create an accurate record of a country's past, provide an honest account of its history, expose patterns of violations (the profile of a regime), and, by obtaining confessions, gain public acknowledgement of what has occurred. Whether an authoritative history of violence prevents the past from being rewritten or deters violence from recurring are open questions.[6] Surely the hope is that official confirmation will begin to heal the wounds, that truth telling plays an important psychological role in reconciliation, that a more knowledgeable citizenry will recognize the signs and resist the return to repressive rule, and that the implementation of recommended reforms will help ensure change.[7] The South African Truth and Reconciliation Commission hopes to realize these and further gains – to achieve reconciliation and a sense of belonging that supersedes ethnic nationalism by creating a culture of human rights.

Until now, truth commissions have not paid special attention to women, as either victims or perpetrators of human rights abuses.[8] In part this is because women's rights were not specifically defined in human rights law until 1993, when the Second World Conference on Human Rights took place in Vienna. The South African Truth and Reconciliation Commission encouraged public debate and input on its terms of reference. Beth Goldblatt and Sheila Meintjes interpreted that invitation as an opening for the consideration of gender issues, and they responded with a lengthy contribution. We are pleased to publish an abridged version of their report, unique in the annals of truth commissions.

The Truth and Reconciliation Commission (TRC) was established at the beginning of 1996 following the first democratic elections in South Africa. The TRC is playing an extremely significant role in shaping South Africa's collective understanding of our painful past. Its task is to investigate and provide as complete a picture as possible of the nature, causes and extent of gross violations of human rights.[9] By viewing our past through a gendered lens, we gain a deeper understanding of how our particular history has shaped the lives of all South Africans. By using a gender framework to develop truth and reconciliation, we contribute towards the building of a new society based on freedom and equality.

A gendered approach requires that we look at the way society locates women and men in relation to all areas of their lives – the workplace, the domestic sphere, and the civic life of the community. Race, class and gender structure social relationships in South Africa. Women's experience cannot be understood in isolation from men's because they are a consequence of the interrelationship of women's and men's roles and statuses in society generally. Women have been and are still subordinated to men, constraining the full development of men as well as women. To transform this

imbalance requires measures directed at restructuring all social relationships in all spheres of society. With this understanding we may be better
able to construct a new society based on a human rights culture that allows
all people, women and men, to contribute fully to society and develop to
their full human potential.

Women's organizations placed gender issues on the TRC's agenda. Using
gender analysis, they made recommendations to the TRC to improve women's
participation in the process and to ensure women's voices are heard in the
history that emerges. The Centre for Applied Legal Studies organized
several meetings with women's organizations, the TRC and others to
explore how this could be done. The result of this process was the submission of a paper on 'Gender and the TRC', and the TRC has since adopted
some of its recommendations. Two all-women hearings have been held so
far where women have come forward to speak about their intimate, painful
experiences.

This chapter is a summary of the submission that was presented to the
TRC. It briefly reviews the history of repression and resistance by women
during the period 1 March 1960 to 5 December 1993 that is the focus of
the TRC. It explores issues relating to gender and political violence in South
Africa and some of the important sites of this violence. It looks at the issues
of amnesty and reparation and lists the recommendations made to the TRC
to improve the process. The paper draws upon written evidence of women's
experiences in the South African struggle as well as interview material with
eight women.[10] We focus on the experience of women alone because we
believe that it is women's voices that are most often ignored. We acknowledge that by not exploring how men's experience was gendered we are
omitting an important aspect of a gender analysis of our past. Failure to
approach the experience of human rights abuses through a gendered lens
will lead to the neglect of women's experiences of abuse and torture, which
are often seen as a male preserve. We have already seen women in TRC
hearings emphasize men's experiences of violence rather than their own.
This distorts the reality which was that women too were direct victims of
past abuses.

The History

The history and development of South Africa since colonial rule is the
history of conquest and the institutionalizing of racial discrimination and
subordination. Less emphasized, but equally important, is the way in which
patriarchal power relations were integrated and used to bolster the power
of the oppressors within indigenous communities. Patriarchy was em-

bedded within the social fabric of apartheid in particular ways and meant that women and men from different racial, class and cultural backgrounds experienced life very differently.

Apartheid, like earlier forms of domination and control, was founded on and reinforced by violence. During the 1960s apartheid policies of 'separate development' which had begun in the 1940s became entrenched. This period had devastating consequences upon the lives of black people. Whole communities were uprooted from their land and were dumped in inhospitable environments – ironically labelled 'homelands' – without adequate infrastructure. Women found themselves in a less secure position than men in relation to opportunities for employment, security of land or farm tenure, and access to housing. Families were torn apart and impoverished. As migrant labour regulations prevented women from joining working husbands in the towns, women were left in rural areas dependent upon remittances. Women in urban areas, with permanent rights of settlement, were prevented from obtaining housing on their own account.

The 1960s were also a period of intense repression, following the vitality of movements to protest the pass laws and the introduction of Bantu education and other forms of apartheid. The ANC and the Pan African Congress (PAC) were banned after the Sharpeville massacre in March 1960, events that significantly altered the scale of public opposition to state controls.[11] Eight women, ten children, and fifty-one men were killed at Sharpeville. A state of emergency was declared during which more than 10,000 people were detained.[12]

Methods of interrogation changed after the state of emergency. State security developed more sophisticated and psychological methods of interrogation, in addition to strategies of banning and even banishment. The introduction of detention without trial – 90 days in 1963, increased to 180 days in 1965 – opened a new, more sinister era for detainees. The Terrorism Act of 1967 entrenched the powers of the state for purposes of deterring all internal opposition.[13] Individuals like Albertina Sisulu spent years restricted by banning orders and house arrest in her home in Orlando.[14] She was held in solitary confinement on several occasions, in 1963 for three months and again in 1981 and in 1985. Active political opponents in trade unions, such as Rita Ndzanga, experienced severe assault. She recounted her experience in detention:

> They dragged me to another room, hitting me with their open hands all the time ... they ordered me to take off my shoes and stand on three bricks. I refused to stand on the bricks. One of the white Security Police climbed on a chair and pulled me by my hair, dropped me on the bricks. I fell down and hit a gas pipe. The same man pulled me up by my hair again, jerked me and I again fell on the metal gas pipe. They threw water on my face. The man who pulled me by the

hair had his hands full of my hair ... I managed to stand up and then they said: 'on the bricks!'... and they hit me again while I was on the bricks. I fell. They again poured water on me.[15]

So acute was the experience of personal disintegration for some, like Ruth First in the 1960s and Jenny Schreiner in the 1980s, both members of the South African Communist Party, that they tried to kill themselves.[16]

By the 1970s methods of torture assumed a much more violent form against those in opposition. Detention and the process of interrogation involved the most callous and vicious forms of assault and did not exclude women on the basis of their sex. Thenjiwe Mtintso, a former journalist, member of SASO (the South African Student Organization) and later a commander in Umkhonto we Sizwe (MK, the armed wing of the ANC), described her experience of detention and interrogation as one of constant physical assault and abuse of her womanhood.[17]

During the 1980s, the context of resistance changed profoundly. International hostility to apartheid had grown considerably and, in spite of the reluctance of Britain, France and the United States to take a strong stand, an international boycott movement was under way. Moreover, internal organization and opposition grew in scale. The South African regime was forced into attempts to reform cosmetically the worst aspects of apartheid. In this context of reform and repression, internal opposition movements became more strategically organized and a strong mass movement emerged. State repression became more violent, with the state increasingly supporting reactionary forces within the 'homelands'. The ANC and PAC began to step up their guerrilla attacks. From the mid-1980s the struggle for competing control escalated into what some analysts term a civil war. In these conditions of war, militarized constructions of masculinity and femininity became more pronounced, in spite of countervailing forces within MK, where it was well known that women were soldiers and commanders. Women increasingly became drawn into the violence that grew throughout South Africa, as activists themselves, or as indirect victims. Although women's role in resistance is often defined in terms of their maternal function, women have used this as a means of lifting themselves out of the private realm and entering the public arena. This has had the effect of politicizing private issues and placing women's pain at the loss, abduction, and attack on themselves and their families on the oppositional agenda.

As large numbers of women became more active in struggles against apartheid during the 1980s, methods of sexual torture assumed greater prominence. Women's sexuality was used to undermine their identity and integrity during interrogations. Lydia Kompe, a former trade unionist and activist amongst rural women and a Member of Parliament since 1994, describes how the police brazenly terrorized and tortured during the 1980s.

They came in numbers. I'm sure there were about 20 well-armed police and in the same village there was a police station which was like a camp where they were torturing people and we were taken to that torture camp.... The majority of us were women and they even took Patsy's young girl of about 15 years, a beautiful young girl I was worried about.... They harassed me at that little office and I was strong, I was very adamant and they got very angry with me. They questioned me saying things like 'You're such an old woman coming from an oppressive country' because they saw themselves as a different country.... 'What do you think your husband thinks about you? This is the reason why all the men are getting divorced. You will sleep for the whole six months alone because we're going to keep [you].' And I could hear the screams [of people] being tortured that were kept in those tents but they would never let me go and see what they were doing. It was worse than the central government torture, so people say.[18]

She describes how electric shocks were administered during torture by means of instruments powered by a generator specially brought to this particular rural area for the purpose. During the course of the night at the police station, each young woman was called in turn to leave the cell. On their return, the women would not speak about what had happened to them but Kompe suspected that they had been abused or raped. She explains the failure of the young women to discuss these incidents in terms of the prevailing cultural view that sexual abuse is shameful and cannot be divulged.

During the later 1980s, in successive states of emergency, women were detained in large numbers. Accounts of women's experiences in detention include a long list of reported sexual assaults and torture.[19] Twelve per cent (3,050) of the state of emergency detainees in 1986–7 alone were women and girls. The violation of their identity and integrity, their sense of themselves as women, were part of the form and content of their interrogation.

During the 1990s, the dying days of apartheid, the old regime worked together with reactionary forces to attempt to destabilize communities and scuttle negotiations for the transfer of power. Large-scale violence occurred in black townships, often ostensibly predicated on ethnic differences. Dispossession and deaths of breadwinners particularly affected women, who were responsible for children and the maintenance of the home and family. Incidents such as the abduction of young women to serve as sex slaves in the hostels occurred during this period of frenzied violence. When the liberation movements finally forced through negotiations and elections occurred, these decades of violence had left many people brutalized and communities in disarray. Many women are still living with the legacy of that social breakdown, including large-scale criminal and domestic violence.

Although it is important to emphasize the killing and torture in our past and the extraordinary suffering of opponents of apartheid, we need also to pause and recognize that the apartheid system itself violated the basic rights of human beings in ways that systematically destroyed their capacity to survive. The gendered dimensions of this system had an added de-humanizing effect on many people's lives. The influx control system, linchpin of the migrant labour system, not only separated families, but also criminalized a huge number of men and women who were merely trying to be together and to find work to support themselves and their families. This experience often violated the integrity of individuals in devastating ways.

Lydia Kompe points to the multiple meanings and subjective under-standings of violence during the apartheid years. She describes her experience of the system which gradually but systematically undermined her identity and her way of life. She lost her rural home and was forced to become a domestic worker in town, where she could not live with her husband nor bring up her children in a family. She describes how the law, and its implementation and effects, were different for men and women. While men's lives were hard under apartheid, women suffered even greater economic burdens and social restrictions that oppressed them and caused suffering. To spend time with her husband meant risking arrest. He was twice arrested visiting her room in the suburbs where she was a domestic worker. Of her experience she said:

> Can one actually say it's violence?... It's not as serious as my husband being killed in jail. One would say, it's not like me having left my own country going to stay thirty years outside. So that's what I always say to myself, what is this violence? How can one express it to somebody who can actually feel sympathetic? What I'm telling you now is a story. I don't think it will be seen as violence. It's a story that this is how we lived in the past. And this was where it actually crippled me in my mind.[20]

The system that Lydia Kompe describes forced her to adopt illegality as a mode of survival and this violated her sense of integrity. She pointed to particular effects the pass laws had on African women. Although these laws also determined the movement of African men, they were even more harsh in their effect on women. Because of the gendered nature of social relations, women had primary responsibility for child care and support, and they were disadvantaged in their access to land and to the labour market. Her story is one of dispossession and impoverishment. The Betterment Laws[21] deprived her family of independent small commodity production on the land, and they were to uproot themselves to seek wages in the urban areas:

> It was an internal violence.... I lived in a society for many years using false identities for my survival because I was a victim of the influx control.... I had to

do away with my own African culture, with my own self and call myself a different thing so that I could come and work, because I was not allowed to work in the so-called proclaimed areas of Johannesburg, because I didn't qualify, I was a rural woman. I had to use false names and false identities. The surname Kompe is not my surname, it is a false one.... I respect that name because it made me bring up my children and send them to school.

For Lydia Komape, the move to the city required violating her rural and African identity. She acquired a false identity as Lydia Kompe: 'Komape was a Bantu name, which would have prohibited me from entering the urban areas.' Yet she was tortured by the guilt associated with her new identity as a coloured woman, which gave her advantages over her black fellow-workers. She discovered that the coloured toilets were better than those for African women, a discovery that led her to begin organizing on the shop floor against the divisions apartheid imposed on workers. Her verdict on the 'internal violence' of apartheid is that 'the system crippled me and my mind. I was committing a crime in order to survive, to avoid the crime of stealing.'

In terms of the human suffering and psychological trauma involved, the entire system was a gross violation of the human rights of a whole society. Lydia Kompe's experience shows not only how apartheid shaped South Africans' lives, but how gender fed into this experience and added to the burden suffered by black women. While both men and women suffered from all of these methods of social control, factoring gender into the apartheid equation produces a more complete understanding of South African history.

Gender and Political Violence: Women as Victims of Apartheid

The definition of victim in the Truth and Reconciliation Act of 1995 includes relatives and dependants of victims. This is very important because it locates wives, mothers and children in centre stage as having suffered 'gross violations of human rights'. It is important to see these women as primary not secondary victims, because they themselves suffered directly. It is difficult to separate the psychological pain of a mother whose child has been tortured from that child's physical and psychological pain. Both are victims in need of support and rehabilitation. This position is supported in the law of delict, developed in South Africa and elsewhere in recognition of the direct harm suffered by witnesses, relatives and others who are able to claim pecuniary damages from the perpetrator.

A further dimension of loss is the economic and material one. Detention, imprisonment, exile and death might have meant the difference between starvation and survival to poor families and communities. Jesse Duarte, the member of the Executive Committee of the Gauteng Provincial Government in charge of safety and security, emphasizes this aspect:

> Women who lost their sons or daughters for example, at the time when they were just beginning to become economically active, have something to say to us as a society about having reared a child to a particular point and then that child is taken away from them without an explanation.... Then there is the cultural perspective of the economic position of that particular family. [Perhaps] that family did not need, or that person did not contribute to the financial security of any family. But in the minds of people right now they lost a potential bread-winner.[22]

Duarte thinks the issue was sidelined because mainly women raised it, women who were seen as wanting to be paid for the contribution that their children made towards the struggle. For Duarte, that is not true; in truth, in reality, their breadwinners had been taken away.

Responsibility for maintaining family life rested very much upon women's shoulders. This was the case for wives of political prisoners or detainees. June Mlangeni's experience echoes that of many women as she describes the impact of her husband's imprisonment in the 1960s:

> We were young when Andrew was arrested and I was looking forward to the future with him ... but it was torn apart by a government which separated two people who aimed to build a future together. After I saw him on Robben Island I became stronger, and I could cope better with the police harassment. Before I used to shiver when the knock came at 2 a.m knocking from window to door, front and back doors ... and they knew that I was a woman alone in the house. When Andrew was arrested I was a housewife. I started to work when Andrew was in prison and I took time off to go to court to listen to Andrew's case ... then my employers found out that my husband was one of the Rivonia Trialists, and I was fired.[23]

The cultural significance of loss is a further aspect. For women, the loss of a husband in struggle had a very significant impact on her status in her community. Widowhood could mean the loss of status. Jesse Duarte noted that it is not so much the economic loss as the cultural loss and the loss of position within the community that has an impact on widows.[24] When women lose their husbands they become doubly repressed by their own community; they become women without standing, almost illegitimate in the present context of South Africa's cultural reality. The son becomes the woman's husband, even if that woman was a very high-powered political activist. The minute her spouse or her partner was taken away, that was the end of her.

In her testimony to the TRC, Sepati Mlangeni, the widow of Bheki Mlangeni, spoke of the awful effects of her untimely widowhood, a mere two months after her marriage: 'I am an outcast in my own society,' she said.[25]

A number of children were taken into custody and detention with their mothers, whilst others were abandoned or left for long periods in the care of relatives or even strangers. Although the scope of this chapter does not extend to examining the experience of children, it is important to remember that they were often also direct and indirect victims of human rights violations. Young people disappeared from their homes, detained by the police who never informed their families where they were. The press reported one chilling example of this kind described to the TRC:

> Maudline Lutya's brother, Wiseman, disappeared during rioting in Guguletu in 1976. She inquired at police stations and hospitals and asked around the local community, to no avail. Nobody told her anything. Three weeks later … she went to the Salt River mortuary…. She found her brother 'shot through the head, some of his brains were coming out'.[26]

Women's role in supporting their detained husbands and children began to take on a political character during the detentions of the 1980s; a support movement comprising families and friends of detainees emerged, the Detainees' Parents Support Committee (DPSC). This movement constantly brought to the attention of authorities and the public the harshness of the deprivations caused by detention. It acted as a counter to the state's attempts to destroy political opposition. Indeed it intensified opposition and made private concerns a political issue. Women, traditionally perceived as second-class citizens located in the private sphere, became key political actors in these struggles against state oppression.

In another context, Jean Franco argues that the meetings at government offices of mothers and families of the disappeared 'constituted a space of memory that also became a counter to the public sphere'.[27] Franco says 'the movement exploited the traditional view that mothers were the vessel of reproduction, but they also went beyond any essentialist definition of "mother" and thus demonstrated that it was possible to transform protest into a broader ethical position, one based on life and survival'.

Many of the people who have already spoken in the TRC are wives and mothers of men who were killed. Many of these women were themselves detained and harassed by the police. Although these women have come forward to speak about their husbands, fathers or sons, they were not encouraged to speak publicly about their own experiences. In the first week of the Truth Commission's hearings in the Eastern Cape, the widows of the 'Cradock Four' came to speak about their murdered husbands. They themselves had been harassed and arrested, yet their stories were not probed and were treated as incidental. Our society constantly diminishes women's role and women themselves then see their experiences as unimportant.

Even Albertina Sisulu, one of the most prominent fighters for justice in South Africa who suffered a great deal of personal repression during the period 1960–91, was more able to talk about her husband and children's experiences than her own.[28] She uses the second person to describe her experience, finding it difficult to speak about herself as a suffering individual. She also locates her subjectivity within the collective – the nation.

The above discussion shows that women, even in acting in support of men, must be seen as both victims and resisters in their own right. We must also recognize, however, that many women were directly active in resistance and were detained, tortured and killed because of their own effective opposition to the state.

Constructions of Gender in Prison: Women Experience Torture

A variety of forms of physical and psychological torture were used against women. Some of these were also used against men, but others targeted women's femininity and sexuality, and all were experienced in a gendered way. This section explores some of the forms of torture developed to undermine women.

Physical methods of torture

Accounts of women's experience in detention recorded by the DPSC in 1987 include assault and electric shocks on pregnant women, inadequate medical care leading to miscarriages, teargassing, solitary confinement, body searches and vaginal examinations, rape and forced intercourse with other prisoners, and foreign objects including rats being pushed into women's vaginas.[29] Jessie Duarte and Nomvula Mokonyane speak of incidents where women's fallopian tubes were flooded with water, sometimes resulting in their inability to bear children.[30] Children as well as women experienced these forms of cruelty. During the states of emergency, girls as young as fourteen were detained, tortured, beaten, and teargassed.

Jean Franco points out that women are ashamed to speak of their torture. First person accounts are often laconic or euphemistic. When recording their experiences for commissions on human rights they merely state they were raped without attempting to describe the event. She shows how pain destroys language. In South Africa, where sexual assault is common knowledge, 'women are afraid to talk about these assaults', according to people who have worked with detainees.[31]

Although both women and men are tortured, it is clear from South African and parallel international experience that differing constructions of gender shape their experience and treatment. Studies of political violence do not highlight men's gendered experience of their torture, but research on ordinary prisoners reveals systematic attacks on their masculinity. Inger Agger suggests an interesting hypothesis, that sexual torture of men aims to induce sexual passivity and to abolish political power and potency, whereas behind the sexual torture of women is the activation of sexuality to induce shame and guilt.[32] Carolyn Nordstrom argues that sexual assaults attack 'the core constructions of identity and security in their most personal and profound sense'.[33] The intent is 'to break down the fabric of society, and … thus to break down political will and resistance'. One could argue that sexual assaults in the context of political detention and war are institutionalized acts that make public the private.

Physical assault was used to break women as well as men. Joyce Dipale, a Black Consciousness leader, was kept in solitary confinement during 1976 and 1977 for five hundred days. Her experience of torture was graphically described by Hilda Bernstein:

> She was subject to many agonizing forms of torture, including the 'horse' – she was handcuffed to a pole and swung round and round until she lost consciousness – electric shocks on her bare breasts, buttocks and genitals ('I got used to the pain but never the humiliation'); beatings; prolonged standing with deprivation of sleep, food and water; and being kept in a dark room, she does not know for how long – 'I lost touch with time.'[34]

Jenny Schreiner, who was detained in the late 1980s, spoke of the shock she experienced as a middle-class white woman who had never known any physical violence until she was assaulted in prison. She mentioned that the power of her oppressor was particularly potent because he was a man.

> Mostert … insisted that I stand up. My response was that all Section 29 said in terms of detention was that they could hold me until I answered questions, they couldn't even force me to answer questions … and that standing up was not part of Section 29 and I was not standing up.… At which stage he walked around the table and physically picked me up and stood me up, but stood me up so that he could slam my back into the wall. Which although, I mean he didn't shatter my skull or anything, but it's a clear statement from step one. 'I am in control of this, I am bigger than you, I'm more aggressive than you and I have no respect for you.' And there I think that it' s also a question of it being a gender thing. There's a man who is physically picking you up and shoving you into a wall.[35]

The fear of rape is always present for women detainees. Thenjiwe Mtintso described a night when the police came to take her away from the police station where she had been detained for the first three months.

> They stopped on the Kei bridge and there were about three men in the car in which I was and about five men in the other car that was escorting us. And when we got to the Kei bridge they asked me to get out of the car and they all got out. And I had not minded being beaten or anything or even killed in the process but rape, just as far as I was concerned, this was it. This was going to be a gang rape and they were just going to leave me here.... I wouldn't leave the car, so they dragged me out ... they beat me up.... I had got a sense then that the others had wanted to rape but I don't know, I can't say whether they were going to rape me but that is when I got the fear that I could be raped.[36]

Diana Russell interviewed Elaine Mohamed who said:

> The way women experience detention is totally different from the way men do. I burst into tears when a security policeman said to me, 'I really enjoy interrogating women. I can get things out of them and do things to them that I can't do to a man.' I was terrified by this statement. I felt horror and pain about it when I was physically hit by the police, and I think the police realised this immediately.... I was body-searched twice a day every day.... I remember policewomen making me strip in front of men and people laughing at me.[37]

Withholding medical care is another form of physical torture. Albertina Sisulu described the near-miscarriage of Winnie Mandela, 'And at one time when we were in jail with Mrs Mandela she was threatening [about to give birth] and they wouldn't let us as midwives attend to her. It was terrible, she was bleeding and she could really lose the baby at any moment, until we had to fight as women, then the door was opened.'[38]

Psychological forms of torture
The police developed sophisticated methods of psychological torture that attacked women's identity. These methods targeted the traditional roles and social location of women to undermine them. Nozizwe Madlala explained why her detention was different from a man's.

> To start with, the attitude of the police towards you. They may try many ways to make you feel that you shouldn't be here. A woman shouldn't be here. You are here because you are not the right kind of woman, you are here because you are irresponsible, you are here because your morals are low. They say all sorts of things to you. You worry a lot about responsibilities outside prison, your responsibilities. This last time I was detained I had a child already and that was my main source of worry and I felt guilty at times. I wondered what was right, but then later I would be quite convinced that I hadn't done anything wrong and in fact what I was doing would eventually benefit myself, my child and humanity.[39]

Jenny Schreiner described how the security police would search for areas of vulnerability in a detainee and use this to undermine her by trying to make her feel diminished as a woman:

> [There was] ruthless prying into an area of a person's personal life that they knew was vulnerable.... That all the kind of personal pain of a marriage that doesn't work is brought to the fore and in a context where they are going to send you back to a police cell to sit with nothing other than the emotions that they've scratched open. You're thirty and you're single, therefore there's something wrong with you as a woman, and that's why you get involved with politics.... They were attacking your identity with their own particular conception of what a woman is.... The bizarre thing is that I had done a lot of work in DPSC. I'd spent a lot of time listening to people who had been through detention, preparing the detention manual, so I knew the methods that they were using.... But although at the time that they're saying it, you know that and you can sit there with your arms folded and kind of stare them back in the face, when you go back into that police cell ... you sit in that cell ... our own self image depends on the affirmation that you get from other people. And that for me was what came through very strongly, because no matter how much at the time that they were saying it (and rationally I knew that they were talking rubbish), you go back into your cell and you sit there and think, 'Well!' You know, I think back over my life, my personal relationships are difficult, maybe I am, maybe that's why this went wrong.... You internalise a whole lot of stuff because there's nobody else to actually say 'OK, so your relationships were difficult, but that doesn't write you off as a person'....But when you're sitting there, it's not so easy to keep your perspective. The emotional barrage that one is under, the extent to which you have access to nobody other than people who are doing everything to undermine your personality, to undermine everything that they can see about you that is positive, they will find a way of undermining.[40]

Targeting women as mothers was one of the cruellest forms of torture. Albertina Sisulu described how the security police told her that her child was dying, and then that she had died. Later they told her that her husband was very ill.

> In '63 ... I was tortured ... the police would come, you know twice or three times a day opening the door [of the cell] and saying 'Are you sitting here, the child is in the intensive care unit with pneumonia she can die any moment. If you are not prepared to give us the statement then you won't bury that child.' Okay, I will remain thinking, let the child die if the nation is saved. Doesn't matter, I'm not going to say anything about what is happening. What my husband did, others are doing. I knew a lot because I was also now involved in politics. The worst was when they came, actually came in the morning to say, 'We've come to tell you that your baby has passed away in the night.' That torture is not for one day, three days, but for ninety days of your detention. You are being tortured by this today and tomorrow.... Torture in jail is in many ways. They may not torture you physically, but mentally they get to your brains.... At one time they said

Walter was in hospital. 'Would you like to go and see him?' I said, 'Oh yes!' 'Not unless you do what we want you to do.' Sitting there thinking my husband is very ill. Sitting there thinking my child is dead.[41]

Thenjiwe Mtintso had a similar experience. The police obviously realized that the best way to weaken women detainees was to make them believe that their children were dead or dying. This would play on their worst fears as mothers and expose their deepest vulnerabilities.

When I was detained my son was nine months and I left him in bed.... One day they came in with a big photo in the *Daily Despatch* that showed a red Volkswagen that had been smashed and I had a red Volkswagen at that time. They said to me 'You see, that is your car ... one of your colleagues was driving your car with your son inside and we were chasing him and that's what happened to your car and your son is dead there'.... That stayed with me for the rest of my stay in prison. They would not say 'No, he is not dead.' They just continued beating me up, beating me up ... I don't know what it would have done to a man, but that was one way of getting to a woman.[42]

The security police attacked women as sexual objects, undermining their sexuality. They accused Thenjiwe Mtintso of being involved in the struggle for sexual gratification and discounted her contribution as a woman engaged in politics. She said that in her second detention, 'The police were beating me up, not because they were torturing me but because I was giving some sexual satisfaction to these men, Steve Biko, Mapethla Mohapi ... those that were in Black Consciousness around King Williamstown.'[43] She then described how the torture changed in the second month of her detention when they stopped focusing on her as a means to get information on the male activists and became angry with her for not breaking down:

Anger at me ... for not fitting the stereotype of this woman who was going to break down ... so they got very angry that I was thinking that I was a man. It was always 'You think you are a man, you think you are strong, we are going to bring you down, we've brought down better people than yourself, men, strong men'.... This is where they actually use your womanhood. For instance, they would let you stand for the whole day and you would not be allowed to go to a toilet or anything and it gets to a point where you can't hold on so you will wee-wee standing there. And all of them will be coming in and out just laughing at this woman who just pees anywhere. Around menstruation – because at some stage you've just got to menstruate. You are just like this in a cell and there is nothing and you are going to come in stinking obviously ... after a month of wearing those pants it is hard here and so as you walk ... and stink. That is the humiliation then where your womanhood is used. 'You are useless. These men who sleep with you. Look at you how you smell.'[44]

Race and class impacted on women's experience of political violence.

Caesarina Kona Makhoere poignantly describes the way in which apartheid structured prison life – food, clothing and prison accommodation were qualitatively different for Asian, coloured and African women. 'If you want to find out what racial discrimination is, just go to any South African prison. The reality is very hard. Here are three people sharing the same table. Yet what they eat is divided on racial lines. And you are expected not to be hurt. Mama Aminah has a "coloured" diet, while the four of us – Aus Joyce, Aus Esther, Mama Edith and myself – have to eat rubbish food.'[45]

The experience of white detainees was also seen to be more privileged. 'Mothers of white detainees speak about their awareness that they have had a privileged position in their access to family members and their ability to afford legal help and access to international pressure.'[46] Jenny Schreiner confirms that she felt she was at an advantage as a white woman in detention:

> There was a very strong line that ran through the [interrogation], they weren't questioning me with any seriousness, because my attitude was that of the group of us that I knew had been detained, being white and middle class and a woman I was in a far more protected position than a black woman and two black men, and I decided that since we all had a fair amount of overlap of knowledge, the best thing I could do was to shut up.

She notes, however, that her sheltered life may have made it much harder for her to deal with the torture and the conditions of detention. She attempted suicide during her detention after having 'cracked' and made a statement:

> I think for me as a woman who grew up in a very secure background in an environment in which violence was just not ever part of it. My Mother gave my brother a hiding when he insisted for the fifty-fifth time on playing with her electric sewing machine, and she burst into tears, I mean that's the extent of violence, we'd get the occasional spank when we were young. So my experience of personal violence has been incredibly limited.[47]

Barbara Hogan was at a particular disadvantage as a white woman during her prison experience. The state segregated prisoners by race and also separated the political prisoners from the criminal prisoners. For a long time she was the only prisoner during her detention and imprisonment. She says:

> You lose contact with the outside world, and inside you don't have a supportive community around you … you know that you can always lose that community, if you are lucky enough to have one, as has happened with many women prisoners … you face enormous social and emotional deprivation under those circumstances. I think that I always found myself very profoundly affected by the threat of loss.[48]

The majority of the victims of repression in the 1970s and 1980s were young, black and from working-class backgrounds. The financial burden of detention was very severe, especially in communities such as the Eastern Cape, where wives of detainees not only lost their husbands' income but were unable to find work for themselves due to the high levels of un-employment. Visitors to jailed detainees felt guilty if they could not afford to take food or clothes to the detainee. 'Some did not visit their loved ones because they had nothing to take to them.'[49]

Our interviews with Albertina Sisulu, Amina Cachalia and Sheila Weinberg highlighted the different responses each woman received from her (racially separate) community. Sheila Weinberg found the white community very hostile to her family's involvement which made them feel isolated and unable to trust other people. Amina Cachalia and Albertina Sisulu were able to rely on members of their community to warn them when the police were coming and to assist in looking after the children. Jessie Duarte spoke of women from the Indian and coloured communities who were ostracized by their families for becoming involved in resistance politics.[50] Lydia Kompe's whole life story (set out above) shows how race has permeated every aspect of people's experience in this country, even going to the toilet.

Women also perpetrated violence; it was not the preserve of men alone. In their capacity as officers of the state women perpetrated institutionalized violence. The press reported women in hostels organizing sex slavery and women central to the necklacing of informers (in which a lighted kerosene-soaked car tyre was thrown around the neck of the victim). Witch burning included as many women as men. A full understanding of the multi-faceted and cross-gendered nature of political violence in South Africa requires an exploration of these issues. Many feminist theorists have attempted to explain why women sometimes collude in their own oppression and are even complicit in the oppression of other women. We do not attempt to outline these debates here but, through the words of some women, we try to shed some light on this complex issue.

Duarte's analysis is that the women who became spies for the system may have a legitimate argument that they were politically or economically unable to resist. They did not need to get involved politically, but economically they were unable to resist the kind of money they received, especially in an era when black women were not employed by the system in other ways.[51]

Nomvula Mokonyane spoke of the devastating effects of fear and uncertainty on family life, where women acted even against family members. She suggested that the state had a conscious strategy of destroy-ing families of opponents:

The worst kind of female perpetrator is where you find wives acting against their husband – inflicting pain on their husbands, partners, sisters, brothers, friends or even their own children. There are such examples in this country. This occurs because of fear, uncertainty or because of survival. Many families have broken up because of this. In many instances the state has actually used what has been perceived as the sexual weakness of women in such cases as where the man has been taken into detention and they bring another man to have a relationship with that woman while that man is detained. The relationship is exposed and the whole fabric of that family is undone. The children are affected and there is divorce. At the end of the day those women cannot be seen as victims because people will just see them as corrupt women who were just doing these things because their husbands were not there and fail to see what actually led to the situation and pardon them and allow them to speak so that they can understand themselves why that other man made those advances, because I think they would be interested to know why it happened and who actually made it happen like that.

But Mokonyane found some acts of complicity inexplicable. The torture of women by women was one example:

When it comes to some women's actions against other women it makes you wonder that you could actually find a woman pumping water into another woman's fallopian tubes or attaching electric shocks to another woman's nipples. The woman may be perpetrating these acts for survival reasons but the infliction of pain and the manner in which that pain is being inflicted this woman knows exactly what the effects of that pain will be on that other woman. It is hard to know if you will be able to reconcile with that woman perpetrator. It may be easy to pardon some women but not some other women such as these. In many instances women tend to be much more harsh and insensitive than men. For example women [prison warders] may see a woman giving birth in a single cell and not intervene until or at all if a man intervenes. A woman [warder] may not help a diabetic detainee who has collapsed in her cell and help only arrives from a man.

Barbara Hogan describes the transformation of a prison wardress who started off as a 'sweet little thing'.

For the first three days her eyes would be standing out and be red because she'd been crying every night at having to lock people into cells.... And in six months that little same wardress would be demanding to see sanitary towels soiled before she'd issue another sanitary towel. If you take a prisoner's side ... you lose all your esteem ... you are socially ostracised, and you don't get promotion.[52]

Women who were spies, informers, warders, and even torturers were all strands in the complex web of our past. Many of these women were forced to act as they did out of economic pressure, from fear, by being tricked or threatened, and because they were brought up in a society that told them cruelty was a necessary response. Some of these reasons do not adequately explain the degrees of cruelty that certain women perpetrated, particularly against other women. Arguably, their anger regarding their own position in society was misdirected at other women who seemed so completely to defy convention and move from the private into the public realm. The resulting confusion within a violent political context may have allowed anger and pain to be transferred onto others through cruelty. Understanding that women were capable of perpetrating violence enables us to see that women are not monolithic in their outlook as a group and are not bearers of certain essential qualities such as kindness and compassion. Women, like men, are divided by race, class, and ideology. Many women supported apartheid and were fundamentally convinced through their experience of the society that racism and violence were necessary mechanisms to ensure order and to maintain stability and a particular way of life.

Sites of Political Violence

The history of women's experience of state violence set out above looks mainly at state political violence such as detention, imprisonment and assassination. That is only part of the story. Women figure prominently in political violence at many other sites – in townships and hostels, in the province of KwaZulu/Natal and on the Reef; there was also gendered violence in the liberation movements, and the South African government sponsored violence against women in neighbouring states.

The province of KwaZulu/Natal, a site of political violence, is described at length in the next chapter. The specific context of the conflict in Natal is a complex one that grew out of the ethno-national politics engendered by apartheid and involved a range of issues related to specific localities and struggles. In rural areas, the threat of removals by the state during the 1980s led to pockets of organized opposition facilitated by the Association for Rural Advancement, an organization initiated by former members of the Liberal Party, and supported by a range of progressive lawyers and individuals. In informal settlements, such as Inanda and Umbumbulu, struggles surfaced around access to resources for survival. In Natal townships, incorporation into KwaZulu became a major issue of conflict with the state, as did the issue of KwaZulu control over education, teachers, and schools. The highly complex war in KwaZulu/Natal and its gendered consequences require further exploration and examination. Evidence suggests that groups such as the South African security establishment, Inkatha, armed vigilantes, and the United Democratic Front punished women by means of gang rape. During the early 1990s, the victims of attacks by groups of armed men were often women, children and the elderly. 'Often the women may be sexually brutalized before being killed. If men are at home at the time of the attack, they are often forced to stand by and watch the attackers brutalize and kill the women and children in the house before they themselves are killed.'[53]

In the refugee centres on the south coast of Natal, sexual harassment appears to have been prevalent.

> The women have no privacy and often become targets for sexual abuse and assault. In one refugee camp on the south coast at least three women were forced to flee the camp after being raped by men in the camp. Confidential discussions with other women in the camp revealed a chain of sexual harassment.

Townships and hostels

The political violence of the 1980s had a wide-ranging impact on all South African lives. In particular, the army and police controlled the residents of black townships. Within this context of heightened violence and fear, tensions developed among township residents. These tensions related to accusations, often by young against old, of collaboration and failure to stand up to the oppressors. Terrible methods of punishing supposed informers developed, such as the infamous 'necklace'. Many women were victims of these forms of violence. Political and sexual conflicts may have been played out in some of these cases where women, the objects of sexual competition between men, became the target of political violence. During a political trial in the Eastern Cape, evidence indicated that a woman whose boyfriend was a 'comrade' was labelled an informer and killed because she was seen taking a Fanta and a dress from a policeman.[54]

One of the campaigns of the 1980s was the consumer boycott of white-owned shops – many women were victims of violence by 'the comrades' for failing to heed the boycott. Viewed through a gender lens, women who had to meet the household's needs on a tiny budget, and thus needed to shop at the cheaper white-owned shops in town, would have found the boycott particularly difficult to observe.

Pule Zwane conducted a fascinating and chilling study linking rape in the townships to the decline of political organization, coupled with unemployment and other factors.[55] A group of youth in Sebokeng formed a group called South African Rapist Association (SARA). One of the members of the group explained why he had participated in forming the group:

> I was a comrade before joining this organisation. I joined it because we were no longer given political tasks. Most of the tasks were given to senior people. I felt that we have been used by these senior comrades because I do not understand why they dumped us like this. Myself and a group of six guys decided to form our own organisation that will keep these senior comrades busy all the time. That

is why we formed SARA. We rape women who need to be disciplined (those women who behave like snobs), they just do not want to talk to most people, they think they know better than most of us and when we struggle, they simply do not want to join us.[56]

The Reef

Large-scale violent conflicts, called 'third force' violence,[57] tore apart townships on the Reef during the late 1980s and early 1990s. New evidence shows that the state sponsored much of this violence in an effort to disorganize resistance and demoralize communities.[58] Many of the victims of the 'third force' war were the poorest communities, predominantly women living in informal settlements. Women are particularly vulnerable to this type of violence because it disrupts the homes from which they work and the streets on which they hawk their wares. It removes their centre of security, their place of work, and their networks in the surrounding community.

The perception that men are the main victims of violence is reflected in assistance provided after the Boipatong Massacre of June 1992. Jesse Duarte notes that 128 people died in that massacre, 48 men and 80 women. Only the families of the men were ultimately provided with legal assistance. 'The single women who died in that incident were completely ignored. They were totally and absolutely ignored as if they had nothing to contribute to society so they didn't need to be given any kind of legal support.'[59]

Many families became refugees in their own country as they were forced out of their homes during the hostel/township wars. The burden of confiscated homes and disrupted families was most often borne by the women of these communities. A woman described how this occurred:

We left our home two weeks ago. Four men from the hostel questioned me about my tribe. I replied that I am a Sotho. Then I was told to consider leaving. They said Mgadi section is only for Zulus. They said that our section is now Ulundi section … the following day … I then phoned my husband to inform him that we have left the area.... On Sunday we went to check the house under escort by the Katlehong police. We took our property and left some of our furniture.[60]

Evidence that men who occupied the hostels abducted women from local townships on the Reef has also come to light.[61] Abducted women were kept for days in the hostels and repeatedly sexually abused. A feature of their abduction was the performance of peculiar rituals, such as drinking blood.[62] The violation of township women humiliates not only the women, but crucially also implicates the men who symbolically have control and are thus responsible for the protection of those women.[63]

Duarte describes 'third force' violence as indirect repression. She argues that there was an absolutely determined attempt to undermine entire communities that were seen to be very firmly opposed to apartheid. The whole purpose of undermining the East Rand, and Katorus in particular, was to bring down the community's morale. It worked to such an extent that today young people in that community have very poor morale and see themselves as potential beneficiaries of the state because 'they deserve to get what was taken away from them'.[64]

Duarte suggests that the hostel system created the brutality that hostel dwellers used in township struggles. It is a kind of political repression to lock a twenty-year-old male behind a fence at nine o'clock at night and later go on to recruit that same young man to become a killing machine; it is absolutely repressive to be forced to live as a single man or a single woman in a hostel situation, and there are long-term effects of hostel dwelling.

The liberation movements and neighbouring states

Gendered criminal acts were committed within the liberation movement's camps, although we believe these were cases of human rights violations, not crimes against humanity. Apartheid was a coordinated system that legally sanctioned horrifying abuses. Abuses in the camps must be understood in terms of individual criminal acts and within the context of the conditions of the camps and the nature of the war being fought. Those involved need to acknowledge and condemn acts of abuse of women in the camps. If South Africa is to become a truly democratic society with a human rights culture, the message needs to be conveyed clearly that the oppression of women, including sexual abuse and harassment, are unacceptable wherever they occur.

We were unsuccessful in our attempts to speak to women about their experiences in the camps. In an interview, Caesarina Kona Makhoere expressed an unwillingness to speak about the camps but intimated that her experience had been terrible: 'At least in prison I knew I was in the enemy camp.'[65] We interviewed Thenjiwe Mtintso, a senior member of the ANC's army, who said she had no personal experience of sexual abuse in the camps, perhaps because 'I had already been in the front command structures so I didn't come fresh from home into the camps. And secondly, I had the advantage of a better understanding of gender and how it plays itself out.'[66] She was aware of allegations of rape in the camps and says that women are reluctant to talk about their experiences for two reasons. Firstly, on a personal level, they are not easily able to talk about rape. Secondly, on an organizational level, they are afraid that their evidence could be used to equate *individual* human rights violations by ANC cadres with the *systematic* violations of apartheid. Some of these women have chosen to participate in an organizational submission being prepared by the ANC rather than come forward individually, but it is not known whether the submission covers acts such as rape.

Mtintso provided some insight into the circumstances in the camps that may have led to sexual abuse or rape. 'There is something about being in a camp situation, about sometimes people feeling the hopelessness of the whole thing and about the frustrations of being in a forest perpetually and not seeing your way ever of getting out. There was always hope, of course, but there was always that bleakness some days and that frustration.'[67] She argued that the men's experiences before reaching the camps shaped their aggression and attitudes towards women:

> And there was also an element in my own view of some of the comrades who, I would say, were dented somehow in terms of their experiences inside the country and everything and you would then say that psychologically they are people that would have needed attention, therapy or whatever. However, that opportunity was not there. So they find themselves in the camp. And that then manifests itself in aggression. For some of them the aggressive behaviour you could actually look at as frustration on the one hand, but the experiences, on the other, which some of them had gone through, and this leaves this dented individual in terms of their psychological make-up, in terms of their view of life. In that context then they hate women.

She also suggested that women's success challenged men's sense of themselves and their male identity:

> I have looked at comrades who just get so angry and frustrated because women performed better than they did. And I can imagine that anger translating itself in one or another way. The man could easily want to prove his manhood, his masculinity in terms of 'I am still a powerful individual' and that could, I'm not saying it did, that could result in rape. And most of the people that were in the camps are people that had gone through the hands of the police and I would then argue that in one way or another this affected them. Even those that had not gone through the hands of the police, the comrades had left their homes very young and therefore they missed out on the proper developmental stages as well as parental guidance in terms of their relations with individuals, particularly with women.

Mtintso saw parallels between the anger of the security police and some of the men in the camps towards independent and strong women:

> And looking at some of their behaviours, their anger with women performing better, I remember the anger of the security police with me not breaking down.... When you are a woman they expected you to break down quickly. And when you don't break down quickly they really get so angry with you because you are beginning to break down their beliefs that women are weak and so on.... So, I can see that the anger of men in the camps with a woman who performs better and the anger of the security police [with a woman] who performs better in terms of resistance than the men, because that then destroys the stereotypes.

And it then means for me, in terms of the treatment that you get as a woman probably is double-barrelled in that you get worse treatment from the Boers because they don't want you to behave in that manner and you still get worse treatment from your own comrades because they don't expect you to perform better. It's a can't-win situation.

Mtintso suggests that the lack of support structures in the camps may have prevented some of these 'dented' people from getting help. She spoke of one comrade who had raped somebody, which he denied, and a few months later committed suicide.

This is one person you want to sit down with and go beyond what the commissars were doing and so on. That support system that says 'talk about it'. 'What is really eating you up?' But he had been tortured a lot and then he raped, I heard. He was tortured inside the country, left the country, joined MK and remained in the camps very sort of reserved and unhappy.

Mtintso also spoke about the rapes and sexual abuse that occurred in the underground structures of the liberation movement. She said the men knew that women would not want to talk about having been raped. One of her comrades said to her, 'You know, it's going to get to the point that I am going to rape you. And it's going to be very easy to rape you and I know that there is no way that you are going to stand in front of all these people and say I raped you.' The prevailing sexism in society coupled with the extreme conditions of the underground lifestyle resulted in men at times taking advantage of women. Mtintso described how 'comrades who were contacts inside the country would come outside to report … these experiences. They would put up a comrade in a particular place and comrades would sleep with them. And that's rape. That for me is rape.'

We have not attempted to research the male gendered constructions developed within the liberation armies and the methods used to ensure conformity and compliance. An understanding of these issues may shed light on some of the incidents committed in the camps. Part of the explanation for what occurred in the camps highlights the link between sexual abuse and domestic violence, in that all these forms of abuse flow from the way society condones, and even supports, the discrimination and disadvantage that women experience. When issues of sexual abuse surface, as when Thandi Modise publicized abuse by her partner, a former MK soldier, they are often censored. The issue of censorship also came up in Zimbabwe where *Flame*, a film that highlights abuse of women guerrillas, was censored.

There is currently a debate going on in Namibia about SWAPO torture of supposed 'informers' during the liberation struggle. The government has attacked those raising the issues as divisive and disloyal opponents who are trying to dig up something which should best be left in the past. In South Africa, too, there is a veil of silence regarding some of the experiences within the ANC. We need to be cognizant of the psychological literature that indicates the difficulties many people face in talking about sexual abuse. But we also need to consider the important goal of highlighting the abuse of women so that change can begin to occur. The only way to do this properly is to explore these issues openly – we do have to lift the veil of silence.

The South African government sponsored violence against women in neighbouring states. RENAMO was a South African surrogate in Mozambique. Research and counselling carried out in Mozambican refugee camps in South Africa produced considerable evidence that women were raped in front of their husbands and that sons were forced to rape their own mothers, amongst a range of horrifying forms of abuse.[68] RENAMO appears to have abducted both women and children to their camps. Children were taught how to kill – first animals, then people – and sometimes they were forced to kill their own parents. Those young boys were also taught to rape. The women abducted to RENAMO camps were made into cooks and carriers of arms, and they were used as sex slaves.

Even more direct evidence of the culpability of South Africa's security forces exists in Namibia, of abuses against SWAPO and other Namibian women. There is a large body of evidence in this regard which must be gathered and further examined. The SADF's strategy, if there was one, regarding rape of enemy women must be researched. The notorious Koevoet Unit and other military personnel, including 32 Battalion, reportedly committed many rapes within a broader campaign of terror to subdue the Namibian people, particularly in the North of the country.[69]

Amnesty and Gender

Referring to the rapes in the war in South Africa, Jacklyn Cock cites a sworn statement made by a 70-year-old woman in Cradock. The woman describes how she was walking in the street and some white soldiers stopped her and lifted her into the military vehicle. After a short distance the vehicle stopped and they pushed her out. Two soldiers then raped her violently. She says 'The two soldiers were very young. The one held my arms while the other lifted my dress and removed my slip and panties. I said, "What are you doing, children?" The one replied, "Ons gaan jou naai. As jy nie wil, gaan ons jou doodmaak."'[70] (We are going to fuck you. If you won't, we will kill you.) This incident suggests that the SADF may have sanctioned rape as an activity, if not a conscious strategy.

Carolyn Nordstrom suggests that rape is a dirty war tactic, often a public display intended to 'break down the fabric of society'.[71] She says 'It is an attack directed equally against personal identity and cultural integrity.' In this interpretation rape can 'be understood as an abuse which targets women for political and strategic reasons'.[72] Rape is a war crime in terms of the Geneva Convention whether or not it occurs on a large scale or is associated with a coherent policy. The Convention also covers individual rapes used as 'torture or cruel and inhuman treatment'.[73]

Section 20(3) of the Truth and Reconciliation Act enables the Amnesty Committee to assess whether a particular act was associated with a political objective. If it is, then the perpetrator may be granted amnesty. The process of examining a rapist's act by the Committee would allow the political nature of rape to be highlighted, whether or not amnesty is granted. We argued to the TRC that, in most cases, such acts would not fall within the criteria of a political act as defined by the Act. Much of the testimony from women who suffered rights violations suggests that rape, sexual assault, and the threat of rape were committed 'out of personal malice, ill-will or spite, directed against the victim'[74] in addition to any political motives or orders from a superior. Given the difficulty of separating the political and the personal motive in sexual abuse, few perpetrators are likely to be granted amnesty. We argued that the TRC needed to focus public attention on the use of sexual abuse within the political conflicts of the past in all aspects of its work.

The major difficulty which may render much of the above irrelevant, however, is the unlikelihood of rapists or rape victims coming forward to the Commission. In conducting this research we found it very difficult to get women to talk about their experiences of rape. In all the already recorded testimonies, we could find no personal account of rape. Yet many of the people we interviewed knew of women who had been raped. Duarte says of women who were raped in prison cells while in detention or in the van that was taking them to detention that they struggled with trauma after these rapes.

> Women could not say they were raped in the 1980s because from the position of the people they worked with that was considered a weakness. If women said that they were raped they were regarded as having sold out to the system in one way or another. Quite frankly speaking, the most vicious people were women themselves. When women who were raped came and told other women about their rapes, those women were quite vicious about those particular incidents having happened. The consequences of these rapes were the same for these women as criminal rapes. A political rape has no different consequences. It has exactly the same reason behind it – a violent act against a woman.... In fact the women were being punished as women.[75]

Mandisa Monakali of the Ilitha Labantu Centre, which deals with female abuse victims, was reported as saying 'the wives and widows of political prisoners are walking around with wounds. But nobody wants to talk about them.'[76] Women do not speak about rape out of shame, for fear of loss of status, because they do not want to relive the pain, and because they are often unwilling to subject themselves to cross-examination by the accused person's defence lawyer. Duarte considered the women who might come before the Truth and Reconciliation Commission to talk about these experiences and asked about the loss of pride they would experience.

> The incident may have happened ten years earlier and the woman may have dealt with the trauma by herself.... Now that woman is being asked to recreate that loss of pride. Furthermore the woman knows that in coming forward to say so-and-so raped me that she may not necessarily see justice being done. All that these women will do is to add to the historical understandings of levels of repression. I think this is fine and many women will be happy to do this. But there has to be consideration for the other side – for the emotional trauma that women have gone through. Some of these women are now in high-powered positions – in government or as executives. How will it impact on them now in the positions that they hold, given the gender bias that people have about sexually abused women and the concept that women always ask for it anyway?[77]

Duarte spoke of these women's need for a support mechanism. One of the 39 non-negotiable items in the new South African Constitution is the right to privacy, but for those women who come forward to tell their stories to the Commission, their privacy is forever violated. How are those women going to be able to deal with their own environment, having elected to violate their privacy in a very public way?

The Act gives the Commission some powers to limit cross-examination, powers to investigate matters, to hold in camera hearings and to keep the identity of witnesses out of any reports. We made a number of suggestions as to how the Commission could make use of the Act in order to address the kinds of problems women would have in revealing their experience of sexual violence. Perhaps the most significant of our recommendations was that separate 'Women's Hearings' be held. The TRC responded positively to these suggestions, and several of these hearings have been held. The outcome of our recommendations with respect to reparations has yet to be seen. Both authors were invited to act as advisers to the committee which dealt with these matters.

Reparations and gender

The Act requires that victims make application for reparation to the TRC, which requires knowledge of those human rights violations before it is able to assist them. Many victims will find it extremely difficult to approach the TRC for help, because women, particularly those who have suffered sexual abuse, find it very hard to speak openly about their experiences. Women tend to define their suffering in relation to other people such as their husbands and children and are reluctant to make public their own experiences of abuse which society often sees as belonging in the private realm.

Women are also indirect victims. A number of women have approached the TRC to explain that losing a husband or child is the loss of a breadwinner in addition to the loss of social status and the obvious emotional pain of loss. Women, like June Mlangeni, lost their jobs because of the imprisonment of their husbands. She had to stop her children's schooling, electricity was cut off, and furniture and property repossessed.[78]

In formulating a reparations and rehabilitation policy the Commission should consider women's specific needs and interests. Despite the possibly limited resources available for reparation, the TRC should actively encourage women to come forward and make claims. The modesty of some of the requests should not deter the Commission from carefully considering an appropriate reparations policy. If the truth and reconciliation process is to aim at healing the whole society, the TRC has a positive obligation to seek out those who are in need of help.

Opinions vary as to how best to rehabilitate and make reparations. Some have suggested that people should receive actuarially quantified monetary compensation as they would in civil damages claims, particularly as amnesty denies the right to pursue civil actions against perpetrators. The arguments against this position vary from the practical (there is not enough money) to the principled (people cannot be compensated financially for their suffering). These arguments should be considered carefully and any assertions such as 'there is no money' should be backed by factual evidence. The policy also needs to be considered in light of the definition of 'gross human rights violations' which we have suggested should be read extremely widely. Finally, the impact of reparations must be looked at not simply from the vantage point of the individual but also from that of the community of which that person is a part.

It must also be noted that the quantification of civil damages claims by the courts has been criticized by gender analysts all over the world for allowing gender bias to limit the size of the awards that women get.[79] Calculation of quantum often ignores the unpaid labour of women and the other caring functions women fulfil, such as looking after the disabled. The calculation that looks at the individual's potential life chances in determining the loss of quality and expectation of life also should be studied for gender bias, because it is premised on a society that affords women little opportunity to improve their life chances and standards.

We believe that the TRC process is aimed at healing more than one generation's pain and that it sets in place the framework for building a human rights culture to be treasured by future generations. Part of the reparation and rehabilitation process is the public acknowledgment of our history and a commitment to a better future. We would stress the need for creative public education that highlights the truth of our past and locates gender as a central aspect of the analysis of our past.

Accommodating gender in the TRC process

In view of its possible usefulness to women in other civil conflicts, we summarize here the mechanisms we proposed to the TRC to incorporate gender in the truth and reconciliation process. We suggest that the TRC actively reject a gender-neutral approach towards its analysis of evidence and incorporate gender into its policy framework. Without this framework, gender issues, and women's voices in particular, will not be heard and accurately recorded.

With respect to human rights violations, the TRC must ask the right questions so as to enable people to reflect their real experience when making statements. Gender issues come into play because, in addition to people's reluctance to revisit the full horror of their experiences of torture, particular difficulties are associated with discussing sexual abuse. Some of the literature observes that women often describe sexual torture in vague and general terms. Questionnaires should be carefully reconsidered and further briefing of statement takers may be required.

While the Commissioners should question victims sensitively and be aware that exploring abuse in graphic detail may not always assist the victim, they should not avoid 'embarrassing' subjects like sexual abuse because this reinforces the way our society often hides such abuse and relegates it to the private realm. Cross-examination of victims should be conducted sensitively and without causing further harm to the witness. The TRC should invite psychologists who have worked with abused women to brief them on how to speak to victims. The Act does not address the issue of expert evidence, but experts may be particularly useful in providing insights because victims of sexual violence often do not talk about their experiences explicitly.

Women who have approached the TRC in the case of another victim, their husband or son or father, should also be encouraged to speak of their own experience where this occurred. Although the Act requires the Human Rights Violations Committee to determine that a person is a victim for the purposes of reparation and rehabilitation, it does not prevent the Commission from asking people about their own experiences.

The Commission should encourage women who have been raped or sexually assaulted to come forward to speak about their experiences. This public encouragement will in itself help our society to understand how abuse of women formed part of a political struggle and that such abuses are considered gross human rights violations. This can be done both through statements to the press and through NGOs and community organizations such as COSATU (Congress of South African Trade Unions) and the Rural Women's Movement. The TRC should call a meeting with the press to encourage reporters to give prominence to women's experiences and gender issues. The TRC should use other media opportunities such as radio and television interviews to highlight gender in the TRC process.

The Commission should publicize section 38 of the Act which binds all members and employees of the TRC to the preservation of confidentiality. Women need to know that they can come forward without other people knowing about it and can give their statement to a person in safe and private conditions. They should be informed that they do not have to repeat their statement in front of the whole Commission in public and under the glare of television cameras. To make it easier for them to speak openly, women should be able to request that their statements be taken by women and they should be allowed to elaborate on their statements in closed hearings, possibly only to women Commissioners.

Because some women relate experiences told to them by women who are unable to speak openly of themselves, we suggest that the Commission arrange for group hearings and invite women in particular communities to come forward. These hearings could be arranged in conjunction with women's organizations and counselling centres that have been working with these communities. They could be attended by women Commissioners only, if necessary, and psychologists or social workers could assist in the conduct of the hearing. Similar hearings could be held for men who suffered sexual abuse during torture and who may also benefit from a single-gender forum. Men should be encouraged to come forward to speak about their wives, mothers, daughters and sisters who were victims of rights violations.

Because the Commission is a quasi-judicial body, it needs to consider judicial bias towards women, including attitudes towards the credibility of women witnesses and views of the probability of their evidence. International legal research has found judicial ignorance of the social context of women's experiences, proven male identification with witnesses and accused persons, and stereotyping of women's position. The Commission needs to consider how to handle the gendered assumptions that creep into judicial fora. A number of NGOs are currently working on judicial training and could be approached for assistance in this regard.

The reparations policy must consider carefully a gendered understanding of past abuses and encourage women to come forward. The policy must be forward-looking in its approach and must provide for the building of a human rights culture where all forms of discrimination and abuses against women are unacceptable. Women's organizations and other NGOs should be involved in the formulation of the reparations policy. Women must be asked about their needs, and the TRC should direct women to existing programmes and resources in communities aimed at providing such assistance as pensions, housing, education and counselling. If some of the reparations are quantified according to the approach used in civil damages claims, research will be needed on the ways gender bias tilts this standard away from compensating women fully for their loss.

We also made some longer-term proposals to preserve our collective memory of past abuses. First, the Commission's final report should include a gender analysis, develop a framework, and periodize our history; it should give due weight to the differing experiences of men and women in recording our country's history. It should also self-consciously consider how the report should be used to educate future generations.

We propose a memorial list of the women who were killed and the circumstances of these deaths. We should like to see a Peace Institute established, which houses a museum and research facilities and ensures that gender is an integrated focus of all projects undertaken there. We also propose a specific research project to look at the role of gender in past abuses.

This submission highlights many facets of the pain and suffering that violence in South Africa caused to women and men in particular ways. It also focuses on the violence and inequality that are an ongoing part of women's lives. Abuses are still occurring, although within an altered political context. Raising these issues within the TRC process does not mean we can put them behind us and assume that the matter of abuse of women has been settled, and that reconciliation has occurred. Examining the conditions that allow women to be harmed and violated should focus our attention on the need to eradicate ongoing abuse. If the TRC is to leave a valuable legacy, it must lift the veil of silence hanging over the suffering of women and must incorporate the struggle to end this suffering in the struggle for human rights in our country.

Although violence and cruelty are depressing and difficult topics to engage with, we should not reduce our subjects to the status of victim alone. We must also celebrate the bravery of South African women and note that the positive aim of this enquiry is to highlight the need for the protection of fundamental human rights so as to work towards our vision of a transformed society. We conclude with an untitled poem by Dorothy Mfaco.

> There is a world where people walk alone
> And have around them men with hearts of stone
> Who would not spare one second of their day

Or spend their breath just to say your pain is mine
That world is not ours.
We will build a new one
Where we wake in comfort and ease
And strive together to create a world of love and peace.

Acknowledgements

We wish to thank Cathi Albertyn, Ilze Olckers, Lydia Levin, Laura Pollecut and Joanna Birenbaum for their comments and their help on earlier drafts.

Notes

1 Hayner 1994.
2 The 13 countries are Argentina, Bolivia, Chad, Chile, El Salvador, Ethiopia, Germany, Philippines, Rwanda, South Africa, Uganda, Uruguay and Zimbabwe.
3 *Report of the Commission of Enquiry into Complaints by Former African National Congress Prisoners and Detainees*, October 1992; *Report of the Commission of Enquiry into Certain Allegations of Cruelty and Human Rights Abuse Against ANC Prisoners and Detainees by ANC Members*, 20 August 1993. Although we follow Hayner (1994) who classifies them as truth commissions, the Sweyiya and Motsuenyane Commissions were really commissions of enquiry into the ANC camps.
4 Pienaar 1995.
5 Robert Block, quoted in *World Press Review*, June 1996, p. 10.
6 Neier 1990.
7 Hayner 1994.
8 There was virtually nothing on gender violence in the reports of the Sweyiya and Motsuenyane Commissions. Meintjes and Goldblatt write that Thabo Mbeki gave a submission to the TRC on behalf of the ANC, which glossed over gender violence, but the 'truth' has yet to come out about those experiences; ANC women (and men) are very reluctant to come forward.
9 Preamble to the Promotion of National Unity and Reconciliation Act 34 of 1995.
10 List of interviews: Amina Cachalia, 12 April 1996, Johannesburg; Susan Conjwa, May 1996, Cape Town; Lydia Kompe, MP, 15 April 1996, Johannesburg; Caesarina Kona Makhoere, 3 April 1996, Mamelodi; Thenjiwe Mtintso, MP, 5 May 1996, Johannesburg; Jennifer Schreiner, MP, 19 April 1996, Cape Town; Albertina Sisulu, MP, 12 April 1996, Johannesburg; Sheila Weinberg, Gauteng MPL, 12 April 1996, Johannesburg.
11 Black Consciousness (BC) emerged during the latter part of the 1960s as a new political and ideological current, to become the strongest internal influence on

black politics until the resurgence of trade unionism after 1973. BC stressed the need for blacks to reject liberal white tutelage, the assertion of a black cultural identity, psychological liberation from notions of inferiority, and the unity of all blacks including 'coloureds' and 'Indians' (Hyslop 1988:185).

12 Lodge 1983:196.

13 See Bell and Mackie 1985 and Foster 1987.

14 Sisulu interview. Other information from IDAF 1981:38 and Russell 1989: 144–52. Orlando is a black township in Johannesburg.

15 IDAF 1981:31–2.

16 First 1988; Schreiner interview.

17 Mtintso interview.

18 Kompe interview.

19 FEDTRAW 1987.

20 Kompe interview.

21 Under 'betterment', tribal areas were divided into residential and agricultural land. Instead of living in scattered homesteads close to fields, people were clustered into villages on poorer soil such as hilltops, while the rest of the land was divided into fields suitable for growing crops, forestry (woodlots) or grazing.

22 Jessie Duarte, speaking at the Workshop on Gender and the Truth and Reconciliation Commission, Centre for Applied Legal Studies, University of the Witwatersrand, 19 March 1996.

23 Schadeberg 1994:25.

24 Duarte 1996 (see note 22).

25 Sepati Mlangeni, Evidence to Truth and Reconciliation Commission, 2 May 1996.

26 Brand 1996:9.

27 Franco 1992:112.

28 Sisulu interview.

29 FEDTRAW 1987.

30 Nomvula Mokonyane and Jessie Duarte, speaking at the Workshop on Gender and the Truth and Reconciliation Commission, Centre for Applied Legal Studies, University of the Witwatersrand, 19 March 1996.

31 FEDTRAW 1987.

32 Agger 1989:313.

33 Nordstrom 1996.

34 Bernstein 1985:100.

35 Schreiner interview.

36 Mtintso interview.

37 Russell 1989:31–44.

38 Sisulu interview.

39 Anonymous 1989:24.

40 Schreiner interview.

41 Sisulu interview.

42 Mtintso interview.

43 *Ibid.*

44 *Ibid.*

45 Makhoere 1988.

46 FEDTRAW 1987.

47 Schreiner interview.

48 Hogan in Schreiner 1992:23–4.

49 Middleton 1991:11.

50 Duarte 1996 (see note 22).

51 *Ibid*.

52 Hogan in Schreiner 1992:31–2.

53 Irish 1993:5.

54 Interview with attorney acting in the case of *S v Gqeba* ECD, unreported case no: 53/89.

55 Zwane 1994.

56 *Ibid*.

57 Some believed that the 'third force' was a cohesive group with state backing at the highest level, but the most widely held assumption was that maverick individuals or small groups within the security forces, often with close links to the white right wing and state protection, were responsible for provoking some of the violence in order to derail negotiations (Human Rights Watch/Africa 1995: 26).

58 The Goldstone Commission of Enquiry.

59 Duarte 1996 (see note 22).

60 Reported in Peace Action Report, August 1993:10.

61 *Ibid*.:7.

62 Personal communication from a counsellor who for reasons of confidentiality cannot be named.

63 On the basis of an understanding of some of the symbolism attached to the historical role of abduction, one can suggest what significance these actions have in the present. Historically, abduction was associated with a ritualized and thus symbolic exchange of women between different clans in marriage. The right of men to control women is asserted in this socially sanctioned action. This was accompanied by the exchange of *lobolo*, bride-wealth, which in effect symbolized the reproductive significance of women. In the current conflict, these actions by hostel dwellers are a travesty of this early tradition, but clearly resonate with it. One might argue that this is part of a strategy to demoralize those engaged in the local political contest.

64 Duarte 1996 (see note 22).

65 Makhoere interview.

66 Mtintso interview.

67 *Ibid*.

68 Personal communication, Tina Sideris, psychologist working with refugee women in Mpumalanga.

69 For detailed evidence of some of the excesses see Cleaver and Wallace 1990 and Konig 1983.

70 Cock 1989:58.

71 Nordstrom 1996.

72 Thomas and Ralph 1994:81.
73 *Ibid.*:86.
74 Section 20(3)(ii) of the Act.
75 Duarte 1996 (see note 22).
76 Mandisa Monakali, reported in *The Star*, 11 April 1996:6.
77 Duarte 1996 (see note 22).
78 Middleton *et al.* 1991.
79 For example, Graycar and Morgan 1990.

3 Women and Violence in KwaZulu/Natal

ASHNIE PADARATH

Editors' Introduction

In one of its most cynical acts, the apartheid regime of South Africa created mythical 'tribal homelands' in the 1960s and then granted four of them 'independence'. Thus were Bophuthatswana, Ciskei, Transkei and Venda created and eight million people stripped of their South African citizenship. KwaZulu and five other homelands never achieved the same level of pseudo-autonomy. Traditional élites dominated these homeland regimes; they were dependent on Pretoria for their budgets and armed with new powers of patronage, policing, and control over the black populations in their juris-diction.[1] Corruption was not uncommon in these bureaucracies. Perceived as collaborators, the homeland governments were widely despised and often had to use high levels of coercion to retain control;[2] their power derived from Pretoria and their influence resided in the essential and scarce resources they dispensed – everything from land, housing, jobs and loans to residence permits, places at school, pensions and social services.

African reserves were created in the nineteenth century, much like the Indian reservations in the United States. But it was the Group Areas Act of 1950, passed after the National Party came to power, that dictated where South Africans could live and determined the massive population removals that dumped people in inhospitable and unfamiliar environments. The artificial drawing of the 'bantustans' on the map of South Africa entailed more than three million forced relocations from the 1950s to the 1980s.[3] Pretoria was never successful in making any area ethnically 'pure' but, by using ethnic identity to measure entitlement in the allocation of always inadequate resources, it was able to pit one 'tribal' group against another. 'The apartheid system was therefore able to use the very deprivation and dispossession which it imposed on Africans to "reinvent" ethnic differences.'[4] Not surprisingly, the system generated fierce resentments among these ethnic groups, a steady escalation of conflict and a cycle of violence. Following Nelson Mandela's release from prison and as a settlement was being negotiated, most of the homeland regimes collapsed; they were slated for reincorporation after the 1994 elections when the homeland system formally ended. The one exception to this transition was KwaZulu, a 'self-governing' homeland created in 1977, dominated by the Inkatha Freedom Party led by Chief Mangosuthu Gatsha Buthelezi, and destined to be reintegrated into the province of Natal.[5] Inkatha's opposition to mass action in the 1970s and 1980s brought it into conflict with the ANC, the Congress of South African Trade Unions, and the United Democratic Front. KwaZulu with some eight million Zulus had the largest population and was the most fragmented homeland. Stretching along the Indian Ocean coast from south of Durban right up to the border with Mozambique, KwaZulu was in constant dispute with the state over what territory it would control. Deliberately, the state gave it the black townships around Durban to administer, areas replete with housing shortages, political discontent and all of the problems of squatter settlements struggling to survive. It was in this environment that a variety of civic, youth and women's organizations emerged to form the United Democratic Front (UDF) in Natal's urban townships.[6] As a potential ally of the banned ANC, the UDF posed a direct threat to Inkatha's hegemony in the region. 'In many areas, people known to belong to the UDF were attacked, their homes burned, many were killed, and survivors became refugees. More than a million people fled their homes in the ensuing decade. The violence has been particularly brutal and sadistic, with considerable evidence of collusion between the South African security establishment, Inkatha, and armed vigilantes known as Amabutho.'[7]

This chapter is a testament to the extraordinary power, strength and endurance of the ordinary women of KwaZulu/Natal. The gendered nature of the experiences of women during the low-intensity civil war that has plagued the province from the 1980s has received scant attention. Violence was confined to the townships and other black areas whilst the rest of the South African population remained insulated from the conflict. While black townships burned, a few kilometres away in the city centres and middle-class suburbs people remained comfortable; their ignorance was maintained, in large measure, by a state interested in concealing the war. The paucity of research and documentation regarding women's experience of the war and violence makes chronicling these events a daunting task. It is known widely that security forces brutalize women in detention; that rape, sexual harassment, and humiliation are not uncommon methods of torture. But while the sexual nature of prison torture is the focus of much attention, the sexual brutalization of women believed to be supporters of opposing political parties has received very little emphasis or even acknowledgement. This phenomenon is especially relevant in KwaZulu/Natal, where the experiences of women have been likened to those of women in Bosnia. The aim of this chapter is to focus on the sexual brutalization of women in KwaZulu/Natal by opposing political forces, to tell the stories of the women who survived this terrible evil, to hold the horror of their memories up to the light, and to celebrate their courage, strength and fortitude.

Overview of the Violence

KwaZulu/Natal has been embroiled in a low-intensity civil war since the 1980s.[8] Such a tyranny of violence pervaded the province that KwaZulu/Natal became known as South Africa's Killing Fields. Violence first flared up in little pockets around the province and then graduated into more sophisticated, coordinated attacks. Countless lives were lost as mysterious massacre followed mysterious massacre. Although two major groups were thought to be involved in this war – the Inkatha Freedom Party (IFP) and the United Democratic Front (UDF) – it became increasingly clear that the state had engineered and fuelled the conflict. The outside world simplistically attributed it to 'black on black violence', a baffling phenomenon that blurred the picture of the struggle for freedom. This oversimplification of the conflict furthered the state's interest in perpetuating an official ideology, that black people were innately savage and had a propensity for violence.

After the unbanning of the African National Congress (ANC) in 1990, and the subsequent dissolution of the United Democratic Front, the conflict polarized ostensibly into a struggle for political supremacy between the ANC and the Inkatha Freedom Party. It was impossible for anyone to establish or maintain political neutrality. Political allegiance was determined according to where one lived or by default – if a person did not belong to one party, the assumption was he/she must belong to the other one.

Night-time raids by gunmen presumed to be security forces and/or members of opposing political parties, in which entire communities were targeted, were commonplace. The numbers of people killed and the extent to which people were displaced are still difficult to estimate. Women and children were also often the unintended victims of the violence.

In the much-publicized 1987 KwaMakhuta massacre, hit-squad members of a Zulu paramilitary unit identified Victor Ntuli, a leader of the United Democratic Front, as a person whose death would have a positive effect on the Inkatha Freedom Party. The South African Defence Force instructed the squad of eleven hit-men on how to attack the Ntuli household. They arranged to have police patrols diverted from the area and to check the site afterwards to ensure that no incriminating evidence had been overlooked. Inside the house in KwaMakhutha people were asleep after a late-night prayer meeting. There was a bang on the door followed by shots. The home was then firebombed. Everything went according to plan except for one small detail: Victor Ntuli was not home at the time of the attack. Of the thirteen people killed, most were women and children. General Magnus Malan[9] and other high-ranking military officers, as well as members of the KwaZulu Police force, later faced criminal charges: they were acquitted in 1996 for lack of sufficient evidence, provoking speculation about political machinations behind the alarming failure of the state to prove its case.[10]

The report on cases heard at the Truth and Reconciliation Commission women's hearing in Durban on 25 October 1996 stated three reasons why women were targeted in the violence in Kwazulu/Natal: some women were violated because of the role of their family and friends, and others because of where they lived. These explanations seem to highlight the dual role that women played during the last 35 years: some were activists, but even those who chose not to be were constantly targeted and violated because they were seen as the support structures in the communities.[11]

'My Experience is not Important'

To say that women suffered disproportionately during this period is trite. The perception was that the struggle for liberation from racial oppression was paramount and that gender issues were subordinate to this process. The importance placed on national reconciliation during the transition has largely overshadowed the gendered nature of women's war experiences.

What is not trite, though, is women's reticence to claim a space for themselves in the catharsis of the national psyche. Yet it was women who faced the security forces, armies and death squads that came looking for their sons, brothers and husbands. It was towards the women that men eventually directed their wrath. And it was through women that men attempted to demoralize their opponents. It was women who faced rape, that particularly gendered form of 'punishment', for belonging to either the ANC or the Inkatha Freedom Party. It was the women who kept families together and hope alive during those dark days. Until recently women did not speak of these experiences and many women carried these incidents as their private shame. Furthermore, women did not believe that they had the right to speak of these incidents or the crucial role they played in protecting themselves and their families. Several activists have spoken of women's reluctance to claim any help or support: 'These women would talk about what had happened to their sons, brothers and husbands. When we would ask them about what they had gone through they would say "Yes, I was tortured in prison, but that's not important."'[12] Women perceived and articulated their experiences as secondary to those of their husbands, sons, and fathers.

In an article entitled 'Once the funerals are over...', an anonymous author wrote of the quality of life of women who lived through the nightmare:

> Of all the suffering rape is one kind that is forever hanging over the heads of women. I know so many women who have been raped, and yet this barely makes news. All the time you have to pretend with the children that life is okay so that they can enjoy their childhood. But some of them who have witnessed or heard of these gruesome murders do see through the secrecy.... But whatever the nature of violence, the women that remain pick up the pieces. I find that I have had to go out of my way to help orphans and widows of the violence, which men rarely do once the funerals are over. The psychological and material care is shouldered completely by women. I find myself going to a funeral virtually every weekend! What a life.[13]

Survivors, not Victims

Women displayed amazing strength and fought back with an intensity and courage that belied the stereotype of women as cowering, passive victims. A member of the Black Sash[14] active in the Imbali Support Group, formed initially in response to attacks on a family, spoke thus of women's strength and courage:

> The women should not only be seen as victims of that war. Besides playing their traditional roles as mothers, wives and housewives and usually wage-earners, they were significantly involved in taking initiatives to promote peace; they were really the organisers of meetings in their communities to plan ways of dealing with crises. At these meetings I think they were more vocal than men.... Their strength transcended the western stereotype of nurturing femininity.[15]

The war in the townships also helped to build and reinforce existing alliances with women of other racial groups. White women, for example, would take turns spending the night in townships and acting as barriers and deterrents to night-time attacks. During the time that white women slept in the townships, no violence would be reported in the area. This temporarily positive effect of white women's involvement probably can be attributed to the perception that they enjoyed access to forms of power and resources that their black sisters did not, and that they were less vulnerable to the retribution faced by women in the townships.

Women of other racial groups were also instrumental in unveiling the killing in the townships, which the government was able to hide by imposing various states of emergency and severely restricting media coverage of the violence. For example, women of other racial groups organized placard demonstrations in city centres to bring attention to the violence. It is significant that these initiatives were either jointly agreed upon or emanated from women who were themselves embroiled in the violence. It is also significant that while the experiences of black and white women were starkly different, the commonality of their gendered experiences is still evident today and has laid the basis for a strong bond of 'sisterhood'.

In her submission to the women's hearing entitled 'An overview of women's struggles and their experience of politically motivated violence in Natal', Nozizwe Madlala Routledge said:

> It would be incorrect to simply see women as victims of violence. The levels of conflict have meant that women had to face the might of the police and the army, and also try to act as mediators and peacemakers while protecting their children and communities from a war they did not start. The night vigils of the women of Chesterville are well documented, where women faced the army and challenged the soldiers and police to arrest or even kill them instead of their children. Women in Mpumalanga, Maritzburg and Kwadengezi played a key role in the peace process even though their efforts were not recognized.... White women joined hands with black women and were supporting their sons who did not want to fight. These women were brutalized and harassed.... Women active in the Black Sash and the End Conscription Campaign and in the students' movement were targeted and harassed. They were thrown into police vans, detained and banned. This was the extent of the war. It did not leave anyone untouched. Women played a key role in ending the war. We want history to be told and these women honoured for the role they played. Their stories and the story of this country's painful history are intertwined. If history is to be fulfilled, women's contributions to the struggle acknowledged, the democracy we are building now must not leave them behind.[16]

The Women's Hearing

On 25 October 1996, a women's hearing was held in Durban, KwaZulu/Natal. Similar hearings were also held in other parts of the country. The hearings were organized by the Truth and Reconciliation Commission, whose brief it is to uncover the causes, extent, and nature of gross human rights violations, grant amnesty to perpetrators,[17] and recommend reparations in respect of victims. In an attempt to create a safe environment, men were excluded from attending or participating in the hearings. Ten women testified at this hearing and a further three gave submissions with an overview of the violence in KwaZulu/Natal.

Here, the invisible suffering of women took on its first bit of tangibility when they spoke, some of them for the first time, of their pain, humiliation, and anguish. The multi-dimensional nature of their suffering was exposed, and the shroud of shame was collectively lifted. They told stories of abduction and rape, sexual harassment and mutilation, bravery and tenacity.

The following two stories which were told at the women's hearing are not unique. They have been included to personalize the theoretical exposition and to illustrate that both of the opposing political parties were equally culpable. Notwithstanding the wide spectrum of political ideology, both sides saw the brutalization of women as a means to an end. It is false and misleading to believe that political parties, led predominantly by men, assumed a moral rectitude that precluded them from wielding a particular form of power that dehumanized and objectified women.

Frieda Majozi[18] was returning home to fetch some supplies after spending the night with her two sons in a school close to their home. She and the boys fled because they had been eyewitnesses to the killing of their neighbours by a group of Inkatha Freedom Party supporters. Her husband had remained at home to take care of their belongings. As she entered her home she was surrounded by a group of men whom she identified as a group aligned with the Inkatha Freedom Party. She describes what happened to her next:

> I was wearing a pinafore, Justice ripped it off with a knife and stabbed me on my feet. The others joined in assaulting me, and then held me down while Justice raped me. My husband was made to watch everything, every time he attempted to avert his eyes or turn his head they would hit him. When Justice was finished raping me they poured water on my vagina. When I attempted to close my legs they hit me. The youths took turns raping me and pouring water over my vagina. When they hurt me and I cried out they stabbed me and hit me. I eventually lost consciousness...When they left they took some chickens...When I regained consciousness in hospital I discovered that my womb was stitched and they had to perform a hysterectomy.

Police personnel refused to take a statement from Frieda or open any docket. Since then Frieda has become a recluse and she moved to an area where she is not known. Her husband is now an epileptic and is unable to work.

Khanyisile Doris Khuyzwayo, whose entire family were known supporters of the Inkatha Freedom Party, was 16 years old when she was abducted by three ANC members on her way to a doctor's appointment. She was late for her appointment and accepted a lift from a man who identified himself as a hospital clerk. Once in the car she was blindfolded and taken to a house where she saw another woman who had been abducted from Richmond (some 150 km away).

Khanyisile spent 38 days in captivity during which time she was repeatedly assaulted and gang-raped by her three abductors. She eventually managed to escape and went to the police. 'The police took me to a government doctor in Verulam. I had fallen pregnant. I was a virgin before my abduction. There was a case at the Durban Magistrates Court. The accused were found not guilty.'

Five years later Khanyisile's mother was visited by one of the men who had raped her daughter. He claimed to be the father of Khanyisile's child. Khanyisile never completed school and is deeply affected by the acquittal of her tormentors. In her statement at the Truth and Reconciliation Commission's women's hearing she asked for counselling and a bursary so she could find work and support her child.

What Did the Women's Hearings Achieve?

The women's hearings have been widely criticized for ghettoizing and sidelining women's issues. Notwithstanding the inherent weaknesses and limitations of the hearings, they gave ordinary women who did not enjoy high-profile political images an opportunity to take centre stage and assert their role in the national struggle for freedom.

The form of reparation that the Truth and Reconciliation Commission can offer survivors has also been the subject of heated debate. Among the many questions that South Africans are grappling with currently are issues such as how best to ensure that reparation does not take the form of the individual *placebo*, how it can be elevated to a level where is it not symptomatic but developmental, how best to articulate Milan Kundera's injunction that the demand for human rights be a struggle of memory against forgetting, and how to ensure that memory is victorious in this context.

The expectations and requests with regard to reparation from women testifying at the hearings are modest. Most witnesses have requested some form of counselling, financial aid for educational purposes or asked for help to apply for an Old Age Pension or Disability Grant. Apart from creating an enabling environment for women to tell their stories, the hearings also gave women a chance to celebrate their strength and highlight the various other roles that women of all racial groups played in the struggle.

Portrait of a Perpetrator

The following case is an example of the mindset of the perpetrators of crimes against women and may shed some light on the complexities of disentangling the personal from the political and sex from gender.

On 14 October 1996 the High Court in Pietermaritzburg passed sentence on former Inkatha Freedom Party hit squad member, 28-year-old Israel Hlongwane Nyoni, who was accused of the rape, murder and attempted murder of two teenage girls in 1988. His defence was that the motive for his actions was political, and he requested forgiveness for behaving 'like a wild animal'. The judge disregarded his claim and described his request as 'mealy mouthed and rehearsed'. Nyoni was found guilty and sentenced to a total of 45 years in prison. Although this was a criminal trial, the matter was coloured by the fact that Nyoni intended to apply to the Truth and Reconciliation Commission for amnesty for his 1994 conviction for the murders of six people. Nyoni is currently serving a 75-year jail sentence for that conviction. The judge, however, held that the issue of amnesty for Nyoni's prior conviction was not pertinent and had no bearing on determination of sentence in the rape case.

In his judgment[19] the presiding judge, Hurt J, said the following:

As far as aggravating circumstances are concerned, the features which appear to us to be most relevant are that the victims of your crime were two young, defenceless girls of about fourteen years of age. You told us that you concluded that they were members of the enemy camp because they were not members of the Inkatha Freedom Party. We may say we harbour a measure of doubt as to whether you genuinely came to a conclusion of this type or whether you were simply on what is sometimes called a 'frolic of your own'.... What particularly gives rise to our doubts in this respect is the fact that you satisfied your lust on the complainant in a manner which you conceded in your evidence was that of a wild animal and there are indications in your evidence that you had made up your mind to kill these two young girls before you even went to get an instruction to that effect from the person whom you regarded as your superior. Our doubt as to whether the apprehension of these two young victims was motivated by a desire to obtain information about the whereabouts of the Amaqabane [members of the ANC or its predecessor, the United Democratic Front] to whom you have made reference in your evidence, is aggravated by the fact that the motive for capturing them was a motive of revenge for the killing of an Inkatha Freedom Party affiliated girl a short while before.

It seems to us that your conduct amounted to what would be described as a serious war crime even in the context of actual military conflict. It is necessary for the Court to make [clear] its total abhorrence and disapproval of this type of conduct and in imposing sentence, to give a clear indication to other members of the community that conduct of this type cannot be treated leniently.

Hurt J's judgment and sentence signify a move on the part of the judiciary to recognize rape as a form of torture that was imposed on women at the height of violence in South Africa.

Conclusion

The indivisibility of women's human rights is a novel concept, especially in South Africa. The country is grappling with trying to reconcile human rights abuses with nation building, forgiveness, and reconciliation. Notwithstanding the marginalization of women's human rights issues, it would be a mistake to assume that there is a reluctance to address gender issues in the country. The newly appointed Commission for Gender Equality, the ratification of the United Nations Convention on Elimination of All Forms of Discrimination against Women, and the establishment of provincial gender offices all signify a consciousness of gender issues and a commitment to addressing them. Although this is encouraging, a great deal of ideological and individual evolution is required before women's rights are seen as indivisible and have the same status as other socio-political rights. The challenge that faces us now is to ensure that the rights enshrined in our new Constitution take on substance and become a reality for all women in South Africa.

Notes

1 Szeftel 1994:192.
2 Turshen 1986.
3 Platzky and Walker 1985.
4 Szeftel 1994:193.
5 For an excellent account of the complicated politics of the 1970s and 1980s, see Szeftel 1994.
6 For a detailed discussion of African women's struggles in Natal, see Beall *et al*. 1987.
7 Goldblatt and Meintjes 1996.
8 For details see Africa Watch 1993, Human Rights Watch/Africa 1994, and Human Rights Watch/Africa 1995; none of these reports mentions violence against women.
9 General Malan was Minister of Defence from 1980 to 1991. He approved counter-insurgencies in Mozambique and Angola and set up the euphemistically named Civil Cooperation Bureau, a covert agency responsible for disinformation and assassination. Despite proof that the South African Defence Force had

trained the gunmen who perpetrated the massacre at KwaMakhutha, Malan was acquitted for lack of evidence linking him directly to the killings. He did not apply for amnesty but volunteered to testify before the Truth and Reconciliation Commission in May 1997; he was the first official of the apartheid era to accept responsibility for all acts committed by forces under his command (*New York Times Magazine* 22 June 1997:38). (Editors' note.)

10 President Mandela appointed an independent investigative team to assemble the evidence against Malan and his co-defendants, but the team then handed its findings to a prosecutor, Tim McNally, an appointment of the old white regime; both McNally and the presiding judge, Justice Jan Hugo, also a hold-over from before 1994, were known to be sceptical of the claim that the state sponsored township violence (Berkeley 1996/7). (Editors' note.)

11 Report on cases heard at assassinations event hearing, 24 October 1996 and women's hearing, 25 October 1996, Durban.

12 Interview with Ann Skelton, Lawyers for Human Rights, December 1996.

13 *Sash Journal*, January 1994.

14 The Black Sash is an anti-apartheid organization that began in 1961; it ran advice offices to assist Africans caught in the labyrinth of state control. It was a small human rights organization of some 2,000 largely English-speaking and middle-class white women, most of whom were not feminists. The organization was nominated for the Nobel Peace Prize in 1987.(Editors' note.)

15 I am grateful to Fidela Fouche who provided me with this information.

16 Routledge 1996.

17 Section 20(3) of the Truth and Reconciliation Act enables the Amnesty Committee to assess whether a particular act was associated with a political objective. If it is, then the perpetrator may be granted amnesty.

18 The names of the women involved have been changed.

19 S v Nyoni (CC 32/96, Natal Provincial Division).

4 Mozambican Women Experiencing Violence

ALCINDA ANTÓNIO DE ABREU

Editors' Introduction

Led by FRELIMO,[1] Mozambicans fought a decade-long war of liberation and in 1975 gained independence from Portugal, which had ruled the country for five hundred years. The civil war that followed lasted from 1976 to 1992. A rebel band known as RENAMO[2] was created and armed by the white Rhodesian government, ostensibly to counter the threat from the Zimbabwean independence movement operating out of Mozambique.[3] After Rhodesia became the independent nation of Zimbabwe in 1980, South Africa took over the sponsorship of RENAMO, providing weapons, training and logistical support. South Africa's purpose was to destabilize the FRELIMO regime, which embraced socialism and opposed apartheid. Imminent change in South Africa, coupled with a devastating drought in 1991–2, gave both sides an incentive to negotiate an end to the military stalemate. An agreement was signed in 1994 and multiparty elections took place in 1994. The civil war cost the country US$15 billion and claimed one million lives; virtually every Mozambican family has at least one member or acquaintance who was killed or mutilated, or who 'disappeared'.[4] In this destructive war fought in the villages of the poorest provinces of the country, RENAMO destroyed or forced the closure of nearly half of all primary schools and a third of the rural health network.

Mozambican women fought valiantly in both wars; on the home front, through the Organização da Mulher Moçambicana, they lobbied for the family law project, which has never been enacted. The personal stories recounted by Mozambican women in this chapter contain all the grief of war. Aida speaks

73

of rape at gunpoint: no one knows how many weapons were brought into Mozambique, but the estimate of experts is ten million, including more than six million AK-47 assault rifles.[5] Cândida was displaced by the war; in her case she was kidnapped and ended up living in another province, far to the south of her home. She was one of tens of thousands of girls and boys kidnapped mainly by RENAMO and pressed into service. Boys younger than eight years old helped in base camps until old enough for military training; girls were kidnapped for the sexual amusement of the men, or to cook, clean and do the laundry.[6] Some 200,000 children were orphaned and another 250,000 separated from their families.[7] The war uprooted over five million Mozambicans, and it is estimated that most peasants were forced to flee at least once during the war.[8]

Rosa describes her revulsion for what RENAMO bandits did to her, their legacy leaving her unable to vote for their candidates in the 1994 multiparty elections that recast the rebels as a political party. Her reaction summarizes the dilemma of reuniting a country after civil war, especially one inscribed so brutally on the bodies of women.[9] The father of a son and daughter kidnapped by the guerrillas, António Sitoe, was resigned: 'If they are elected, you have to accept. They are going to govern us, and we must accept them.'[10] But the mother of one boy kidnapped when he was ten years old was having none of that; Marta Matusse said, 'Myself; I will never forgive them. If they were living among us in the village, in time we would forgive them, though we would not forget. As it is, I cannot forgive what they have done.'[11]

Aida had to carry the uneaten remains of a stolen cow, an example of how these unpaid armies ate off the land, impoverishing and starving the peasants. In fact nearly all of Mozambique's cattle were slaughtered during the war.[12] Rosa talks about losing more than material possessions, of assaults beyond the physical one of rape: she speaks of the loss of her dignity. The wording of the first article of the United Nations Universal Declaration of Human Rights is rarely quoted in full: 'All human beings are born free and equal in *dignity* and rights.' Governments can work to create or reinstate a culture of human rights, but how does society compensate a woman for the loss of dignity, and what do we even know about the mental, physical and social consequences for a woman's health of the violation of her dignity?

In the 16-year armed conflict that followed Mozambique's independence in 1975, many people were driven out of their homes and displaced. The majority of the refugees were women and children. This chapter gives a brief overview of the situation of women in the country and then the testimonies of three women who experienced rape during the conflict. A section on intervention follows; it describes the preventive and supportive measures put in place by three organizations to help women and the families of victims of rape. These organizations provide legal protection and promote respect for women's rights.

The Situation of Women in Mozambique

Women constitute 51.5 per cent of the population of Mozambique, which was estimated at 16,613,877 in 1994.[13] Women are also the majority of workers, constituting 60 per cent of the workforce.[14] The majority of Mozambicans are poor peasant farmers living under very difficult circumstances that include a high level of illiteracy, poor health conditions and excessive workloads. The peasants remain the main producers of food, which means they also provide for the survival of the rest of the population. The annual gross domestic product has grown in the last few years; it is now around US$100 *per capita*. The resettlement of people who had been refugees or were internally displaced is helping in the recovery of both marketed agricultural production, which grew by about 26 per cent in 1993, and subsistence agricultural production, which grew by about 23 per cent in 1994.

When the war came to an end in 1992, more than five million Mozambicans, mainly women and children, who had fled to safety on the outskirts of cities and towns or in neighbouring countries, returned home. It was in their home areas that thousands of women had been violated and killed and children kidnapped during the war; over one million people had been murdered; and houses, hospitals, schools and stores had been robbed, burnt and destroyed. Many of the children were used as soldiers, and those who experienced violence are nowadays violent too. But the women, the children and the elderly in all of the families touched by the conflict are trying to heal the wounds of war.

The war created many widows and female-headed households.[15] Restricted access to resources – credit, land, capital, technology and extension services – aggravates the situation. The poorest are burdened by unemployment and low wages. In urban areas, more and more women work in the informal sector. They are vulnerable to competition from cheap imports because of the currency devaluation that keeps the prices of imported goods artificially low and crowds out local goods.

Within this environment and as a result of armed violence, women must now deal with the increased presence of guns and of rape inescapably linked to those guns. Although we do not yet know the exact number of women who were victims of violence and experienced rape during the war, it is generally agreed that hundreds of thousands were seriously injured. Many women faced harassment and immense insecurity. They complained of being forced to have sex with soldiers during the conflict. Since the end of the war, rape has become a new social problem in the country. We used to have incest and domestic violence but not rape by groups of young people. At the same time, we are neighbours of South Africa, which has been declared one of the most violent countries because of high levels of car theft, robbery, and rape.[16] Many of our unemployed young people go to South Africa, and in my analysis I see violence as a generalized problem in our subregion.

Women Testify about Violence

The brutality and bitterness of the armed conflict undoubtedly caused immeasurable suffering to women. It has also changed their perceptions and expectations about Mozambican society. The rights to life, liberty and security of person are fundamental; these rights and freedoms were strongly violated and this experience colours women's hopes for the future.

I collected the interviews reproduced below in Zambezia and Maputo provinces in 1994 for a survey on women in conflict situations.[17] Zambezia is situated in the centre of the country and is one of the most densely inhabited areas. Maputo Province is in the south; it contains the capital and shares borders with South Africa and Swaziland.

Aida
Aida lives in Maputo. She is married, has four children and a grandson. She describes the atrocities she endured during the war and her feelings about her experiences.

It was in 1992 when they took me and my husband to Matsequenha where we stayed for three days. They had stolen food and clothing from my house and did the same in the neighbourhood. Afterwards they compelled me to carry everything and follow them. They were eight armed men. We walked for hours and mid-way they forced us to have sexual relations with them and they repeated it on the way to the base in front of everybody, including my husband. They beat me on my head with the butt of the gun because I was refusing to have sexual relations with them and because I didn't want to talk.

On the third day of our journey, we arrived at a base where we rested. Here they killed, cooked and ate a cow. They asked me why I wasn't talking and I said nothing and kept quiet.

On the fourth day I had to load the rest of the meat that they didn't eat. We left early in the morning and walked about three hours, arriving at another base, bigger than the first one. They put us all together and seated us on the ground.

Then they separated boys and girls from women and men. The bandits[18] ordered the adults to leave and they stayed with the young people. My husband, the others and I, after leaving the load, walked back home where I arrived full of pain with my feet swollen.

I would like peace to be a reality because I don't like to see such suffering anymore! If I lay my eyes on the bandits who made me do this, as a woman I can't do anything, but the government should send them back to their original areas. We can forgive them if they will put an end to all these cruelties!

Cândida

Cândida is a 20-year-old woman living at Matola-Rio without any prospects for her future life. She describes how she suffered when she was kidnapped during the war.

I was kidnapped in 1984 and came back home in 1994. I lived in Gaza province when I was ten years old. I was sleeping when I heard the scary noise of the door being forced open. I woke up in a hurry along with the rest of my family. The attackers took also my mother and grandmother who were assassinated later on. My brother was also kidnapped. On the way to the place of captivity I saw people being brutally killed and houses and stores burnt. In captivity I witnessed a woman dying after being raped.

When I arrived in captivity I was given to a couple with whom I had to live. But that man's woman later handed me over to him for 'sex work'. That man violated me without any pity!

We tried to escape once but the soldiers shot at us and we were kidnapped again. I never saw the beginning of my periods. When I came back I had stomach aches. Now I live with my father who took me to the health centre where I was treated and the pain stopped.

MULEIDE (the Association of Women, Law and Development, a national NGO) sent Cândida to the hospital, although at that time the organization was only doing research to define strategies to deal with violence against women.

Rosa

Rosa is a peasant living in Zambezia province. She is married and has six children. She was captured at three different times. She talks about how revolted she is by what she saw and experienced.

The first time I was forced to follow them they raped my daughter. The second time two men compelled me to have sexual intercourse. And the last time they tried it on the way to the camp and I refused because I'm old and very tired of all those things. So they ill-treated me.

They had already pillaged all the crops I had produced on my plot. The captors asked me how I could cultivate maize that year when the other peasants couldn't manage to grow anything.

I am disgusted and I can't vote for these people. They did me a very bad deed. They took everything from me including my dignity and I lost my brother. Till now I don't know whether he is alive or not.

When they raped my daughter they were many. She cried out and their commander ordered them to stop. He was concerned about the sacked goods.

Intervention

When the war came to an end, some of these women were able to benefit from the treatment and legal advice developed by different institutions and organizations. Others tried to find solutions to their traumas and problems by using traditional healers.

In this section we explain what Kulaya, MULEIDE and Kurarama are doing in relation to violence against women. Before these organizations and institutions were established, victims of violence didn't benefit from any support other than routine legal and medical procedures. Neither the police nor the courts[19] were sufficiently sensitive because discrimination against women still exists in Mozambican society.[20]

Kulaya
Kulaya is a word in Changana that means counselling in terms of education. It is the name of the psychological rehabilitation centre that was created in November 1995 to deal with issues related to violence against women – physical, psychological and sexual violence. Kulaya functions as a psychological rehabilitation centre for children and young people; it is located at the Central Hospital of Maputo and is linked to the Faculty of Medicine.[21] Kulaya works with MULEIDE, and with the legal and medical services and networks, to take cases to the police and the courts.

Researchers at Kulaya have carried out five studies of violence experienced by people treated and assisted by the unit. Four studies were carried out by Manuela Almeida: one of psychological issues in adolescent victims of sexual abuse seen at Maputo Central Hospital (1996); another of young victims of violence seen at Maputo Central Hospital (1996); a third of the ideas and manifestations of violence in students at the Eduardo Mondlane University, carried out in 1993–5; and a fourth of psycho-social issues affecting women victims of violence attending the psychiatric and psychological services at Maputo Central Hospital in 1995–6. A fifth study of the use of physical and sexual violence against women was done in 1994–5 at Maputo Central Hospital by Dr António Anchonfok Lee (March 1996). On the basis of this research we came to realize that sexual abuse is a taboo subject in Mozambique, since there is no database and a lack of information about the incidence and prevalence of this problematic issue.

In examining the causes of violence, we concluded that all of the problems and effects are related to the war, and that the war is responsible for the increased violence against women in our society. The actual conditions of life in low-income families aggravate the rate of violence. These families suffer joblessness, which creates emotional disagreements; the adult members of the household are so busy trying to survive that they don't plan time to care for and talk to their children, and this creates developmental problems.

With regard to the characteristics of the sample we studied, all of the subjects are female; they are young girls, adolescents, and women between the ages of four and 35 years who attended Kulaya from 1993 to 1996. In 1996 the average age of victims of sexual abuse was 13 years. The majority of the victims are single; most are students at the first level of primary school; others are young people not in school and housewives. Most acts of sexual violence take place in the evening, but some occur during the day. Most of the attackers are unknown to the victims, but some are neighbours, friends or employers.

We found a range of symptoms. One of the psychological effects clearly shown by the victims is traumatic stress syndrome. The victims have various levels of anxiety, depression, anguish, fear and insecurity, among other symptoms. We asked them about their life perspectives and prospects. Only 22.9 per cent want to study and follow up their studies; 35.4 per cent want to go on living at home, selling informally what they manage to make there; 14.6 per cent were housewives in their childbearing years. One of the feelings they express is the desire to forget what happened, to be happy and build a home of their own, to buy clothing, bedding and a television set. They want life to return to normal, to have friends and play with them and eventually get married. Some of them said they would like to be nurses, medical doctors, lawyers, journalists and teachers.

It seems to us, looking at women victims of violence, that their universe is very restricted, and that these restrictions are linked with their limited potential. The limitations are imposed by the marginal conditions in which they live, by their lack of information, and by their primary reactions in terms of their ideas and immaturity.

What Is Kulaya doing? Based on our studies and other observations, Kulaya is taking measures to address the problems faced by the victims and their relatives. Kulaya intends to improve its services so that it can contribute to the restoration of personal dignity. Concretely, this means that Kulaya would like to connect with other institutions and NGOs to integrate the victims who attend their centre into literacy campaigns, professional basic training, non-formal education, and programmes to access credit to reduce their level of poverty and improve their living conditions.

The victims of sexual abuse are temporarily hospitalized while Kulaya tries to arrange for their reintegration into family and society and to provide for their mental and physical welfare. Among the teenagers, the psychological trauma leaves them with a slight incapacity in their school life and personal relationships. Their insecurity and weak self-control sometimes give rise to impulsiveness and the explosive release of pent-up tensions and aggression, which increase the difficulties of readaptation. These teenagers are trying to express their feelings about the lack of contact with their parents and relatives who are so busy just surviving that they don't have time for the children.

The principal activities undertaken by Kulaya are testing of intellectual capacity and psychopathology; the study of personality features; medical examinations followed by consultations; individual and group therapy; psychopharmacology; and sexual, social and civic education.

A large number of parents who accompany their children during the consultations demonstrate interest only in the police report so that they can ask for reparation. Our work with parents focuses on their need to inform their children about the risks of talking to people they don't know and accepting invitations from strangers, the dangers of walking alone in the streets, about proper hours to go out, and about sexuality. Kulaya is trying to make parents understand the need to collaborate in their daughter's treatment and to explain to them the nature of the victim's trauma and incapacity, so that parents will be the first to help and find support for their daughters.

Kulaya analyses preventive measures and believes they should deal, on one hand, with issues related to the cycle of violence in society and, on the other hand, with sexuality, starting with pre-adolescents at the first level of primary school, including sexual and social education. It is important to explain the life cycle according to Mozambican cultural realities, taking into consideration the contents of initiation rites and other ceremonies, so that treatment programmes and education campaigns can realize their objectives. The initiation rites are part of the rite of passage (the ceremony and rituals that accompany changes of status that occur in the course of a lifetime). The initiation ceremony is used to integrate the adolescents into adult life.

MULEIDE

MULEIDE[22] is a national NGO with the goal of empowering women through the law. MULEIDE was constituted on 7 December 1991; its main activities are legal education and training, publications, counselling, and a legal aid clinic.

MULEIDE provides the initial care for victims when they escape from their attackers. The association has offices for counselling and legal assistance in three provinces covering the northern, central and southern zones of the country. There are professionals in these offices to assist the victims. The specialists work with a core of activists against violence. An activist is a person, male or female, who works at the grassroots level where she or he lives and who is trained to give the first assistance to the victims.

MULEIDE has developed materials on concepts with a gender perspective as well as a methodology and a working method for assisting victims of violence. The activists have a manual and 'The Victim's Book' is also available to victims, relatives and friends, and others experiencing violence or wanting to help. Among other things, MULEIDE IS trying to promote local cooperation between police, judicial authorities and organizations for human rights education and protection of victims.

Since the Fourth International Conference on Women held in Beijing in 1995, MULEIDE has been trying to prevent violence against women by making the 'private public', that is by bringing taboo issues like sexual abuse into public forums for discussion and by making battering a crime and a violation of women's human rights. MULEIDE organizes seminars, workshops and dramatic productions to educate people and change societal attitudes towards violence against women. In the past, women were educated to obey their husbands, and when a man battered his wife, she had to accept it as a proof of his love because it was 'her fault'. It is becoming common to hear some men say during counselling sessions: 'After Beijing I don't beat my wife anymore!' Others say: 'I didn't know that it was a crime to batter my wife, you know, I thought it was part of our culture!' That is the reason why drama and popular education, as well as the media, are so important in civic education for change.

It is interesting to note that initially MULEIDE brought to the seminars young people whose parents were violent or who lived in or created a violent environment; now these young people are among the activists against violence.

Wife beating is one thing; it was culturally accepted by the society. In the past girls were educated to respect their husbands and husbands had the right to beat their wives to instil discipline and respect. But rape has a different impact on society. Rape is something that shocks Mozambicans.

Kurarama

Kurarama, a word that means 'to live' in the Chindau language, is a nongovernmental organization constituted to deal with relationship therapy. Kurarama organizes educational and training materials and programmes to teach self-esteem, self-confidence, and assertiveness to victims and other people interested in improving their selves and their social welfare. It is a new, nonprofit organization at the national level with headquarters in Maputo. Both women and men are members. The family and the individual are the focus of Kurarama, which approaches gender relations in the household and all the problems related to it. The chairperson of the General Assembly is Maria Elisa Pinto and the President is Cecilia Abreu, my sister. I am a member.

'All Against Violence'

Due to the increase of violence against women, last year women's NGOs and government institutions organized a campaign, 'All Against Violence'. The organizations involved wanted to have a multidisciplinary approach so they coordinated a set of activities. Tasks were distributed as follows: Forum Mulher (The Women's Forum) coordinated activities and the dissemination of information; MULEIDE worked on legal reform and offered counselling and legal aid to the victims; Kulaya offered counselling and psychological services; the Ministry for Social Action Coordination and OMM (the Mozambican Women's Organization) created shelters for victims; AMME (the Association of Women Educators) worked with girls and teachers; and CEA, the African Studies Centre at the Eduardo Mondlane University, studied the dimensions of the problem of violence.

The campaign began on 12 September 1996 with a concert. Members of the government, leaders of political parties, Members of Parliament, religious groups and NGOs participated. The role of media during the campaign was crucial in sensitizing society to the issues of violence against women.

It is time to follow up that initiative, spreading information on preventive measures. There is a mental health network that brings together governmental institutions and NGOs that could analyse these problems and make proposals for prevention. NGOs must play a more important role in terms of intervention, and local associations and institutions organized at the community level must be involved. The mechanisms that connect these institutions and organizations with the police and courts must be reactivated.

Conclusion

The government that was constituted after the general and multiparty elections in 1994 dedicated its first five-year programme to the principle of non-violence against women. The Ministry of Social Action Coordination and the police are starting projects to enable social workers and members of the police force to support and protect women from violence.

Although the war ended in Mozambique, its brutal impact on society is still alive – the violence, the destruction of prospects for development, the inability of families to be economically productive, the tearing of the social fabric and human solidarity. Five years of peace are not enough to rebuild society and restore the social fabric. We cannot repair the years of suffering when in their minds people are still screaming, when they feel hopelessly burdened with a disabled child or wife who reminds them that there was a war that has ended but is still alive.

There is need for a more comprehensive group of instruments to address the problems faced by women in armed conflict and a need to analyse their problems in a gender perspective. Beyond that, we have to contribute to the creation of a society with more humane qualities.

Notes

1 Frente de Libertação de Moçambique.
2 Originally called the Selous Scouts and trained by Ian Smith's regime to fight against Zimbabwe's liberation movement, RENAMO is the Portuguese acronym for the Mozambique National Resistance. It was a warlord army detached from any state apparatus, with no other goal than warfare (Luckham 1994:19).
3 For a history of the colonial period see Newitt 1995; for the post-independence history of the war see Hanlon 1991.
4 Harsch 1993:5.
5 Daley 1997.
6 Keller 1994.
7 Harsch 1993:3.
8 Hanlon 1996:99.
9 Mozambique has never considered convening a truth and reconciliation commission like the one in South Africa. An official at the United States Department of State commented: 'There is a need to empty wounds of all the old infection before healing can start. But in some countries, like Angola and Mozambique, I'm not sure you'd have anything left if you cleaned out all the infection.' (Quoted in Hayner 1994:6.)
10 Keller 1994.
11 *Ibid.*
12 Hanlon 1996:99.
13 CNP/DNE 1994:7.
14 MINEC 1995:5.
15 Officially, 23 per cent of Mozambican households are headed by women, but many men migrate in search of work, and if migrant husbands were taken into account, the figure would probably be much larger (Hanlon 1996:72). (Editors' note.)

16 In the cases of car theft, the police from Mozambique and South Africa are working together.

17 Some of the women in Maputo were interviewed by a BBC journalist during the multiparty and general elections.

18 It is common for Mozambicans to refer to RENAMO guerrillas as bandits.

19 For an analysis of the courts, see Welsh, Dagnino and Sachs 1987. (Editors' note.)

20 One of the basic objectives of Mozambique after independence was the elimination of colonial and traditional structures of oppression, including traditional relations between men and women (Welsh, Dagnino and Sachs 1987). (Editors' note.)

21 The Portuguese acronym for the centre is CERPIJ.

22 In Portuguese, *Mulher, Lei e Desenvolvimento*.

5   Attack with a Friendly Weapon

ASMA ABDEL HALIM

Editors' Introduction

Although the British were the *de facto* rulers of the Sudan, Egypt and Britain jointly ruled the country through an arrangement called the Condominium. Sudan was granted independence in 1956, inheriting a colonial policy that divided the Christian and animist black south from the Islamic and Arabic-speaking north. Civil war broke out almost immediately between the government, which was controlled by northerners, and southerners who demanded autonomy. The first phase lasted from 1957 to 1972, when an agreement was signed in Addis Ababa. Ten years later, the government of President Colonel Jaafer Nimeiri provoked a renewal of the conflict by breaching the Addis Ababa treaty. He subsequently extended *Shari'a* law[1] to the non-Muslim south, adding more fuel to the war, and paving the way for the current government to launch a religious war. The Sudanese People's Liberation Movement and Army have been the major opponents of successive northern-dominated governments; their objective is self-determination for the southern Sudanese.[2]

The civil war in Sudan is now Africa's oldest conflict and it continues with no sign of abatement. The war has destroyed the pastoral economy of the southern region and has impoverished, displaced and slaughtered southern Sudanese. Estimates of the numbers of dead, most from the Dinka tribe, range from 1.3 to 2.3 million. Famine is a recurrent theme, the result of raids by the Sudanese military and by government-armed militias drawn from ethnic groups in competition with the Dinka. The use of militias proved cheaper than deploying the regular army. The famines were directly manipulated by militias, merchants and government personnel, who profited from their control of grain markets and their ability to raise prices artificially in Dinka areas; to that end, they were not above sidelining railcars filled with food relief. Cattle markets were similarly manipulated.[3]

Along with this decimation and dehumanization of southern tribes has come the return of slavery, as tribal militias capture women and children as war booty. The numbers are unknown. One Swedish missionary estimated that at least 50,000 girls had been enslaved in the north.[4] When the National Islamic Front took power in 1989, it restricted daily life and political activity. Severe punishment is meted out to anyone who breaks the rules and expresses his or her political or civil independence. Not all northerners want this war or condone this genocide. But it is dangerous to criticize the war openly. The National Security Act allows security agents arbitrarily to detain anyone for up to six months without judicial oversight in secret detention centres referred to as 'ghost houses', where torture and ill-treatment are commonplace. Many intellectuals have been forced into exile. In February 1997, Asma sent us this message concerning the military trial of the 21 Port Sudan defendants, ten of whom are civilians, including seven who were never in the military.

> The past month has just been a nightmare. I am trying to keep my sanity by looking at other things but there is no escaping the fact that I am losing sleep over this. Human Rights Watch did a good job on this trial.[5] But they cannot address unsubstantiated 'facts'. The facts are that there are at least 30,000, yes, thirty thousand detainees around the country. They are mainly students, lawyers, doctors, and other professionals, especially trade unionists. Some of them are being tortured and others are suffering from the fact that the government cannot provide enough food and water for them.... The unprecedented violence of this government in the north was never treated in the way it deserves.
>
> Everywhere that people are concerned with Sudan I keep stating that if the infrastructure of justice is lost in the north then the south is more vulnerable than ever. The power is concentrated in the north. The south just became a battleground that everyone is using for their own purposes.... One idea is to separate the south from the north. It turns out the southerners do not want a separation. When the war was started by southern rebels, they were not saying let us go and kill the Muslims! The religious overtone was this government's way of attracting arms from Iran and Iraq.
>
> All the universities and higher institutes have been closed for the past four weeks and may remain so indefinitely! Everyone who can stir up any opposition is stashed safely in an unmarked jail.... This may be the time to direct all eyes towards the storm hanging over Khartoum, which could easily turn into something worse than Mogadishu.

Little is documented about sexual violence against women in the war-plagued southern Sudan, although women are the daily victims of phallic warfare aimed at checking their participation in public discourse. Through mass rape and other forms of torture specific to the female population, perpetrators of these heinous crimes believe they can inflict debilitating blows on women's psyches. The international community has unfortunately remained taciturn about the plight of these invisible women and has treated them as a disposable class of humanity. Forsaken by their own government, ignored by the international community, some women in the war-torn areas of the Sudan have abandoned their traditional locales and have ventured into the northern cities where they fall victim to further marginalization and near dehumanization. Others have crossed the border to live in refugee camps that do not protect them from gender-specific crimes.

Southern Women Seek Refuge in the North

The city of Khartoum daily receives new faces from all of Sudan's provinces. Racially and religiously diverse, the Sudan reflects all that Africa suffers from; it is its microcosm. The capital city, Khartoum, has inhospitably housed populations fleeing the war-devastated southern Sudan. Major streets of Khartoum are now thronged with dark, tall, dignified women who have fled the south for dear life. But in their new haven, things are hardly any brighter. Winning a piece of bread is another battle to wage in their new urban setting. At noon, under the blazing sun of Khartoum, these women gingerly entreat drivers for a little something to help them fuel their flickering lives through another day. Fortunately, drivers don't speed by because the traffic is usually bogged down in rush hour by temperamental traffic lights; drivers have no choice but patiently to inch their way forward on the tarmac. Novices to vagrancy, the women are not insistent in teasing a penny out of reluctant givers; they knock once, but no more.

Several things seem to set them apart from the rest of the population. They look racially distinct from most northerners. Khartoum has also witnessed a wave of Arab-speaking, drought-stricken women and children who have taken to begging as a means of survival in the all-consuming environment of the capital city. But because of their religious, racial, and linguistic ties with the mainly Arab urban population of the capital city, life is not nearly as hard for them as it is for the women from the south. Facility with the Arabic language allows women from drought-stricken areas who beg to engage in long drawn-out conversations with some of the most skinflint urbanites. To buy time to attend to traffic matters, drivers usually trade money for peace with these loquacious Arabic-speaking mendicants.

The southern women, on the other hand, are not known to have been beggars, and they are not good at it. Traditionally, they lived in tightly knit social structures where the community lent unfettered support to all its members. Wherever their itinerant life style carried them, they unselfishly shared whatever resources were available to them with their less fortunate relatives and friends. Houses of relatives in the north, big or small, would host relatives coming from the south. One southerner noted that the war and the consequent displacement have created many radical changes in behaviour:

> war has affected our traditional behavior that is distinctive to us. We are doing many things that should have been the responsibility of the community but are now individual responsibility.... Failure to share and live together as family or as tribe has encouraged adoption of individualistic behaviors which are not helpful to our communities. Even eventual help that we could receive from organizations are not meant for groups but for individuals, e. g. UNHCR identity cards, grants, jobs or even problem solution. The community oriented behavior turned into an 'I don't care for the others' attitude.[6]

Women find this behaviour frustrating and painful, especially when they realize that all the changes brought by being uprooted, whether bad or good, are permanent.

Times have changed and the dignity of the southern women has been swept away systematically, right under the unobservant eyes of the international community, leaving these victims disappointed and tearful. People who did not have to beg when they were masters of their destiny have been reduced to moral nonentities. The northerners ask, 'Can't they just go back home and leave our streets in peace?' But the homeland these women left is shipping soldiers' bodies back to the capital city, while after each attack by the army, the government militias or other combatants, still more bodies are left to feed the vultures. And amidst this tragedy one senses a mounting will among the women and a determination to continue living in spite of the odds.

The war in southern Sudan is the oldest civil war in the world, yet it is the least known. This tragic tale began on 18 August 1955 when some southern soldiers in the town of Torit waged an armed protest against the British-instigated policies that discriminated against southerners. The Torit uprising was, in fact, symptomatic of a greater social malaise that plagued the nation prior to independence. That malaise laid the roots for the discord which was to tear through the social fabric, demoralizing the nation and shattering its very existence.

Most northerners wish away the objective reality of the southern question. They elect to listen instead to the more sedating media rendition of the issue. The media version tends to brush the problem of the south aside as a creation of western-educated southern Sudanese. But experience teaches us that the problem of the south rests on deeply ingrained injustices suffered by the south at the hands of successive Sudanese governments. The civil war in the Sudan has been raging for 32 of the 42 years of independence. There has not been an equitable power-sharing mechanism that would guarantee the south its central role in the affairs of the country. In the past 30 years, southern resistance to the north's monopoly of power has resulted in the displacement of nearly four million people from their homes. In these circumstances, women and children have no choice but to migrate north to the centre of power. Displaced persons, blessed with the gift of proximity to an international border, would not miss the opportunity of taking refuge in those neighbouring countries rather than fleeing to Khartoum.

Women caught up in the war zone endure both mental and physical violence in a situation where killing and maiming of civilians are everyday occurrences. Research by uprooted southern women living in Cairo shows that mental suffering not caused by physical violence is no less severe than that caused by physical violence.[7] Often women do not know the whereabouts of their spouses; they could as well be soldiers on either side of the war, or dead, or simply alienated from their families. Left to fend for themselves and their children, these women flock to the most accessible areas in the region in the hope that they will find some peace and security away from their devastated homes. Migrating to northern Sudan becomes the obvious alternative. But once in the north, they have to adjust to city life. They wrap themselves in whatever clothes they have and under those clothes they bear their wounded honour and dignity. They press the wrappers against their bodies and start the day that usually takes a genius to get through.

While in the cities, these unfortunate women quickly become the dartboard on which the morally righteous Islamic government of the Sudan tests the efficacy of *Shari'a* law, the so-called immutable divine law of juridical Islam. Islam outlaws the consumption of alcohol and punishes those who violate this sacred ordinance with up to 80 lashes. Displaced southern women are known to brew liquor to provide for their children. Under no circumstances will the government, charged with the protection of public morals, allow these morally suspect women to corrupt the Muslim community. They must be punished in accordance with the provisions of the *Shari'a*, no matter what factors impelled them to break the law. Daily, the system sends out its representatives in a frantic hunt for these sociocultural pariahs; it catches and incarcerates them in filthy custody cells. Soon, they will be taken to the court to answer criminal charges of brewing and selling liquor or prostitution, because women's resistance to rape merits a charge of prostitution. At the criminal court, divine justice seems to reinforce the sense of injustice suffered by the southerners in the civil war. The courts interpret the southerners' attempts to make ends meet as criminal conduct punishable under the penal code. The court summarily sentences them to imprisonment, and in prison they are subjected to further forms of degradation.

The situation of the women's section of Omdurman prison, which a UN Special Rapporteur visited twice in 1993, is indeed desperate.[8] Most of the inmates are southern women sentenced for making or selling alcoholic drinks. The prison was designed to house less than one hundred prisoners, but during the last three years the number of inmates was constantly over six hundred, in comparison with the years before 1989 when less than a dozen women were detained in the prison at any one time. Except for periodical releases,[9] it appears that the competent authorities did not undertake any of the measures requested by the UN to improve the situation or to deal with the social causes of this phenomenon, which over-whelmingly affects southern women living in Khartoum.

War and displacement also have contrary, unexpected and positive effects. Displaced men have found it hard to forget about their degrees and higher education and to accept manual work that brings in an income. Women immediately feel that their families have to survive and they go out to work as housemaids or nannies or workers in different institutions. The men are content to baby-sit the kids while women go out to work. One interesting result of these responses is the change in women's status due to their changed role from housewives to breadwinners. Women have vowed never to give up this change and never to revert to the status of being owned or inherited or of being revered only as mothers and wives without having any property or freedom of movement. Many Sudanese, especially men, are not optimistic about a future with women who have real power. Women are predicting that violence could result if women insist on their newly acquired status.

The War in the South

The women who have made it to the north seem to be luckier than those who have stayed in the war-shattered areas. In the north, they live on the outer fringes of the cities where city dwellers shed the scum of the earth and the damned. In the south, their daily existence is bedevilled by the fear of being raped, enslaved or killed, or by the horror of witnessing their loved ones expire in routine aerial bombardments carried out by the Islamic government against southern villages.

'Why should a woman feel injured if she is raped?' The rhetorical questioner believes it is the same physical act a woman would experience with any man. Her husband or her father or her brother are the ones who should feel injured because rape is an act against their honour. There is only one honour at stake here, and the woman, who lives vicariously through others, just carries that honour for the males in her family. When the fathers and the brothers and the husbands go out for revenge, it is to avenge their honour, not hers. There is very little realization that

> A woman's self-respect, sense of dignity and physical integrity is shattered when at the hands of her captors she unwillingly becomes the participant observer of the planned and enforced destruction of her culturally defined womanhood. In every sense of the word, in every level of her being, the torturer's invasion involves radical disorientation.'[10]

These women have no one to whom they can tell their true stories. The official who bulldozed their makeshift homes is not going to hear their stories; he is there to clear them out of the place. They must move literally to the middle of nowhere, not knowing which hell is better – the indignity of being an inferior and treated as a stranger in a place that is part of what they call home, or the war that burns the life out of them or sends them to be captives in the hands of neighbours who think that they are entitled to capture the women and take them away. The pain of slavery can be survived when there is still hope that they may be reunited with families if they stay alive, but their very desire to go back is shattered by those who take possession of their lives.

Patriarchy is no historical contingent to the culture; it is intrinsic to the Sudanese social make-up, well grounded by reason of religion and custom. The strong authority that males wield over females is turned into a relationship tainted with ideas of ownership because men consider women as representatives of culture and bearers of the family honour. In both northern and southern Sudan, a woman fulfils a prescribed and well-defined role, specifically where sexuality is concerned. Men's ownership of women's sexual conduct positions women as the first property to be attacked and violated in times of conflict. Violations of other property may be rectified, but the damage to the owner caused by the violation of 'his women' cannot be. Society is constructed in a way that negates women's presence as human beings who have their own existence. This situation is not unique to the Sudan.

Until recently, women's bodies were seen as private and were not of concern to the international community, with the exception of sexual assault against women civilians during armed conflict. Humanitarian law requires occupying powers to protect the civilian population, and soldiers who rape may be punished as war criminals. This is the case whether sexual assault is part of an international strategy to suppress or punish the civilian population or the result of failure by commanders to exercise proper discipline over their troops.[11] Therefore sexual assault of women is never a 'private' matter. Yet rape was almost universally considered a private act in the sense that it should be kept at home and be dealt with by men rather than by states or the international community. It was only in 1996 that rape was recognized as a human rights violation and as torture. 'Rape has never been the concern of the international community,' Justice Goldstone of the International Tribunal for War Crimes in Former Yugoslavia said in an interview at an early stage of those investigations. 'We have to deal openly with these abuses.'[12] This European civil war has created a precedent. The use of rape and forcible pregnancies as a genocidal weapon in Yugoslavia highlighted rape as a heinous crime against humanity. Perhaps the fact that Yugoslavia is a European country made it a strong focus of the Western media, which helped create this outrage against rape. The Fourth International Women's Conference at Beijing and the demands of women for accountability of states that violate the rights of women or fail to prevent violations of their rights also echoed throughout the world and the international bodies. Women's voices and actions left a tremendous impression on those who heard them and highlighted the suffering of women as human beings.

Slavery: Women as War Booty

Since 1989 the war has taken on a religious nature. A military coup in June 1989 brought to power a leadership that vows to reconstruct the social and religious life and institutions of the population of the whole country. Chants of *Allahu Akbar* fill the air, and able-bodied youth are being recruited with promises of *Shahada* or martyrdom. Only 5 to 10 per cent of the population of the predominantly animist south is Christian; religion has added a new dimension to the war they are fighting. It may be argued that this dimension was already there, but without doubt it is the dominant feature now.

Women, who represent the honour of the enemy, have always been captured to degrade opponents. In this new religious battle, women are considered legitimate spoils of war. The idea that women are booty and, as such, are rightfully owned by those who capture them, stems from centuries-old *Shari'a* law regarding slavery and war booty. The belief that this practice is religiously sanctioned in a religious state caught on quickly with the Muslim groups living in the territories adjacent to the southerners. The fact that the southerners are 'infidels' – either Christians or animists – lifted any doubts from the minds of those holding women that they were entitled to enslave them after winning a battle. The legacy of slavery in the Sudan still persists and taking southerners for slaves apparently poses no problem in the minds of those who think it is legal. Women were enslaved in the past, a past as close as the 1930s and 1940s when women were the most valuable of chattels. In the first half of the twentieth century, the colonial powers outlawed slavery; slave owners resorted to *Shari'a* courts to establish a marriage between them and their women slaves. Women's status as concubines was turned into the status of marriage so that the masters could keep their women slaves.[13]

The *Shari'a* courts failed to establish any anti-slavery laws because, to this day, slavery is thought to be legal in *Shari'a* law, as An'Naim has pointed out:

> In my view, it is utterly abhorrent and morally indefensible for *Shari'a* to continue to sanction slavery today, regardless of the prospects of its practice. Moreover, the fact that slavery is permissible under *Shari'a* does have serious practical consequences not only in perpetrating negative social attitudes toward former slaves and segments of the population that used to be a source of slaves but also in legitimizing forms of secret practices akin to slavery. In the Sudan, for example, images of slavery under *Shari'a* and Islamic literature continue to support negative stereotypes of the Sudanese from the southern and the western parts of the country, which were sources of slaves until the late nineteenth century. Moreover, recent news reports indicate that Muslim tribesmen of southwestern Sudan feel justified in capturing non-Muslims from southern Sudan and keeping them in secret slavery.[14]

There is a history of failure on the part of Islamic law to outlaw slavery or frown upon it. The only way out was to resort to secular law to outlaw slavery. An'Naim further stresses that slavery will 'remain lawful unless we find an adequate and systematic reform methodology to implement the original intention of the Qura'an.'[15] The case of Sudan proves that the forgotten practice of slavery may be revived in the minds of the believers unless it is actually abolished.

With the revival of the religious state in the Sudan, a revival of the traditional *Shari'a* is inevitable. Despite the fact that there is a clear prohibition of slavery or any type of forced labour in the Sudanese penal code (Criminal Law of 1991), the traditional ideas are what stick in the mind rather than what is written in the books. Turning the civil war into a religious war waged against infidels under the chants of *Allahu Akbar* made it that much easier for citizens to perceive of the south as the land of unequals who may be treated in any way sanctioned by religious norms. The women taken out of the war zones were taken mainly by the armed militiamen from southwestern Sudan. In April 1996, for example, armed militiamen captured scores of villagers from different locations in the Aweil-Wedweil area, along the Babanusa–Wau railway, who had gathered in the hope that a UN train distributing food was approaching. Similar events had taken place in that area under the same circumstances in previous years. At the end of October 1996, raids and abductions were again reported while a government train guarded by the military and armed militias proceeded northward from Wau. Six villages were reportedly destroyed on the eastern side of the railway line, between Ariath and Maker, with five people killed and 20 women and children abducted.[16]

The women are raped either to show the southerners how they were defeated or because the women are thought of as booty and do not have the right to object to the masters' whims. Southerners believe that this is a genocidal war. Men from the west or the north intentionally impregnate women so as to bring into the south children fathered by other men and change the demography of the whole area. Ethnic lines that hold southern tribes or ethnic groups together will be destroyed in the region forever. The women endure mental violence when they become creatures without rights and are forced to bear unwanted children fathered by the enemy. At the same time they suffer separation from their own children. They also suffer the physical violence of forced labour and forced reproduction, over and above the rape that destroys their souls and their self esteem.

Women in certain areas suffer these forms of violence at the hands of both government militia and rebels. In zones where rebels and militias drive each other out, women suffer a double jeopardy when government militias treat them as rebel property and when the rebels treat them as property in the government territory. This happens mainly in the southwestern regions. When rebel troops raided Kurmuk and Gaisan, two major cities in southeastern Sudan, in May 1996, the General Women's Union of Sudan, a government-sponsored body, issued a statement condemning the rape of women in the district. SUNA, the official news agency, carried reports that the high school students, all girls, were either abducted or raped by rebel troops. The international community did not respond to their appeal, and the women's union sent faxes around the world seeking support. As usual, both sides, government and rebel, exchanged accusations and both denied, not just their responsibility for such acts, but the sheer fact that any rape took place. The resolutions passed by the UN Commission on Human Rights regarding the human rights situation in the Sudan, 1996/73 and 1997/59, both failed to mention rape among the atrocities of the civil war. Even human rights organizations that follow slavery of women and children in the Sudan do not seem to treat rape as a proven atrocity against all parties to the war. Human Rights Watch/Africa did not address rape in its elaborate report on the region.[17]

Louis Farrakhan, the African-American leader of the Nation of Islam, challenged journalists to verify the rumours of slavery. An NBC television programme, *Dateline* (24 October 1996), investigated acts akin to slavery in southern Sudan, and the *Baltimore Sun* confirmed that a form of captivity and release for money does exist.[18] Although portrayed as a duel between the media and a controversial African-American leader who denies the existence of any wrongdoing in the war, the investigation gave the issue of slavery much-needed attention. This criminal behaviour goes unpunished: the government flatly denies the existence of the practice. When cornered by news agencies and other investigators, the government formed its first investigative committee in February 1996. *Dateline* produced scenes of children lined up to be exchanged for money and interviewed men who were exchanging the children for money. The men claimed that they were just getting their expenses for helping the women and children get back home. Women talked about their plight, their stolen souls, their treatment as objects, their unwanted children from the sexual abuse they endured at the hands of their keepers. At US congressional hearings in March 1996 about human rights abuses in southern Sudan, Father Macrum Gisees, a Sudanese Catholic Bishop, testified that holders of southern Sudanese women and children argued that the women are war booty as a defence in court. That defence is legitimized by the people's perception of *Shari'a* and what it says about a war with infidels.

Francis Deng, UN Special Representative for Internally Displaced People, tells about a prominent religious leader who intimated to him that 'he and other leaders were receiving letters from their Arab followers inquiring whether it was ordained or forbidden by Islam to kill a Dinka'.[19] Deng, a Dinka himself and a son of a leading Dinka family, says that northerners dominate the Dinka through burning villages, destroying the crops, and looting livestock. The issues of rape and captivity for forced labour were not mentioned. The Dinka are not the only tribe affected, although they are the most affected by reason of their proximity to and interaction with the north.

There is a history of Sudanese women caught up in war, but it is hardly told except as anecdotes by grandmothers. They tell the stories of women who committed suicide by throwing themselves in the Nile during the civil wars of Sudan's Mahdist state, wars which lasted from 1885 to 1889.[20] In this religious conflict, warriors raped women as war booty, and many women avoided the humiliation of capture and preserved the honour of family and tribe by tying themselves together and throwing themselves into the Nile River. The stories relayed by grandmothers about the incident are full of pride in those women who protected their honour and would not let the enemy violate them. These women were said to have felt a responsibility towards the men who were unable to protect them. In other words, women's losses were counted as men's losses.

Women don't have to be combatants to be violated physically and mentally. It is almost common knowledge that women will be dragged into combat areas to be violated by soldiers. It is as if women have a duty to satiate the sexual urges that drive men in wartime. The story of Asian comfort women during World War Two[21] is but one example of how regular armies may violate women and bring them into the combat areas for that purpose. An Algerian woman testifying at the Fourth International Women's Conference held in Beijing described how young women were raped by Islamist rebels and forced into 'marriages'.[22] Their stories bear witness to the fact that a woman's sexual life and organs are nothing more than a commodity to be taken from enemy territory. Women's work as housekeepers, as cooks, cleaners, and nurses, are not services to be purchased in the same way as men's service as combatants. Women's work seems to accrue to men as an entitlement and is extracted from women as responsibilities towards men rather than towards the cause they are fighting for. Even when women join the fight because they believe in the cause, they are not excused from women's work.

Women Combatants

It turns out that women combatants do not have better luck than civilians. Within the rebel forces women served in different military ranks. For the Sudanese women, north and south, service in the military was available only in civilian ranks and the medical profession. Only in the rebel factions in the south are women known as combatants. The southern rebels are no exception when violence against women takes place. Gender relations are based on the subordination of women, and the same relationship survives in the different climate of war. A change of the role of the man from a breadwinner to a combatant entitles him to more rights. The change of the role of the woman from a housewife and mother to a combatant causes a further decline in her status. Forced marriages and rape seem to be common amongst combatants. Women are reminded that whatever additional roles they are entrusted with, their original role as providers of sex comes first.

A recent news article carried a first-hand report from two former woman combatants, Aroghu and Aliza, who talked about the violence against women at the war front.[23] The main faction of the Sudanese People's Liberation Army (SPLA) is estimated at 800,000 and, according to Aroghu, there are some 354 women officers below the rank of commander. Lack of promotion was not the only problem faced by women rebels, said Aroghu. They were also forced to put up with human rights abuses. 'I remember during our training in 1986 in the bushes of the Equatoria region [in the south], some of us were sexually abused not only by the Sudanese trainers, but also by Ugandan soldiers who were training us.'[24] Another woman fighter, Aliza, told the same reporter that she was tortured and detained when she refused to go to bed with the local commander. She said her rank meant little to the men. She felt that women counted for nothing in the eyes of the rebels. Aliza said that 'women must begin to fight their oppressor on all fronts. Women should prepare the ground for demanding equality and justice even through the use of armed struggle. For how long are we going to face this oppression?'[25] Her statement has nothing to do with which side she was on or whether she has changed her mind about fighting for the cause she initially took up arms to defend; it is about her being a woman and her right to do her share for her community without being violated. The leaders of the SPLA have yet to make a statement or investigate the matter. At least in the case of these military women, it is clear that they do not intend to postpone the fight for their rights till the war or peace is won. The practice of subordinating women's issues to nationalistic priorities does not seem to keep these women from demanding their rights, for which they are prepared to resort to armed struggle. The situation with women combatants seems to repeat itself whenever women attempt to be involved in what is classified as a man's place.[26]

Aliza's statement is one of the rare expressions by women of their readiness to go into an armed struggle for their rights. Throughout the nationalist movements, including the armed struggle, there seems to be a recognition of women's issues, but at the same time there is no reluctance in relegating those issues to a minor status and no hesitancy in postponing them as secondary issues that can wait till the men are done with their issues. The sheer fact that a woman's right to her bodily integrity is violated at will by the men around her shows that even what men seek to protect women from, that is honour, could also wait, since the satisfaction of men's sexual desires is more important than women's bodily integrity. The women's bodies are needed in the form of supplies that would keep the men strong and in a fighting mood. The violation of the woman by friends seems to be part of her duties, her violation by the enemy is her responsibility. She should give that body willingly for men in her quarters and be ready to protect it with her life in the case of attack by others, because a violated body is a symbol of violated honour.

State Responsibility

The international community seemed finally to acknowledge the interpretation that rape is a violation of human rights and humanitarian law when in June 1996 the International Tribunal for War Crimes in Former Yugoslavia indicted eight Bosnian Serb military and police officers in connection with rapes of Muslim women in the Bosnian war. This marked the first time sexual assault was treated separately as a crime of war.[27] Now that atrocities against women are being investigated and tried in Bosnia and Rwanda, the international community should not make any exceptions. A similar investigation and tribunal is needed in Sudan and other countries. The different rebel factions in southern Sudan should be alerted to their responsibility for their atrocities against women, and they should be told that they can expect to be called before any future tribunal.

Women's organizations around the world should support domestic organizations dealing with the rights of women and pressure the international community to pay attention to a war that is not any less atrocious than the other wars that are dominating media attention. International attention to this longest of wars should expand beyond providing food.

Although women's issues cut through all aspects of war and peace, the only debate that seems to concern the world now is whether what is going on in the Sudanese war should be called slavery or tribal rivalry. Before anyone else adds to the vocabulary of conflict, let us say that women want out of the bloody and inhumane situation, regardless of what it is called. The state should take responsibility under the law and in the name of the religion it is using to 'rescue' women and investigate all accusations. The charges being made in the international media about slavery and other violations should be openly discussed and put on the table.

The UN Special Rapporteur has reported on the situation of child soldiers and on the condition of women in Sudan. If the Sudanese state was in the dark before, this report brings the situation to light. Instead of condemning the anti-Islamic sentiments of the Special Rapporteur, the state should disseminate the results of this investigation – and the state, as well as individual perpetrators, should be held responsible for their crimes on the same basis as the tribunals in the former Yugoslavia and Rwanda. As the Sudanese saying goes, 'there is no smoke without fire'. The charges of slavery, considered by the state and the international community as only smoke, should be traced back to their origin.

In all war zones around the world, women are holding social life together; they are keeping the markets open and they are longing for peace. But do we see them at any table where peace is being negotiated? The decision to go to war was taken without consulting them or obtaining their consent, and the peace process is taking whatever direction it is taking without their input. Not only that, but we have yet to see a woman in a decision-making position at any level in the opposition. Women suffer doubly from war atrocities because they did not participate in the decision to go to war and are not party to the peace process. The government should be pinned down to its international responsibility to treat women and women's rights as integral parts of the peace process. The state should take responsibility for seeing that women are represented and their human rights protected.

Notes

1 The *Shari'a* is a body of formally established sacred law in Islam, based primarily on Allah's commandments found in the Koran; in theory it not only governs religious matters but also regulates political, economic, civil, criminal, ethical, social and domestic affairs in Muslim countries.

2 For a history of this position see Ruay 1994.

3 For a critical account of the famines see Keen 1994.

4 Keen 1994:101.

5 Human Rights Watch 1997.

6 Malou 1997.

7 Reported at the International Sudanese Studies Conference, Cairo, 11–14 June 1997.

8 Reports of the UN Special Rapporteur on the Human Rights Situation in the Sudan, E/CN/.4/1997/58 and E/CN/.4/1996/62.

9 On 5 December 1996 the President of the Sudan ordered the release of nearly 200 women from Omdurman prison. State television reportedly showed the prisoners, some carrying babies, shouting with joy when the Justice Minister announced the presidential decree that night.

10 Barry *et al.* 1984:98.

11 Fitzpatrick 1994.

12 *New York Times,* 28 June 1996.

13 Sikainga 1995; see also Mahmoud and Baldo (1987).

14 An'Naim 1990:175.

15 *Ibid.*

16 Reports of the UN Special Rapporteur on the Human Rights Situation in the Sudan, E/CN/.4/1997/58 and E/CN/.4/1996/62.

17 Human Rights Watch 1997.

18 Gilbert Lewthwaite and Gregory Kane from the *Baltimore Sun* and the Sudan Ambassador to the United States, Dr Mahdi Ibrahim, interviewed by Charlayne Hunter-Gault, Newshour segment ' Shackled Youth', 19 August 1996.

19 Deng 1993.

20 Sudan fell under Egyptian-Ottoman rule in the nineteenth century and was governed from 1874 by an Englishman, Charles George Gordon. It was this administration that Mohammed Ahmed, the Mahdi (a title traditionally used by Islamic religious reformers), challenged in 1882. He led a revolutionary uprising,

capturing Khartoum and killing Gordon in January 1885. In June 1885 the Mahdi died and was succeeded by the Khalifah, Abd Allah, who tried unsuccessfully to extend Mahdism in a holy war. For four years the Khalifah waged war to the east, west, north, and south, till the expansionist drive was spent in 1889. The Madhist state met its nemesis in Kitchener who defeated their army at Omdurman in September 1898. (Editors' note.)

21 See Hicks 1995 and Howard 1995.

22 Sadou 1996:28–33.

23 Interpress Service, April 1997.

24 *Ibid.*

25 *Ibid.*

26 Fifteen years after independence, the Zimbabwean film *Flame*, which depicts violations of the human rights of women combatants at the hands of their comrades, is being attacked by former combatants. One of their criticisms is that the film should have depicted the hardships faced by combatants in general, such as hunger, land mines and exploding petrol tanks. Even after the war women's issues that had been 'postponed' did not seem to be important.

27 *New York Times*, 28 June 1996.

6 'Favours' to Give and 'Consenting' Victims:

The Sexual Politics of Survival in Rwanda

CLOTILDE TWAGIRAMARIYA AND MEREDETH TURSHEN

Editors' Introduction

From the fourteenth to the end of the nineteenth century, Rwanda was a centralized kingdom. Europeans arrived only in the 1890s, when Germany conquered Rwanda and Burundi and ruled them as part of German East Africa to the end of the First World War. After the German defeat, the League of Nations mandated the two landlocked central African nations to Belgium, which had already colonized neighbouring Congo. Although a social revolution was in progress from 1959, Rwanda regained its independence in 1962 before its problems were resolved.[1] Today Rwanda is a poor, densely populated, fertile but mountainous country, smaller than the state of Massachusetts. Illiteracy still handicaps half of the women and one-third of the men. All Rwandans without exception suffered and are still suffering from the atrocities of the civil war that started in October 1990 when the Rwandan Patriotic Front (RPF) invaded from Uganda. Hundreds of thousands of people have been killed and thousands are still being killed today, all of them Banyarwanda killed by other Banyarwanda.[2] Half of the country's eight million people[3] were uprooted: two million were displaced within the country and another two million fled to neighbouring, not always friendly, nations. A group of extremists in the country turned the power struggle between the government, its opposition and the RPF, which was on the verge of resolution following the signing of the Arusha Accords in August 1993, into a vicious and bloody ethnic war.

On 6 April 1994 all on board died when the plane returning President Juvénal Habyarimana from negotiations in Tanzania was shot down in Kigali, the capital.[4] Seemingly on cue, the RPF, extremist militias,[5] the Presidential Guard and the national army, implementing a plan apparently developed long before this event, began to eliminate their enemies and systematically exterminate moderates who favoured reconciliation. Hutu-dominated ultra-nationalist groups used the ethnic card to inflame animosities entrenched by Belgian colonists in classic divide-and-rule ploys that pitted the majority Hutu against the minority Tutsi.[6] In 1994, the military, militias and civilians murdered between 500,000 and one million people. While both groups killed people of the opposite group as well as members of their own group, ethnic Tutsi sustained the largest numbers of deaths – 600,000, representing 70 per cent of all Tutsi in the country. The intensity and ferocity of the slaughter stunned the international community as well as Rwandans themselves.

Both national and international factors are involved in the Rwandan civil war. The international community failed in many ways in regard to this conflict. At a time of acute political and social crisis, the World Bank applied austerity measures which, combined with the impact of the currency devaluations imposed by the IMF, contributed to the impoverishment of the Rwandan people and the destabilization of the society.[7] The international community not only failed to stop the war and the genocide in 1994, but in fact withdrew United Nations forces stationed inside the country on 22 April 1994. Then it failed to separate the people responsible for the genocide from the mass of refugees.[8] And finally, the international community encouraged host countries to force refugees to return to Rwanda and pressured the RPF government to accept them, even though it was clear that no preparations had been made for their return and that many of them might be jailed arbitrarily or assassinated.[9] As one commentator noted in April 1996,

> The two million Rwandans cramped in camps in Zaire and Tanzania have nothing to return to, nothing to look forward to: agricultural markets have been destroyed, local level food production and the coffee economy have been shattered, urban employment and social programmes have been erased.[10]

Rwandan men and women have been implicated in the killings, but investigations show that women bore the brunt of the civil war. It is estimated that 20 per cent of the male population died, leaving 60 per cent of women widowed; 70 per cent of Rwanda's population is now female.[11] In the chaos of the crisis in the spring of 1994, sexual violence occurred on a massive scale; reportedly more than 250,000 women were raped.[12] As this chapter makes clear, violence against women is still continuing in overt, brutal, subtle and ambiguous ways.

This chapter is a condemnation of the rape of women in time of war, and it draws attention to the plight of women in the aftermath of war. It presents the case of Rwanda, in which the manipulation of ethnicity obscures the power struggles taking place and impedes any lasting resolution. Simplistic explanations of the conflict render invisible the real suffering of Rwandan women who were and are still being raped by all parties in the conflict. Women are targeted partly because of their ethnicity but mainly because of their gender, and 'their bodies are used as the figurative and literal sites of combat'.[13] The rapes described here demonstrate that all sides in the Rwandan conflict have their 'bad guys' and that women are suffering another kind of Calvary, beyond their ethnic labels, just because they are women.

The press's oversimplified rendering of 'evil Hutu' versus 'good Tutsi' reinscribes an ethnic division that is largely artificial and hinders the construction of a reconciliation that transcends power struggles disguised as ethnic conflict. The media presented the civil war in Rwanda as a Hutu-versus-Tutsi struggle, the Hutu labelled as 'killers' (the bad guys who should be prosecuted) and the Tutsi as 'victims' (the good guys to be helped), while in reality there are simply good and bad men and women everywhere. As one close observer of Rwanda wrote:

> The Rwandan genocide from April to July 1994 was conducted live on television. Images showed Hutu extremists manning roadblocks and wielding machetes, killing Tutsi and Hutu opponents. Clearly, these were the 'bad guys' at work. The then rebel Rwandan Patriotic Front (RPF) was seen to wage a war against those genocidal killers and eventually to prevail over them, assuming power in mid-July 1994. These had to be the 'good guys' who merited our support. What no one knew then was that the RPF too was engaged in massive and systematic killings of civilians, out of the sight of cameras or external observers. There is an impressive amount of prima facie evidence that the RPF has massacred tens of thousands, possibly hundreds of thousands of unarmed persons. While most of that killing took place during the period of April–October 1994, it has continued and continues on a smaller scale.[14]

The Manichean portrayal of good versus evil minimizes the acute suffering of Rwandan women because during this conflict 'Hutu militia and military did rape Tutsi women, but they also raped educated Hutu women, targeting members of the intelligentsia'.[15] After the victory of the Rwandan Patriotic Front (RPF), Tutsi soldiers of the Rwandan Patriotic Army (RPA) raped Hutu women in revenge for Tutsi women who were raped by Hutu militia, in a never-ending cycle of revenge. According to Amnesty International, Tutsi soldiers guarding women in Butare prison reportedly told their rape victims 'that they were avenging the rape of Tutsi women by the former government's militia and soldiers, most of whom were members of the majority Hutu ethnic group.[16] So Hutu women were made to pay for what Hutu men had done! Tutsi soldiers of the RPA also pressured surviving Tutsi women for sex, arguing that they had fought and won the civil war for them and that now the women owed them.

The focus on tribal identity also obscures the suffering of women in mixed marriages and women who are the product of mixed marriages. Intermarriage between Hutu and Tutsi became increasingly common in areas outside the north after 1973.[17] These women came to be regarded as a fifth column in the political violence of the 1990s and were at the mercy of both sides.

When rape is politicized and used for ethnic cleansing, it can destroy a woman's chance of marriage. 'Will anyone marry a woman who has the child of a [Hutu] militiaman?' is a question being asked in Rwanda today.[18] Both sides used women as 'reproductive vessels'; they raped women to make them bear babies of the rapist's ethnic identity, which follows patrilinearly. 'In the immediate wake of genocide both ... the former Rwandan army and the RPF rounded up young women and kept them as incubators of a new generation, in what amounted to a race to propagate.'[19] In cases where men on both sides believed that their military and political power was linked to their numbers, the ethnicity of the women captives was irrelevant. In other cases, the conquering RPF soldiers held young Tutsi women in Kigali as 'walking wombs'. One explanation is that this was a response to nationalistic jingoism, 'the yearning of youth mixed with the strategies of statesmen to capture women of reproductive age – especially women of one's ethnicity'.[20]

Rape does not have to be genocidal to aggravate women's terror and future stigma, or to produce a class of outcast mothers and children. This fate awaits any woman identified with the losing side in a war. Women are raped by an enemy who is fully aware of how unacceptable a raped woman is to the patriarchal community and to herself. Both mother and child, writes a Rwandan editor, 'will be seen by society as a curse and relic – visible reminders of the bitter memories of a past that everyone loves to forget'.[21] Not only are the mothers cast out, but their children suffer the same trauma.

> Rwanda now has between 2,000 and 5,000 children born of rape. Commonly considered Hutu despite their mothers' ethnicity – and the Government's almost absurd insistence that ethnicity is now irrelevant – the babies are called 'little *interahamwe*' or 'devil's children'.[22]

One woman who had the courage to keep her child is branded a collaborator for doing so; she said of her life and that of her daughter: 'The community isn't interested in me or her. I am alone here, and I have nothing but a child from the men who killed my family.'[23]

Another woman recounted the bitterness of her decision to give birth.

Antoinette, a 25-year-old widow, said that both of her children were killed by the *Interahamwe* and the Presidential Guard 'before my eyes'.

> Then they gang-raped me and left me for dead. My husband, my mother, my father, my sisters and one of my brothers were also killed. Two little brothers survived and I could not risk my life having an abortion. The boys would be abandoned if I died. I have resolved to keep this child. He will be a cross I have to carry for the rest of my life.[24]

Hutu militiamen used rape to destabilize Tutsi society and to break its resistance. Extremist propaganda specifically identified the sexuality of Tutsi women 'as a means through which the Tutsi community sought to infiltrate and control the Hutu community'.[25] Tutsi women were portrayed as 'arrogant and superior', rape as a political act to terrorize communities.[26] Rape was 'a way of inverting all social norms and destroying society'.[27]

During many of the guerrilla wars for independence in Africa, women were abducted to serve the insurgents in their camp – hideouts in the forest where the women cooked and washed clothes during the day but were often gang-raped at night. The RPF did this in the north of Rwanda from the time of their invasion in October 1990.

The Rapes and Killings Continue

Some of the original material presented here was obtained through a journalist, S. Musangamfura, who worked as chief of the Information Service in Rwanda from July 1994 to August 1995. He was told these stories by the victims, who complained to him directly. He has said that he was receiving up to twelve cases a day.[28] Such testimonies are few and far between because those victims still in Rwanda are in danger of finding themselves 'swimming against the current'. Complainants against the RPF government risk having their grievances turned against them, so they prefer to keep silent. Those who escaped to Kenya said that the RPA had certainly committed many more rapes than the few cases recounted here, but the victims are not talking to avoid dishonour or the wrath of their aggressors. Many returned to the journalist to withdraw their story and beg him not to make it a public court case. Women in Rwanda believe that even if they were allowed to complain, their rapists would not be punished. The prosecution of deaths during the genocide has taken precedence, and few charges of rape are being documented in the Rwandan courts.[29]

In the years after the genocide, cases of rape with violence and even sadism are still being reported. In August 1995, M.M.H. was raped, decapitated, and thrown into the latrine of Lieutenant N. in Nyarugunga,

Kanombe Commune. Young girls accused of being *Interahamwe* were savagely violated: stripped naked, they were kicked with boots, beaten with wooden sticks, and knives were used to cut their genitals.

M., the wife of S.J.P. who owned a bar, was imprisoned in several different places, notably in the house of an officer, where she was repeatedly raped and tortured from July 1994. She was then sent to Muhima squad where she was released with the help of a relative, a member of the RPA. Threatened again with imprisonment, she took refugee in the house of Seth Sendashonga, then Minister of Internal Affairs and RPF member. After many failed attempts to protect her, she was able to escape to Nairobi in August 1995, but she is so traumatized that the latest news is she has been struck dumb.

A 19-year-old woman, returning from the burial of three women neighbours in Gafunzo Commune, Cyangugu Prefecture, was attacked by four soldiers of the RPF. Pretending to search for *Interahamwe*, they broke into her house where she was alone caring for her sick brother; her parents had fled to Zaïre by boat in mid-August 1994. One of the soldiers stabbed her repeatedly in her right breast and left her for dead.[30]

Rape is also used as a form of torture. Amnesty International reports that women detained by the RPF government in a store at Gisenyi Technical School were repeatedly raped by soldiers. In one case, Marie Mukamazimpaka, a 46-year-old mother of three, was 'arrested at the end of 1994 and was transferred to Butare prison at the start of February 1995'.[31] She was badly beaten, leaving wounds on her buttocks. She was 'taken on 12 February 1995 to a building occupied by soldiers who raped her for two days'.[32] Other women were also reported to have been raped in Butare prison but were too afraid or embarrassed to describe their ordeal to Amnesty International representatives.

RPF soldiers know no bounds, they respect no limits. They even intrude into the residences of Hutu ministers to take young female relatives (sisters or sisters-in-law). That is how the young sister of one Hutu minister came to be raped by members of the ministerial escort. When the victim complained, the accused soldiers were interrogated; but after some behind-the-scenes deal, the young girl had to withdraw her complaint and deny that she had been raped. The same soldiers were again appointed to their jobs on the staff of the same minister, and they were rotated some time later.[33]

In Rwanda, women cynically say of men in arms (whatever their affiliation), 'they are all alike'. The RPF prided itself on its military discipline, but women say it is a past memory because women and girls are still subject to rape, which the RPF military commanders no longer punish. Even Tutsi women are pressured with psychological arguments by RPF soldiers who claim that they fought and won the civil war for these women who now owe them 'le repos du guerrier'. These attitudes and acts are another source of the people's frustration and discredit the new government.[34]

Until the mass return of refugees at the end of 1996, armed groups of Hutu based in Zaïre and Tanzania were crossing the border to kill witnesses who could testify to the participation of known individuals in the massacres of 1994, to kill or evict people in order to occupy their property, or to press-gang men into the militias. Women caught in the middle were murdered:

... in the night of 3 September 1995, in Rukira district in the prefecture of Kibungo, the house of a 30-year-old cattle keeper was attacked. The cattle keeper's wife and his six-year-old daughter were killed; the girl had her head split open with a machete.... The cattle keeper survived alone with a very young daughter. The attackers were recognized by a neighbor as former inhabitants of that village. They escaped with three extra men from the village.[35]

Or women themselves are the targets. One woman, Savina Mukacyibibi, a 50-year-old widow whose husband and five children were killed in the genocide, was beaten and strangled to death in Taba commune at the end of 1996, allegedly by five local Hutu men who wanted to prevent her from identifying those responsible for the death of her family.[36]

Some women were killed incidentally to the political murder of their husbands or employers who were the real target of the attackers.

On 27 July 1995, Placide Koloni, his wife Immaculée Nyirambibi, his daughters Marie-Claire Umutoniwase, 15, and Carine Unwamahoro, 9, and his servant Séraphine Murekatete, were killed at their home by unidentified attackers, who then set their house on fire with the five bodies inside. Soldiers of the RPA were reportedly seen very near the house. Placide Koloni was the sous-préfet (sub-administrator) of Ruhango in the prefecture of Gitarama. On 14 February 1995, he had been arbitrarily arrested and accused of taking part in the 1994 massacres. He was imprisoned in Gitarama prison, where the conditions are notoriously harsh. On 24 July, he was released on the recommendation of a ... screening committee ... which found that there was insufficient evidence against him. He was killed three days later.[37]

Other women were killed in reprisals, acts of personal vengeance.

In another case in the district of Kanzenze in Rural Kigali prefecture, a woman and her four children who had recently returned from Zaire were attacked by a group of four men. Only one child managed to escape: the mother and three other children were killed. The attackers were described as survivors of the genocide acting in revenge for crimes reportedly committed by the woman's husband, who was in prison for alleged participation in the genocide.[38]

Sex and Survival

Some women survived the civil war only to confront new, more subtle, forms of sexual violence. The coercion is not always overt, and the women are easily accused of complicity, compliance, or even solicitation. Drawing the line and defining rape in these patriarchal communities is complicated by men's power over the means of women's survival in situations of extreme scarcity and insecurity.

Forced cohabitation

M.A., the security officer in charge of information for the 'displaced' in the town of Byumba from April to May 1994, detained the daughter of S. and forced her to live with him. Byumba is an area to the north of Kigali near the Ugandan border that was under RPF control from the early 1990s. She had gone to his office with her sister who was inquiring about the fate of her husband who had been kidnapped in Byumba. S.'s daughter was raped by M.A. as well as by other members of the RPF, notably S.A., another security officer, and Captain D.K., before M.A. took her to live with him.

This was also the experience of J.D.'s spouse when she returned home after exile to stay with her brother; she was taken by an officer who forced her to live with him. Likewise, Captain J.M., member of the Directorate of Military Intelligence, sequestered a young girl who was still a high school student and kept her at his place as a 'wife'. Some soldiers repatriated from Uganda explained those forced marriages by saying it was the custom to kidnap brides in that country.

Other young girls, mainly Tutsi, commonly called 'ceiling girls' because they were found hiding in the ceilings of huts when they were rescued by the RPF in July 1994, were considered 'war booty'. The soldiers who found them sent them to their superior officers. In some cases, the girls attempted unsuccessfully to escape their 'liberators/abductors'. This was the case of A.M. of Nyamabuye-Gitarama, saved and detained as war booty by the local RPA detachment. She faced resistance when she expressed her wish to join her fiancé, also a survivor.

'Favours' to give

Wives whose husbands are in jail are often victims of extortion. For an authorization to visit or to bring food to their jailed husband, these women have to pay the soldiers or other responsible authorities with 'favours' – by agreeing to have sex with them. Some of the most dishonest soldiers searched for women in difficulty in order to offer them services, and the women, often desperate, were caught in the game. Because these women may be considered as consenting victims, evidence of these cases is kept strictly secret; in effect, the victim is forced to protect her aggressor.

Many other women had to exchange sex when claiming their family property. In the Remera area of Kigali, a woman who tried to claim her house was forced by the officer occupying it to stay as his concubine in her own home. Some women who pursued their claims were raped and threatened with death. This happened to A.M., whose house was appropriated by a captain who was living in it with a 'ceiling girl'. When she dared to claim her house, the captain raped her and threatened her with death if she tried it again. As of August 1995, A.M. has not been able to get her house back.

'Consenting' victims

After the RPF took power and formed the new government, what had been commonly called *intsinzi* (in which young girls and women offered themselves to the military to congratulate them for their victory) was not always a consensual act. Many young girls were obliged to offer themselves to the soldiers; otherwise they would be accused of collaboration with the deposed regime and put in jail. People jokingly reported that after so much pressure to give 'favours' to the RPF, some Tutsi women started to complain and said: '*Abagabo ni abagive*, the real men are those who left the country, at least they were paying for "favours" and were not expecting women to offer themselves for free!'

Health and Social Consequences of Rape

There are many health consequences of rape: physical and mental injury, shock and paralysing fear, sexually transmitted diseases including HIV infection, and pregnancy. If abortion is not an option for material or religious reasons, pregnancy may inflict further mental trauma including denial, severe depression, and neglect or rejection of the child after birth. Wartime rape carries additional trauma associated with war: 'death of loved ones, loss of home and community, dislocation, untreated illness, and war-related injury'.[39] Rape by familiars is particularly detrimental and leaves women fearful, distrustful, paranoid. The physical, moral and psychological suffering of women who have been raped is not taken into consideration by their families or communities, who accuse them of deserving what they endured and make them feel guilty.

Rwandan victims of rape are now suffering the worst time of their lives; they are being isolated by their own communities in spite of the mental and physical pain they endured and are still enduring. Most survivors of violence are faced with overwhelming problems such as severe health complications, children born of rape, social isolation and ostracism. The psychological trauma of rape is intense. Health workers have noted that with the return to normalcy, as schools and markets open, the problems of rape victims are manifest. 'Many widows we see now are withdrawing and dysfunctional, not capable of properly looking after their children.'[40] Many Rwandan women who survived rape contemplate suicide; some feel guilty for having submitted, and some are accused of having chosen life over death. A Rwandan testifying at the Fourth International Conference on Women at Beijing said:

Raped women are doubly punished by society. First, judicial practice does not grant them redress for rape as long as graphic evidence is not brought out into the open. Second, from society's point of view there is little sympathy, for at the moment that men and children died without defense, these women used the sex card, 'selling their bodies to save their lives.' Thus, they are judged from all sides, and even among their families they are not easily pardoned. Even worse, people reproach them for having preferred survival through rape.[41]

Many women who have been raped need health care but cannot afford it, or cannot afford the stigma attached to rape, or cannot bear public acknowledgement of the shame. A gynaecologist at University Hospital in Butare has examined hundreds of rape victims since the genocide.

It has been two years since the war, but these patients are very difficult to cure. Initially, they come in with infections, vaginal infections, urinary tract problems – problems that are sexually transmitted. You cure the direct illness but psychologically, they are not healed … they continue to be sick. And there are no services that specifically deal with the problems these women have. There are some groups for widows, and the like, but there are no groups to help women who have gone through this [rape].[42]

In Rwanda, sexually transmitted diseases including HIV are highly prevalent and, as is well known, more than half of AIDS cases in Africa occur in women. Before the war, 45 to 60 per cent of Rwandan soldiers and an even higher percentage of the officer corps were infected with HIV.[43] Thousands of pregnant girls and young women who were raped between April and July 1994 have tested positive for the HIV virus.[44] Some of the rapes were said to be 'tantamount to attempted murder because the perpetrators knew they were carrying the Aids virus'.[45] The Rwandan Minister of Health, Dr Joseph Karemera, alleged that captured Tutsi women were deliberately taken to HIV positive Hutu soldiers to be raped.[46] But Human Rights Watch concluded:

It is impossible to reach any firm conclusions about the transmission of AIDS during the genocide because of the difficulty of ascertaining when a given individual was exposed to the virus....An AIDS awareness center based in Kigali asserts that the national percentage of HIV carriers has remained the same since the genocide – 25 percent. The director, Janvière Mukantwali, noted that a large influx of returnees[47] came from Burundi, Zaire and Uganda – all high-risk countries for the HIV virus, and this population has contributed to keeping the percentage the same despite the widespread killings of the genocide.[48]

What is clear is that, with one of the highest incidences of AIDS in Africa, Rwanda is unable to provide adequate health services for women with this debilitating, usually fatal, disease.

Women in Mixed Marriages

Intermarriage between Hutu and Tutsi was common, but more Tutsi women married Hutu men than the reverse. The marriage of Hutu women to Tutsi men did occur, despite class differences and the possibility that their in-laws would treat them as inferiors.[49] The plight of Hutu women who were married to Tutsi is close to that of Tutsi women raped by Hutu militiamen. Both groups of women have to answer to the question, 'Why are you still alive?' Both experienced the loss of their loved ones, their husbands and children killed. And both encounter strong mistrust and even rejection by the community. During the genocide, ethnicity divided families and turned members against one another: children killed mothers, husbands killed wives, brothers and cousins killed each other because one was Tutsi, the other Hutu. 'For some it was done willingly; others were forced to do it upon pain of death.'[50]

Béatrice is a Hutu; her Tutsi husband and five children were killed during the massacre and thrown in a latrine. She denounced Hutu members of her own family to the Tutsi police, including one of her brothers-in-law as one of the killers. As a result, she says she has been ostracized by her parents and her life has been threatened on at least two occasions.[51]

One Hutu survivor, Thérèse, was married to a Tutsi in Taba commune. Her husband was killed by the *Interahamwe*, some of whom she recognized. They spared her life because she was Hutu and she stayed with her natal family until the end of the war. When she tried to return to her marital home, her sister-in-law drove her off the property.

> She accused my three brothers of being *Interahamwe*, even though they were not, and she had them arrested. They have been held in Gitarama prison since March 1995. I have not tried to go back since because my sister-in-law said that she will get me arrested for taking food to my brothers in prison. I have not gone back to my home because I am afraid for my security. I fear that my sister-in-law will do something to harm me. I know three other cases like this.[52]

Tutsi women married to Hutu were targeted by RPF soldiers, who forcibly took other men's wives as well as their property. The RPA asked Tutsi women to quit their Hutu husbands, saying that those marriages must have been the consequence of rape and not love matches. When there was any resistance, the husband was put in jail, where he would soon find death. This is the case of A.R. from Kinyamakara Commune in Gikongoro. He was imprisoned in Ririma prison where he died a few months later. The same happened to R.A. who was also imprisoned (when last heard of, he was still in jail). His wife, a Tutsi, was forced to marry a young soldier; and the twins of her first marriage with R.A. were given to R.A.'s sister.

Loss of Husband = Loss of Property

Rwandan law stipulates that refugees who return to the country after more than ten years in exile cannot automatically reclaim their property. Nonetheless, Tutsi returnees and their descendants, in the cities as well as in the countryside, are illegally occupying properties that belong to Hutu refugees, most of whom fled during the 1990–4 war. This situation poses special problems for Rwandan widows who cannot inherit their husbands' property, house, cattle, or anything else. Hutu widows or Hutu women whose husbands are currently in prison on genocide charges are vulnerable to being forced off their property. A Hutu woman survivor working with an NGO, who was interviewed in Kigali by Human Rights Watch, identified a range of problems facing Hutu women:

> Genocide survivors, who are mostly women, are being accused of collaborating by the returnees so the returnees can keep their house. The returnees from Burundi are particularly extremist about blaming all Hutu indiscriminately. Many Hutu women returned to their homes only to find that returnees have occupied their houses. When they try to get their homes back, accusations of collaboration are made against them. Other Hutu women whose husbands are in prison for having participated in the genocide have the same problem. They are being implicated by extension. Hutu survivors are being put in the garbage. There is no place for moderates in this country. I know of cases where the military put a family in someone else's house. You don't dare challenge it. I also know of six people who were imprisoned for trying to get their houses back. One was a woman whose husband is in prison.[53]

Many people have been jailed without any charges filed against them. Women bear the burden of that situation. They face all the problems of feeding their families alone, with no resources, no rights, no protection. 'Many of the women left alone are having trouble making ends meet. Some are living in abject poverty, hiring themselves out as day labourers to farmers. Every afternoon, they must walk three miles to the commune headquarters to bring food and water to their husbands in jail.'[54]

Prosecution of Rape

With little debate and almost total unanimity, the UN Security Council voted on 8 November 1994 to create a war crimes tribunal to prosecute Rwandans responsible for the genocide.[55] In September 1996, Rwanda's parliament approved a genocide law to prosecute the 60,000 to 80,000 Hutu held in Rwanda's putrid jails.[56] The International Tribunal covers only the year 1994 and excludes the death penalty; the Rwandan law extends back to 1990, the beginning of the civil war, and includes the death penalty for those who planned, instigated, or supervised the genocide.[57] The International Tribunal can handle fewer than one hundred cases per year; its slow, inefficient and corrupt practices have been the subject of criticism and an official UN enquiry.[58] The massive backlog of accused must be dealt with by the Rwandan courts, which have been criticized in equal measure by the international community for their lack of justice: summary trials, defendants without lawyers, evidence limited to eye witness accounts.[59]

Both the International Tribunal and the Rwandan genocide law cover the crime of rape. Rape is also prosecutable under Rwandan criminal law, but few inspectors, and few women themselves, are aware of this; and there is a lack of female judicial investigators to whom women might speak more easily about being raped.[60] Human Rights Watch investigated the reluctance of women to talk about rape at the International Tribunal. The Deputy Prosecutor of the Rwandan tribunal told Human Rights Watch that the reason they have not collected rape testimonies is because African women don't want to talk about rape. 'We haven't received any complaints. It is rare in investigations that women refer to rape.'[61]

Human Rights Watch blames the insensitivity of tribunal investigators for this failure. Special interview conditions of safety and privacy are necessary if women are to talk, and they must believe that telling their testimony will help bring about justice.

> If women agree to testify, effective protection for rape victims must also be guaranteed by the Tribunal. Many women fear reprisals if they testify. These fears are not unwarranted. Witnesses and survivors of the genocide continue to be killed in the country and abroad. For other women, the stigma of rape will deter them from coming forward if they cannot be assured that their privacy will be protected. Unless the Tribunal takes steps to ensure that adequate privacy and security is provided to rape survivors who agree to testify, it is unlikely that women will agree to testify. Without such measures, there is also a likelihood

that the effort to bring the perpetrators to justice through the Tribunal could further contribute to the trauma already experienced by the women.[62]

Conclusion

The Women's International League for Peace and Freedom reported that Rwandan women approached WILPF International at the Fourth International Women's Conference held in Beijing in September 1995 for teams to go to the refugee camps and help with reconciliation.[63] Such efforts are needed now inside the country. The Rwandan crisis provides an opportunity for Rwandan women to step forward in the search for a lasting solution, one that allows all Rwandans to live together in peace, sharing everyday life. Women must make an effort to bring about reconciliation. The international community can help women initiate a meeting and help in the implementation of their recommendations.

Women in Rwanda suffered and are still suffering the many consequences of the crisis, and many of them are left to face alone the tremendous responsibilities of reconstruction. These women need to get together to use the few resources they have left to end the state of war in the country. Everybody is tired of the endless killings, especially women. More men than women were killed in the conflict, and women are facing added responsibilities now that many of them are either widows or have their husbands in jail and find themselves heads of household.

The civil war changed the roles of Rwandan women, forcing them into what traditionally were men's roles, and many of them are demonstrating remarkable ability to handle the problems of the aftermath. This is the time for Rwandan women to step forward and show what they can do when they work together as women. Before the civil war, every commune in Rwanda had a *foyer social*, a formal women's organization responsible for collective child care, firewood collection, health issues, care of the aged, etc. Women can once again initiate these programmes to bring back confidence and trust. Rwandans need this confidence to function effectively, and it can be achieved only by restoring peace and stability to the country.

The ethnic groups cannot be separated because, for many families, intermarriage exists since the generation of the grandmothers, and it is difficult now to tell who is who. Many Rwandans are linked together as a family. Beyond ethnicity, there are other values and ties related mainly to families, marriage, and friendship that are stronger than ethnicity, and many Rwandan women happen to fit better in those categories.

There is a strong need for national solidarity, if both groups are to be able to live together in peace. A new behaviour of tolerance and mutual acceptance of the other needs to be developed in order to rebuild the country. Rwandans must learn about peace, about respect for each other, and especially about respect for life, a value that was jeopardized by the war. Women, as the guarantors of society, need to invest in teaching these values to the future generation. This long-term project should be included in all school curricula so that young people will learn the values of self-respect and respect for life and other people's rights. Rwandan women can help save the population, and they cannot wait for the international community to do the job. The ones being killed are women, and it is up to the women's movement to find a way to stop all kinds of conflicts and wars, because all are inhumane.

Notes

1 For the history see *inter alia* C. Newbury 1988; Lemarchand 1970. For the background on the ethnic aspects of the civil war see Newbury and Newbury 1995 and *Issue: A Journal of Opinion*, Vol. XXIII, No. 2 (1995).

2 The word for 'Rwandan' in the national language.

3 UNICEF gives a 1995 population figure of 8 million; the UN estimate is lower, 5.9 million.

4 The assassins have not been identified but one of four hypotheses is that Hutu extremists, who opposed Habyarimana's peace agreement on power sharing, brought the plane down. Others are that Burundians did it, as the president of Burundi was also on the plane, that it was a democratic coup that backfired, and that the RPF did it (Reyntjens 1995).

5 The extremists consisted of the *Interahamwe*, associated with the MRND party of President Habyarimana, and the *Impuzamugambi*, associated with the CDR, a hardline ally of the MRND. The Western press identified the *Interahamwe* as an extremist Hutu militia (cf. Royte 1997:38), but young Tutsi were also members and the chief of *Interahamwe* at the time of the genocide, Robert Kajuga, was a Tutsi.

6 The Belgians issued ethnic identity cards, a practice in use under Habyarimana, who ruled Rwanda from 1973 to 1994.

7 Chossudovsky 1996:22.

8 Human Rights Watch 1995.

9 Amnesty International 1996.

10 Chossudovsky 1996:22.

11 Royte 1997:38.

12 The most comprehensive report on sexual violence during the genocide is published by Human Rights Watch 1996a.

13 Bunch and Reilly 1994:38.

14 Reyntjens 1996.

15 Desouter and Reyntjens 1995:19 ff.

16 Amnesty International 1995:6.

17 C. Newbury 1995:13.

18 Hilsum 1995.

19 D. Newbury 1995.

20 *Ibid.*

21 *Umuhuza: Monthly Newsletter Dedicated to Serving All Rwandese*, 1995.

22 Royte 1997:38.

23 *Ibid.*

24 Reuters News Service, Kigali, 6 February 1995. Abortion is illegal in Rwanda and nearly half the population is Roman Catholic. Hundreds of raped women obtained risky abortions from village healers, others from qualified doctors; the government and the medical community made a tacit agreement to ignore the law (Royte 1997:38).

25 Human Rights Watch 1996a:2.

26 Royte 1997:38.

27 Hilsum 1995.

28 Musangamfura then fled to Kenya together with the Minister of Internal Affairs, Seth Sendashonga, in August 1995. He passed these stories to a former Member of Parliament, now a refugee in Kenya, who relayed them to us.

29 Human Rights Watch 1996a:89.

30 Testimony gathered by a Rwandan intellectual and a Canadian sister, quoted in Desouter and Reyntjens 1995:17.

31 Amnesty International 1995:6.

32 *Ibid.*

33 See note 28.

34 Ntezimana 1994.

35 Amnesty International 1996:21.

36 McKinley 1996.

37 Amnesty International 1996:18–19.

38 *Ibid.*:24. From May to June of 1996, Hutu extremists killed 99 witnesses in order to prevent them from testifying before Rwandan or international courts, according to UN observers (Magnarella 1997).

39 Swiss and Giller 1993:614.

40 Royte 1997:38.

41 Layika 1996:40.

42 Quoted in Human Rights Watch 1996a:73.

43 WorldAIDS, quoted in *Civil-Military Alliance Newsletter* Vol. 1, No. 2 (April 1995), p. 3.

44 *Umuhuza: Monthly Newsletter Dedicated to Serving All Rwandese*, 1995.

45 Crary 1995.

46 WorldAIDS, quoted in *Civil-Military Alliance Newsletter*, Vol. 1, No. 2 (April 1995), p. 3.

47 Returnees or 'old caseload' are terms used to refer to Tutsi who lived in exile,

some from 1959, and came back to the country after July 1994 when the RPF took power. Hutu who fled at that time are usually referred to as refugees.

48 A study of 500 pregnant women who had come in for pre-natal counselling was conducted at Kigali Central Hospital in May 1995. Of the group, 25 per cent tested positive for HIV – the same as before the war. Sixty per cent of this sample were living in Kigali before the war and 40 per cent were living abroad. Of the 127 women who tested positive, 96 of them had been living abroad before the war. 'This study underscores the difficulty of making any firm conclusions about the transmission of AIDS during the genocide.' (Human Rights Watch 1996a:76).

49 See Twagiramariya 1995:14 for a fuller explanation of intermarriage.

50 Laykia 1996:40.

51 McKinley 1996.

52 Human Rights Watch 1996a:87.

53 Quoted in Human Rights Watch 1996a:86.

54 McKinley 1996.

55 Human Rights Watch 1996a:92.

56 Amnesty International 1995; Lorch 1995; Magnarella 1997. The number rose to over 120,000 in 1997.

57 Magnarella 1997. The death penalty is contrary to the UN Universal Declaration of Human Rights which guarantees the right to life.

58 Crossette 1996.

59 Magnarella 1997. Forensic evidence, which provides irrefutable physical evidence, is not introduced, although the Boston-based nongovernmental organization Physicians for Human Rights has sent teams of pathologists to Rwanda.

60 Human Rights Watch 1996a:89–90.

61 Quoted in Human Rights Watch 1996a:95.

62 Human Rights Watch 1996a:95–96.

63 Clement 1995:5.

7 Women Denounce Their Treatment in Chad

WOMEN'S COMMISSION
OF THE HUMAN RIGHTS LEAGUE OF CHAD
& THE EDITORS

Editors' Introduction

Chad, the fifth largest country in Africa, is a typical colonial creation: none of its borders coincides with either natural or ethnic boundaries. The great diversity of peoples, cultures, and religions is reflected in more than one hundred languages and dialects. The northern and central regions are Arab and Muslim by culture and the people are largely nomadic pastoralists;[1] the southern region is animist and Christian and the people are settled farmers cultivating cotton, Chad's main export crop. These details are important because the internal strife, which began in 1965, just five years after Chad obtained its independence from France, is widely characterized by the Western press as a north–south conflict[2] like the one in Sudan. But many Chadians believe this is a dangerous oversimplification, one that creates the very duality it purports to describe.[3] As in Rwanda, forty years of independence have seen successful integration and intermarriage, but politicians like Hissène Habré (president of Chad from 1982 to 1990) are always willing to exploit differences to promote their bids for power.

The north–south dualism is also inaccurate because the recent history of Chad is characterized by warlordism – the rise of regional centres of power based on personalized rule and military force.[4] The consequent prevalence of a politics of conflict and war following the collapse of central control makes warlordism even worse for women than civil war. Under warlords, women lack even the nominal protection of the rule of law guaranteed by a central state, and they are caught in indeterminate fighting as warlords resort to force to settle disputes and compete for territory using their private armies.

118

A significant date in Chad's 33-year conflict is 12 February 1979 when France, which used Chad as a base for its military domination of its former African colonies, engineered a *coup d'état* that put Habré in power.[5] Eventually, Cameroon, Congo (Brazzaville), Congo (Kinshasa), France, Nigeria, Senegal, and Sudan all took part in the conflict, with Libya (which shares a border with Chad) occupying and trying to annex the northern part of the country. The civil war of 1979–82 tore the country apart; it tore apart the social fabric, broke up families, and forced women to the forefront of the struggle for survival. Whether married, divorced, single or widowed, the women, especially those who lived in the large urban centres of administrative, commercial, and economic activity, were affected.[6] To the cumulative devastation of internal conflict from 1965 to 1979 and civil war from 1979 to 1982, was now added the chaos of warlordism. Women's resources would be stretched to breaking point. In response to our request for information on the impact of the conflict on women, the Women's Commission of the Chadian Human Rights League sent us an important brief on violence against women in two southern provinces of the country. This chapter incorporates that report and supplements it with information provided by the Chadian Human Rights League (La ligue tchadienne des droits de l'homme, hereinafter LTDH)[7] and other resource materials such as publications of Amnesty International, reports in the nation's leading independent newspaper, and secondary sources.

Chad has been at war since 1965, a civil war that reached a climax between 1979 and 1982 but is still continuing: the country has never returned to normal. The situation has not improved since General Idriss Déby seized power in 1991. The struggle between government forces and the many armed opposition groups has increased, generalizing insecurity and heightening the vulnerability of women. Arbitrary arrest, detention and torture, abuses of women and other violations of human rights documented under the regime of Hissène Habré persist under Déby, but all parties to the conflict are responsible for deliberate and arbitrary killings, hostage taking, and rape.[8]

As in many other conflicts in which opposition groups are fighting against governmental forces, Chadian women and girls have been victims of sexual violence. Most cases of sexual abuse documented by Amnesty International, which represent only a tiny fraction of the total number, are cases of rape, usually committed by several men acting together. In other words, these are not individual acts, an important distinction in international law.[9] Amnesty International has also received information on other forms of sexual abuse including forced sexual intercourse between partners in front of others and men forced to participate in the collective rape of their female relatives. In some cases the victims are singled out because of the real or perceived political activities of their partners or male relatives. Sometimes they just have the misfortune to live in areas where armed groups are active and government security forces automatically consider the population to be sympathizers or supporters of the rebels. Sometimes the reasons given are ludicrous ('they booed the President'), or no reasons are given and the rapes seem to have nothing to do with the war. And some patrols are there to protect the interests of multinational corporations like Exxon, which is prospecting for oil in southern Chad.[10]

Rape by Government Forces

Amnesty International has collected evidence of the routine rape and other sexual abuses of Chadian women by government security forces, usually members of the Force d'intervention rapide (FIR, Rapid Intervention Force) and the Gendarmerie, often operating at night when all village activities have ceased.[11] Government forces use the pretext of counter-insurgency operations to mistreat the civilian population indiscriminately. Local political and military authorities are aware of systematic abuses of women and girls, which they condone as part of war tactics, although Amnesty International has repeatedly pointed out to them that rape is an act of torture prohibited by international human rights treaties. Rarely, if ever, have effective measures been taken against the perpetrators. Overcoming social pressures and feelings of shame and modesty, a few women have tried to prosecute both security forces and rebels, but none has been successful. In other words, rapists act with complete impunity.

The following are examples of the testimony collected by Amnesty International. R., aged 30, was raped in August 1995 in her village in Western Logone. She was one of a number of women, including a twelve-year-old girl, who were raped when the security forces surrounded their village, ostensibly looking for suspected members of armed opposition groups.[12]

> It was 20 August 1995 when the troops surrounded our village about five o' clock in the morning. People were starting to run away; as I was a bit sick I wasn't able to. Then two soldiers came into the hut. They asked me if it was me who was married to a 'codo'.[13] I said no and one of them immediately slapped me, and when I fell over, the other tore my wrap and the one who had slapped me aimed the gun at my head, telling me if I screamed they would kill me. And when one had finished, the other took his place, one after the other; each of the two soldiers had me twice before leaving me. Afterwards, when they'd gone, I had no strength left and couldn't get up.[14]

In September 1995, after parking their vehicles, a combined patrol of troops and gendarmes surrounded the village of M. in Western Logone.

> When they arrived, they started firing in the air and we ran off into the bush. I was very frightened, I had to hide in my father's room. I'd closed the door with a *secko*[15] and the four soldiers who had come broke down the door. Two came in and the other two were in front of the door. They spoke in Arabic and one of them hit me with a rifle butt. It was in that room that the four soldiers raped me one after the other.[16]

Accounts of rape by soldiers are also published in the independent national press. *N'Djaména Hebdo* reported on 7 September 1995 that for the previous two weeks, the population of Mailao (70 km from N'Djaména, the capital of Chad) have been living a Calvary. About 150 soldiers were sent there from N'Djaména, ostensibly to look for rebels of the Mouvement pour la démocratie et le développement (MDD, Movement for Democracy and Development). According to informed sources, the soldiers were extorting goods from the local population, beating people and raping women. At dusk, the streets were deserted, but the villagers lived never-ending nights because of frequent 'impolite' night-time visits from the soldiers.[17]

In a similar operation in southern Chad in May 1995, the president of the Bébedjia branch of LTDH explained that soldiers enter villages they suspect of supporting rebels, they fire into the air, causing everyone to flee. Then they break down doors and loot the huts, down to the last kitchen utensil. In these raids, women are frequently raped. 'Mrs Thérèse Lelem, an older woman, wife of the Békaroua village chief, was seriously wounded in the stomach for refusing to give in when sexually assaulted by soldiers. She was admitted to hospital at Bébedjia, where her days are numbered.'[18]

In August 1994, the Republican Guard massacred many people in Western Logone for daring to boo President Déby when he visited the town of Moundou; among the victims was Mrs Manondji, a pregnant woman who was killed and eviscerated.[19]

Sexual abuse of women in government custody has also occurred in Chad. This case was reported by Amnesty International.[20] A woman was arrested in 1993, possibly because she made inquiries about her husband and son who were imprisoned and believed killed in 1986 or 1987. She said she was taken with ten other women prisoners to a military post in north-east Chad. She said they were forced to do hard labour at the barracks there and that soldiers forced the young women among them to perform as prostitutes. The women were then subjected to similar treatment at a second barracks. None of the women had been tried or sentenced.

Security forces have also raped outside of armed conflict. One young victim, whose relatives lodged a complaint, told the judicial police officer:

On 25 September 1995 I was asleep when my mother was brought from Béboto into our village. I was woken up by the soldiers with my eyes full of sleep…. Unaware of the problem, I immediately had my arms tied behind my back. I was beaten, being worn out, and taken into the bedroom to be searched. That was how I came to lose my virginity to three soldiers…. They told me not to cry out, otherwise they'd kill me.[21]

The doctor's certificate states that on examination the victim, aged fifteen, presented 'lacerations of the hymen, vaginal injuries, numerous wounds and scratches on the arms, consistent with being tied up.'[22]

Rape by Armed Opposition Groups

Women in this situation do not know what to do: 'they find themselves between the hammer and the anvil'.[23] They are raped by government forces as a punishment for hiding members of the opposition, they are also raped by opposition groups on the assumption that they are denouncing rebels to the government. These rapes by rebels are less well documented, which does not mean they are less frequent, but in the absence of a legitimate government, they are less often reported or recorded.

The current government of Chad faces armed opposition in the south, west, and east of the country. The main armed groups (among a dozen or more) are the Forces armées pour la république fédérale (FARF, Armed Forces for the Federal Republic), le Front national du Tchad rénové (FNTR, Renewed National Front of Chad), l'Armée nationale tchadienne en dissidence (ANTD, the Dissident Chadian National Army), and the MDD.[24]

FARF, which operates in the southern provinces of Eastern and Western Logone on the Cameroonian border, uses rape as a tactic of intimidation and reprisal against a population suspected of denouncing them or their activities to the authorities, but sometimes it is merely an opportunistic act by an armed aggressor.[25] In September 1995, three members of FARF intercepted and raped four young women as they returned on foot to their village from the market at Moundou, in southern Chad. One of the victims, J., gave this account:

they asked where we were from and we said we were from Tilo. They asked us if the chief was there. They said they had been to him and asked him to give them and their comrades food but he had run away. They said that if we had been men they'd have killed us … they insulted us and said we were dirty. Then they went with us one by one. One of us resisted but they put a knife against her neck and she had to give in.[26]

The girls lodged complaints with the judicial authorities, which enabled them to make an arrest.[27]

Appeal from the Women's Commission of Chad

So much violence against Chadian women, so many sexual abuses and rapes were committed, the situation was deemed so critical, that the Women's Commission of the Chadian Human Rights League launched an appeal to the international community.

The following communiqué was broadcast in N'Djaména on 20 December 1995; it exemplifies many others that the Women's Commission has sent out asking that action be taken to put an end to rape with impunity.

> *Zara, Fatima, Kaltouma, Agnès, Milamen, Domgang ... whose turn tomorrow?* For some time, reports, written and oral testimonies from branches of our organization mention frequent cases of individual and gang rapes of women, both young and old, and of young girls between the ages of nine and 15. Yesterday, it was the branch in Ouaddaï, today it is the branches in the Logones, Chari Baguirmi, and particularly N'Djaména. The evil keeps growing regularly and is spreading with worrying speed. This vile act is used as a tool of war, but it is also a simple act of banditry. The perpetrators are always the same ones who are used to extortion, namely the Republican Guard and rebels of all tendencies.
>
> The Chadian League for Human Rights has always denounced and condemned these vile and barbaric acts against Chadian women and girls that are throw-backs to another age. We make this pressing appeal to all women's organizations, asking them to assume their responsibilities and to undertake any actions liable to end those behaviours that are harmful to the individual and collective development of Chadians.[28]

The appeal was reinforced by the following tables, which detail many cases of rape during a five-month period in Western Logone, a southern province on the Cameroonian border. Investigations in other areas of the country would certainly reveal the same level of abuses against women. Note the wide range of ages at which women are the victims of rape.

Table 7.1 Cases of rape in Western Logone[29]

Name	Age	Date	Place	Source
Arcelle Yotassem	15	9 v 95	Miladi	Moundou branch
Deubnodji		5 v 95	Mbikou	–
Soumian		5 v 95	Mbikou	–
Collette Monodjimel	28	5 x 95	Mbaïkoro	–
Mbaïnodjimel		v 95	Bodjama	–
Béatrice Naïde	18	27 vii 95	Deli	LTDH of Logones and Tandjilé
Marceline Ndongorne		4 viii 95	Moussoum/ Da djilé	–

Table 7.1 cont.

Name	Age	Date	Place	Source
Pauline Maoundoé		4 viii 95	–	–
Dossem Masmbaye		11 viii 95	Mankoula	–
Ida Yorassem		–	–	–
Mrs Hawa		–	–	–
Mrs Naomie		–	–	–
Mrs Rosalie Massyoel	30	29 viii 95	Laobessa	LTDH of Logones and Tandjilé
Mrs Toïdom	40	20 viii 95	Kar-Koung	–
Miss Clémence	10	21 viii 95	Biramanda	–
Agnès Dénembaye	55	21 viii 95	Niam II	LTDH of Logones and Tanjilé
Martine Makouyonodji	27	21 viii 95	–	LTDH of Logones and Tandjilé
Béatrice Népitimbaye	14	–	–	LTDH of Logones and Tandjilé
Damaris Yondiguissiel		23 viii 95	Djam I	LTDH of Logones and Tandjilé
Rachel Nodjikouael	35	19 viii 95	Krim-Krim	–
Jeanne Neloumbaye	14	2 ix 95	Lara	–
Henriette Larnaïbaye	15	2 ix 95	Lara	–
Gouadjé	12	21 viii 95	Nian II	LTDH of Logones and Tandjilé
Mrs Thomas Mbaïherem		16 ix 95	Nam-Goré	–

A national newspaper gives some additional information about these women: Agnès Dénembaye is the mother of ten children, Damaris Yondiguissiel the mother of seven, Martine Makouyonodji was pregnant at the time, and Béatrice Népitimbaye and Gouadjé were gang-raped; faced with these horrors, the village chief committed suicide.[30]

Table 7.2 Rapes perpetrated by outlaws

Name	Age	Date	Place	Source
Miss Mbaïnaïssem Kilta		6 ix 95	Bague-Dialla	LTDH of Logones and Tandjilé
Miss Koitedje Sourmal		–	–	–
Miss Florence Bekouam		–	–	–
Miss Blanche Guesta		–	–	–

Table 7.3 Rapes perpetrated by regular army forces in western Logone

Name	Age	Date	Place	Source
Roudette Nodjimbadem		14 ix 95	Binde	LTDH of Logones and Tandjile
Odette Balikem		22 ix 95	Doramti	–
Valentine Maoudene	13	–	–	–
Béatrice Djereyom		23 ix 95	Kou-Doholo	–
Mrs Yvette		–	–	–
Mrs Ndoudjinang		–	–	–

Table 7.4 Rapes perpetrated by members of FARF

Name	Age	Date	Place	Source
Ngaryo Nodjilar	15	25 x 95	Komé Ndolebé	LTDH of Logones and Tandjilé
Koïngar Toundemne	11		–	–
Kayalengar Modeal	10		–	–
Djimtoloum Netounanyo	9		–	–
Denise Lonodji			–	–
Laounoum			–	–

The Women's Commission sent an update on 30 May 1997 in which they detail the ongoing violations of women's rights: on 24 October 1996, Fatimé Saleh, a 25-year-old woman, was murdered and her body dumped between the military camp and the police station of Amzoer; on 3 March 1996, Koubra Mahamat, a three-year-old girl, was raped by Mahamat, a 21-year-old man; and on 27 November 1996, the homes of eight women were pillaged and torched.[31] The LTDH has reminded the Chadian government that rape and sexual abuse are forms of torture or cruel, inhuman or degrading treatment clearly in contravention of international human rights standards ratified by Chad, as well as in contravention of international humanitarian law.

Impact of the Conflict on the Status of Women in Chad[32]

Oxfam's Women's Project Officer in Chad, Achta Djibrine Sy, notes that, paradoxically, the conflict has also had a 'positive' impact on Chadian women, empowering them in unexpected ways. The war forced women to provide for their families in situations where men had become unproductive and dependent. As a result, women are more aware of what they can do, of their essential role in the survival of their families and their communities. Women are no longer only dependants but also providers.

Until the outbreak of civil war in 1979, Chadian society was patriarchal, recognizing only men as heads of household and sole decision makers. Men were responsible for providing for the family, women for receiving orders and carrying them out. All household goods belonged to men. Women were confined to biological and social reproduction, which alone gave them status in society. Women's every act and movement was under men's authority and control. Certain women, particularly Muslim women, lived in seclusion, and a wife who went out during the day or engaged in commercial activity would attract the mockery of both family and friends, as she would be exposing her husband's inability to meet her needs. Only widows, divorced women, and women married to very poor men could challenge these social constraints by engaging in income-earning activities.

During the civil war, many men went into exile in the Central African Republic, Cameroon, Congo (Brazzaville), Libya, Côte d'Ivoire and elsewhere, sometimes abandoning their wives and children. Other men remained in Chad but were unable to earn money, because the state ceased to function and many other activities were suspended; the majority of wage-earners were state employees or worked in the private and informal sectors. Some had difficulty adapting while others started to fish, hunt, or work the land. Women were deemed fortunate if their husbands were still alive, even if the men were away or unable to make a financial contribution.

The social disorder brought by the war transformed gender relations. Women invented new ways of making money in order to enable their families to survive. These survival strategies were as varied as the social position of the women concerned. Faced with the increasing needs of their families, some women traded over long distances both inside and outside the country, buying and selling grain, beans, groundnuts, and other foods. They defied danger, fatigue, and other constraints to bring in an income and increase it. Opportunities to make money were very limited; for example, women did not take up activities requiring new technology. Instead, they generally chose food processing, making use of their domestic skills. They also developed commercial networks, resolving problems of purchasing and marketing by trading amongst themselves, women with a surplus selling to those in need of that particular product. As there was no access to banking institutions, women developed *tontines*, a compulsory saving system established by groups of women who each agree to put in a certain sum of money for a given period. The total is then paid out to the members of the group in rotation. The security of the money is assured, and the sums collected allow the women to improve their business and reinvest significant amounts, as well as improve the material conditions of their lives.

In other words, the conflict enabled women to leave the private sphere and participate extensively in the public domain. Although the conflict has increased the numbers of women living in poverty and has exhausted women physically, financially and psychologically, it has also been the foundation of women's awareness of their ability to ensure the survival of their families and communities. Women are no longer regarded only as consumers but also as producers. The war helped them to break with their traditional submission, to acquire more autonomy and personal self-confidence. Today, women's role as producers receives, and reinforces, consideration from their husbands and from Chadian society as a whole.

Even though women and children suffer in armed conflicts, these circumstances also allow them to gain other kinds of power and resources they wouldn't be able to acquire in normal times. Women have demonstrated that they are able to cope and to survive. Of course we deplore the fact that women have to go through these trials to gain their autonomy and independence.

Notes

1 Nomadic pastoralists constitute less than 5 per cent of the population of Chad.
2 See, for example, Michalon and Moyrand 1991.
3 *Tchad 'conflit Nord-Sud': mythe ou réalité?* 1996.
4 Charlton and May 1989.
5 Baroum 1996:71.
6 Sy 1993:11.
7 The LTDH is an independent nongovernmental organization affiliated to the International Federation for Human Rights (*la Fédération internationale des droits de l'homme*). It is a founding member of the Interafrican Union for Human Rights (*l'Union interafricaine des droits de l'homme*), winner of the International Prize for Human Rights in 1992, and Observer Member of the African Commission for Human Rights and Population.
8 In 1991, the President convened a Commission of Inquiry on the Crimes and Misappropriations Committed by the Ex-President Habré, his Accomplices and/or Accessories. Even as the commission was finishing its report, the government was accused of trying to whitewash its own abuses (Hayner 1994:608). (Editors' note.)
9 The reference is to rape as a crime against humanity. For an act to qualify, there must be proof of government participation in or approval of systematic atrocities or persecution; an isolated case is not sufficient (Niarchos 1995:677–8). (Editors' note.)

10 *N'Djaména Hebdo*, No. 186, 1 June 1995, p. 7.

11 The information in this paragraph is taken from Amnesty International 1996a.

12 *Ibid.*

13 'Codo' is a diminutive of the French 'commando' and refers to members of the armed opposition in the two southern provinces of Eastern and Western Logone. (Editors' note.)

14 Amnesty International 1996b:24.

15 A hurdle made of straw supported by wooden stakes, generally used as fencing.

16 Amnesty International 1996b:23.

17 *N'Djaména Hebdo*, No. 199, 7 September 1995, p. 9.

18 *Ibid.*, No. 186, 1 June 1995, p. 7.

19 *Ibid.*, No. 146, 25 August 1994, p. 8.

20 Amnesty International 1991:23.

21 *Ibid.* 1996b:24.

22 *Ibid.*

23 *Ibid.*:43.

24 *Ibid.* 1996a.

25 The information in this paragraph is taken from Amnesty International 1996a.

26 *Ibid.* 1996a.

27 *Ibid.* 1996b:44.

28 Ligue tchadienne des droits de l'homme, commission des femmes, appel au collectif des associations féminines au Tchad (CAFET), N'Djamena, 20 December 1995. (Translation by the editors.)

29 It is interesting that the Women's Commission has published this list, whereas Amnesty International withholds the names of victims and the places where rapes have occurred 'on account of the social stigma involved'. (Editors' note.)

30 *N'Djaména Hebdo*, No. 201, 21 September 1995, p. 11.

31 Letter dated 30 May 1997 from the Women's Commission of the Chadian League for Human Rights.

32 The information in this section is taken from Sy 1993.

8 Hundreds of Victims Silently Grieving

ASSOCIATION OF FEMALE LAWYERS
OF LIBERIA (AFELL)
& THE EDITORS

Editors' Introduction

Founded in the nineteenth century by former American slaves who became the ruling élite of the country, Liberia escaped colonial rule but not foreign interference or political upheaval.[1] In 1980, noncommissioned officers mounted a bloody *coup d 'état,* and Master Sergeant Samuel Doe took power as head of a military junta, initiating seasons of corruption, brutality, and human rights abuses. Fratricidal civil war erupted at the end of 1989, with Charles Taylor of the National Patriotic Front of Liberia (NPFL) and Prince Johnson of the splinter Independent National Patriotic Front of Liberia (INPFL) challenging Doe's Armed Forces of Liberia (AFL). Taylor and various ethnic militias were armed by Burkina Faso, Côte d 'Ivoire, Guinea, Libya and Nigeria (the NPFL, in turn, helped create and arm the Revolutionary United Front in Sierra Leone, plunging that country into civil war).[2] ECOMOG (the Economic Community of West African States Monitoring Group, a peace-keeping force) intervened in August 1990 with UN backing and, in 1992, the UN Security Council voted unanimously to impose an arms embargo. ULIMO (United Liberation Movement for Democracy in Liberia), was among the new groups joining the war; it quickly split into ULIMO-J and ULIMO-K. An estimated 60,000 combatants were bearing arms in 1996.[3]

The lack of discipline in these armies, the reliance on violence and terror as political instruments, the scorched earth policy of the AFL, the wanton atrocities of the NPFL against unarmed civilians, its gruesome use of children as young as six as mine-detectors and soldiers,[4] the massive displacements affecting nearly half of the country's population, the ability of so many outside the country to profit from and prolong this conflict, the abundance of guns despite an embargo, and the increase in armed robberies combine to make this war among the most dreadful in Africa – and ghastly for Liberian women. Too many women are widowed, too many teenaged girls are giving birth and are forced to terminate their education abruptly (even where schools are open), and far too many women and girls have been raped, tortured, kidnapped, and killed. The number of people who have succumbed in this war is unknown. One group estimates that 200,000 civilians, or almost one-tenth of Liberia's population of 2.3 million, have died.[5] Civilians accounted for 90 per cent of the estimated ten thousand deaths in 1990.[6] Only the cynicism of the United States and France matches the inhumanity of the slaughter.[7] Yet Liberia is a signatory to conventions of both international humanitarian law, which is supposed to protect civilians in times of civil war, and international human rights law.[8] Again and again the government and the militias were widely criticized for violating the rights of civilians as the war dragged on. The transgressions of Doe's government deepened the rebellion, precipitating a breakdown in law and order that eventually brought intervention by ECOMOG, itself not blameless.[9] But it is unlikely that the restrictions of Protocol II of the Geneva Convention were on the minds of Doe and his commanders when they launched their initial response to the uprising in 1989, at least in part because there was little prospect that they would be punished for any violations.[10] The violence turned Liberia into a patchwork of armed fiefdoms; most factions appeared to have no particular purpose other than sustained fighting and looting, with civilians as their primary targets. Each successive peace agreement (there have been 33 attempts and 14 agreements so far) seemed merely to give the armies time to rearm.

The Association of Female Lawyers of Liberia (AFELL) responded to our request for information on the impact of the conflict on women by sending us the results of research done by a special committee consisting of M. Masa Kamara, Annie W. Swen and Juanita K. Jarrett. Included is a first-person account by M. Masa Kamara, who is also a magistrate. This chapter incorporates their report and supplements it with information provided by Physicians for Human Rights, the US Committee for Refugees, Human Rights Watch, and other secondary sources.

I interviewed a young Liberian refugee woman in Danane, Côte d'Ivoire, just before my visit to Monrovia. She had been arrested by Charles Taylor' s soldiers in October 1990 and jailed for 65 days. During that time she suffered torture and humiliation of the worst kind. She told me that in jail her head was shaved, and she was whipped with a rope and repeatedly tied up in taipei position.[11] I saw scars on both arms where she said she had been tied and also cut with a knife. In addition to this, she told me that for three days she was naked and had a 15-

inch stick repeatedly thrust up her vagina until she bled. She received no medical treatment and was finally released in January 1991 after a relative interceded on her behalf.[12]

AFELL reports that the women of Liberia are no exceptions when it comes to violations of women's human rights in time of conflict. Between 1990 and 1993, a study conducted by the Center for Abused Women and Girls, a nongovernmental organization,[13] showed that about 80 per cent of victims of sexual abuse were women and girls between ten and 36 years old.

The majority of these assaults occurred far from the seat of central government in Monrovia, in remote areas of what was referred to as 'Greater Liberia' – the rest of the country that was under the nominal control of the NPFL and other rebel soldiers. As the civil conflict was prolonged, the reports of rape showed a change in the age of the victims; between 1990 and 1993, victims were from all age groups, but between 1993 and 1995, the majority of victims fell between the ages of 40 and 65 years. The reason seems to be that with the passage of time, younger women were able to flee from displaced persons camps to relatively safer areas, leaving behind the older women who became prey to rapists.

The trauma of the older age group is compounded by the breach of tradition. The perpetrators of these rape crimes are mostly young men, and in the African tradition, older women look upon young men as their sons. To be raped by a young man is to be raped by one's own son, hence the experiences of this particular group of victims are more shameful and unbearable. The young age of the combatants is remarkable – in one estimate, more than one thousand child soldiers, girls and boys under the age of 15, were active, and perhaps as many as thirty thousand fought for short periods of time to guard their homes and families.[14]

In preparing this report, AFELL consulted with the Center for Abused Women and Girls, which had visited refugees and internally displaced Liberian women in order to ascertain the facts. The women interviewed had been sexually and forcibly abused; some were set free immediately after the incident, but some were forced to become 'wives' of their rebel attackers. The truth of these victims' narrative was confirmed by physical examination.

Shana Swiss, a physician who went to Monrovia on a fact-finding mission in 1991 for the Women's Commission for Refugee Women and Children, a US-based NGO, was also told that some women were held captive and raped repeatedly for weeks until they were able to escape. A Liberian physician told her that village girls as young as ten were 'chosen' by conquering commanding soldiers and forced to leave their villages and accompany them.[15]

AFELL also had access to a study on Liberian rape victims completed in 1995 by a Liberian psychiatrist, Dr B.L. Harris.[16] For his report, Dr Harris chose several centres for displaced persons in Liberia. Interviews with several women again showed a range in the ages of victims between ten and 70 years. This study showed that 33 per cent of the respondents claimed to have been raped, while 18 per cent were reported to have witnessed the rape of their relatives or companions.

Women told Swiss that soldiers forced them to watch the murder of fellow Liberians and required them to applaud or laugh; they were shot if they did not comply. Women who showed any emotion while they were forced to watch the murder of their own or others' children were shot. Several women described seeing the murder of pregnant women and their unborn babies. One woman told Swiss that she was forced to watch while a pregnant woman was held down, her belly cut open, and her unborn baby removed and cut up. This woman said that 40 people were forced to watch and applaud while three soldiers committed this atrocity. Swiss spoke to several women who had witnessed similar incidents in other parts of the country.[17]

Dr Harris confirmed that rape cases were on the increase in areas where there was active fighting and where the conflict was intense and protracted. According to his study, the victims explained that their attackers used threat or force with weapons, especially a gun. The study further showed that pregnancy was reported to have resulted in 6 per cent of the cases with 2 per cent of such cases ending in abortion. Further, Dr Harris confirmed that the psychological trauma can be serious and stressful, not only to the victim, but also to family members. In 45 per cent of these rape cases, the victim did not and could not discuss it with family members because of shame, guilt and self-blame.

M. Masa Kamara, a member of AFELL, who is also a magistrate, witnessed the confession of one attacker who was caught by civilians and taken to court. The crime was committed in 1991 at the onset of the renewed civil war. The first ceasefire had just taken effect, but the area in which the attack occurred was isolated. The victim was a twelve-year-old child. On another occasion, the magistrate learned of brave civilians who arrested one of three armed men of a warring faction and took him to court. These armed men had lured two young female vendors, holding one at gunpoint and raping the other; the nine-year-old victim was thought dead, but she later recovered in hospital.

Neither age nor youth deterred the rapists. Swiss reports being told of an incident in which armed fighters took all but one of 26 schoolgirls from their residential school for one night. They took the girls to a nearby town occupied by a large group of soldiers and returned them to their school only the next morning. Two school staff members and another adult living on the campus told Swiss that many of the girls were crying and extremely upset when they returned and several of them reported that they had been raped.[18]

According to AFELL, it is an established fact that even when there is a lull in fighting, the fighters wait in readiness for the ceasefire to be broken, and then immediately begin to take advantage of the situation, making women their targets. The husband of another rape victim narrated this story in April 1996. The man was a petty trader and the rebels wanted to loot his home; they surrounded his house, held him at gunpoint, and then raped his wife and daughters, forcing him to watch.

With the prolongation of the Liberian civil war, more and more women have suffered indignities and human rights abuses. AFELL notes that its report represents only a minute percentage of the rapes that have occurred. 'Somewhere out there are hundreds of victims silently grieving.'

The Role of Women in Peacemaking

Liberian women have not only been victims of this war; they have also tried to play an active role in ending it. The Liberian Women's Initiative, an umbrella group of religious and social organizations under the leadership of Mary Brownell, a respected educator, took a unified stance at the October 1994 Liberian National Conference: they wanted the disarmament process speeded up.[19] They complained that the UN had ignored a plan they formulated in mid-1994 to provide incentives for disarmament directly to the fighters. They mounted a series of protests, rejecting the roles of former US President Jimmy Carter and UN Special Envoy Trevor Gordon-Somers, who, they felt, were undermining the conference's relevance by encouraging the warring factions to meet separately. They opposed any move that granted new relevance and power to leaders of the armed factions. Inspired by Maureen Shaw, an alliance of women's groups took to the streets of Monrovia demanding the recall of the UN envoy. A group of 17 women led by Mrs Amos Sawyer organized a demonstration in Monrovia against the just-initialled Akosombo Amendment.[20] They opposed it because the amendment, which prolonged the Liberian National Transitional Government, signalled the failure of the factions to reach a permanent agreement.

Liberian women are also playing an active role in politics at the national level. In July 1996 Ruth Perry was appointed chair of Liberia's interim, civilian, largely powerless Council of State. Her position was created by the Abuja II peace accords, the most recent agreement, which seems to be holding. Perry, a 57-year-old widowed mother of seven from Dia in western

Liberia, is the first woman to lead Liberia and the first woman head of state in Africa. She is surrounded on the council by wealthy warlords who constrict her authority by denying her staff and money. Despite their best efforts to silence her, the warlords have not been able to stop Perry from using her office to oppose them publicly and to lead an anti-war campaign. Her goal is to force the factions to give up their guns and submit to an elected government. Perry has travelled around Liberia educating people about their political rights and demanding that the factions implement the peace accord. She gets most of her support from women.[21]

Under the peace agreement, Perry was not permitted to stand in the mid-1997 presidential and legislative elections. There was, however, a woman candidate for president: Ellen Johnson-Sirleaf, 58 years old, a former international banker and senior United Nations official. Mortgaging her UN pension to finance her candidacy, Johnson-Sirleaf ran against Charles Taylor, who started the civil war seven years before and allegedly financed his campaign with wealth siphoned from the resource-rich areas under his control.[22] Taylor, it is feared, will run the country much as Mobutu Sese Seko ran Zaire.[23] Johnson-Sirleaf's unsuccessful campaign relied on borrowed vehicles and volunteers; she represented accountability, institution-building and the ability to attract foreign aid.

The Post-war Humanitarian Situation

At the end of 1995, some 725,000 Liberians were refugees in Guinea, Côte d'Ivoire, Sierra Leone, Nigeria and other countries, and an estimated one million Liberians were internally displaced.[24] Ileana Ros-Lehtinen, Chair of the Africa Subcommittee of the International Relations Committee of the United States House of Representatives, said in hearings on Liberia held on 8 May 1996 that almost every single Liberian no longer lives in the home s/he lived in prior to the war in December 1989. In December 1996, Friends of Liberia, a nongovernmental organization of 800 members based in Washington, DC, reported that at least 200,000 civilians, or almost a tenth of Liberia's population of 2.3 million, have died. Among the dead are fifty thousand children; 300,000 children have been uprooted from their homes, another 30,000 to 50,000 are abandoned or orphaned, and 15,000 are dependent on drugs and/or forced to carry arms. Competing warlords have ravaged Monrovia, the capital city, three times. Churches, hospitals and schools have been burned to the ground.[25]

In September 1996, the Justice and Peace Commission of the National Catholic Secretariat based in Monrovia reported that more than 4,000 young children are suffering from severe malnutrition, while about 20,000 persons are referred to as 'walking skeletons' in the Grand Cape Mount and Bomi counties of western Liberia.[26] Hostilities prevented food and other humanitarian assistance from reaching this region from December 1995 to September 1996.

The Commission noted that respect for human rights is unimpressive. The courts are gradually reopening, but in an environment of prevalent corruption. Law and order have not been stabilized; wrongdoers are not accorded due process and are not punished for crimes committed. For example, the Commission reported that two young women were found dead in Congo Town just outside Monrovia: Christiana Cheeks and Josephine were killed by unknown gunmen, their bodies discovered on 5 August 1996. Suspects were identified but the Justice Ministry has been reluctant to make arrests in spite of repeated calls from members of the public. Generally, the Commission notes, there is a lack of confidence in the local security apparatus; the public perceives all of the agencies to have become appendages of the various factions, making it difficult to provide guarantees for the respect for human rights. There have been constant calls to defactionalize the various security organs. The courts are fraught with factional appointees, compromising the independence and impartiality of the judiciary in the dispensation of justice. The Commission found reports that some factions are operating their individual prison cells outside the framework of the unity government. Escapees have reported gruesome experiences at these illegal prison cells.

ECOWAS continues to guarantee security in Liberia. Some 11,000 ECOMOG forces were on regular patrols in 50 towns and villages where previously they had not been deployed. Victor Malu, commander of ECOMOG, said this was meant to enable them to 'completely dominate the security situation in the Liberian hinterland, thereby making the entire country safe and conducive for election campaigns and other political activities'.[27] ECOMOG disarmed over 30,000 fighters and recovered more than 32,000 weapons – from rifles to anti-aircraft guns and mortars – along with three million rounds of ammunition. ECOMOG has also deployed troops to all of the 13 county capitals 'to encourage internally displaced citizens to return to their homes in the hinterland'.[28] In May 1997 alone, two thousand Liberian refugees returned to the country through 11 border towns. Malu added that the idea behind the deployment was to enhance the restoration of economic and commercial activities and general normalcy in Liberia.

Notes

1 For a detailed history and an account of events from 1980 see Reno 1996 and Tarr 1993.
2 See Volman in this volume for more details.
3 Riley and Sesay 1996:429. For a description of the various armed factions see *New African*, March 1995:10–14.
4 UNICEF (1996:17) reports that a quarter of the combatants in the various fighting factions were children – some 20,000 in all – and that the NPFL had its own 'small boys' unit', ranging in age from six to 20.
5 Friends of Liberia 1996.
6 Swiss 1992:11.
7 The United States supported the corrupt regime of Samuel Doe, sending US $500 million from 1980 to 1986; in the 1980s Liberia was the largest recipient of US aid in sub-Saharan Africa. From 1990 the US contributed over US$440 million in humanitarian aid and US$60 million to support ECOMOG, but it took no part in negotiating a truce (*West Africa*, 10–16 October 1994:1743). Meanwhile, US companies with interests in timber, diamonds, gold, iron ore and natural rubber allegedly continued to do business with Charles Taylor (*West Africa*, 30 November–6 December 1992:2053).
8 Liberia ratified both Geneva Conventions in 1954 and the Additional Protocols in 1988. In 1982, Liberia ratified the African Charter on Human and Peoples' Rights and in 1984, the Convention on the Elimination of all Forms of Discrimination against Women. In 1990, Liberia signed the Convention on the Rights of the Child. See Chapter 1 for a description of the protections conferred by these instruments.
9 Human rights groups accused ECOMOG of committing human rights abuses and some ECOMOG soldiers of assisting and equipping Liberian factions (US Committee for Refugees 1996:54), and a relief worker reported seeing a young boy pimping Liberian teenaged girls to West African soldiers in Monrovia (he received $10 for each girl) (Swiss 1991:5). ECOMOG is dominated by Nigeria; for a description of Nigeria's role in the Liberian crisis see *New African*, March 1995.
10 Copson 1990:6.
11 *Taipei* is a form of torture that involves pulling the shoulders back and tying the elbows together; it causes nerve damage leading to complete and possibly permanent paralysis of both hands. A variation used in Chad is called *abatchar*; the legs are pulled up and bound to the arms, which draws back the head and arches the back. (Editors' note.)
12 Swiss 1991:6.
13 Center for Abused Women and Girls: 'Study on Rape in War-torn Liberia', unpublished report.
14 Swiss 1992:8.
15 *Ibid.* 1991:6.
16 Harris 1995.

17 Swiss 1991:6.
18 Swiss 1992:4.
19 Barrett 1994.
20 Named for the Ghanaian town of Akosombo (55 miles north of Accra) in which the debates took place, the document amends the peace accord signed in Cotonou in 1993 (*New African*, November 1994). (Editors' note.)
21 'Perry Leads Liberia with Power Only to Persuade', Akoromoa <597864@ICAN.NET> 31 January 1997.
22 French 1997.
23 *Ibid.*
24 US Committee for Refugees 1996:53.
25 Friends of Liberia 1996.
26 National Catholic Secretariat, Justice and Peace Commission 1996.
27 Quoted in Oyo 1997.
28 *Ibid.*

9 We Left Our Shoes Behind

TECKLA SHIKOLA

Editor's Introduction

The following account by Teckla Shikola should be read against the history of Namibia's long and bitter struggle for independence, which began with German colonization in 1890. After the defeat of Germany in the First World War, Namibia (then called South West Africa) was mandated to South Africa by the League of Nations. South Africa annexed South West Africa in 1948, a move that eventually led the United Nations in 1966 to withdraw the mandate and call for South Africa's immediate departure. The South African National Party government ignored the UN resolution.

The United Nations recognized the South West Africa People's Organization (SWAPO) as the sole authentic representative of the Namibian people. In 1966, SWAPO's newly formed military arm, the People's Liberation Army of Namibia (PLAN), launched a guerrilla campaign against South Africa. The International Court of Justice ruled in 1971 that South Africa's occupation was illegal, but the war continued. With the end of Portuguese rule, Angola opened up to SWAPO forces, giving them access to the northern border. In 1973, the South African Defence Force carried out a series of attacks on SWAPO camps in Angola. South African forces invaded Angola in 1975, escalating the conflict and turning northern Namibia into a heavily militarized zone. SWAPO stepped up its campaign from bases in Angola and Zambia in 1978. Four years later, Angola signed a nonaggression treaty with South Africa, but SWAPO continued its guerrilla activity in Namibia. In 1988, following the defeat of South African forces at Cuito Canavale, Angola, Cuba and South Africa signed an agreement providing for Namibian independence. UN-supervised elections were held in November 1989. Namibia gained formal independence on 21 March 1991.

Women were active in all aspects of SWAPO's work, including active combat in PLAN. Integration in the military came about as a result of constant pressure by the SWAPO Women's Council to be fully and equally involved at all levels of the struggle.[1] This memoir by a woman combatant is based on a recorded conversation we held with Teckla Shikola in June 1996 at the end of her year as a fellow of the Hubert H. Humphrey programme at Rutgers University.

I left Namibia in 1977. I was sixteen years old. I fled with six girlfriends from secondary school in Oshaha, which is about 100 km from the Namibian/Angolan border. The education system was bad and the conditions at our boarding school were not good. Sometimes we used to have classes only once a week because South African soldiers disrupted the schedule. They would come to our school and beat us. Things were really very bad. It was a government requirement that you had to go into military service either before you went to school or after you finished. You went to be trained by the South Africans. So we just decided to escape from school.

On our way, we stopped at my father's place in Outapi, about 20 km from the border. We spent the night there, but he didn't know where we were going. I left Namibia without my father's knowledge. If he had known, he would not have allowed me to go. People had been leaving the country since 1974 and nobody came back; you didn't hear anything about them, whether they were still alive or not, nothing. No, my father couldn't allow it.

So that my father wouldn't be suspicious, we decided that we would each leave a pair of shoes. Everybody had to leave a pair of shoes at my father's place, so that he would think that we were coming back.

We were not the first school kids to go: SWAPO used to come looking for people who were ready to leave the country, to escape. It was easier when SWAPO came, because they would take you with them across the border.

When we left school we were afraid that the South African soldiers would stop us.[2] We knew we would be reported missing from school and that the South African army would come looking for us. So we changed our clothes at my father's house, and we went toward the border to cross into Angola. But the soldiers caught up with us and asked us where we were going. We said we were going to the North to meet a woman. They asked us questions, 'Are you going to Angola?' They said, 'We hope you are not going to Angola.'

They let us pass and we went to the border and crossed into Angola. And on the other side we were arrested by Angolan soldiers, members of the MPLA.[3] They took us to Kalwecke, about 50 km north of the Namibian border. Language was a problem: we couldn't speak Portuguese and they didn't speak Afrikaans, our official language. They took us to a certain place in Kalwecke, and they separated us. We were seven girls. They sent four to jail. That left me, my friend, and another girl. There were three MPLA chiefs and three of us. They said, 'We are going to marry you so you are not going to join SWAPO.' Of course they meant they wanted to have sex with us.

But we were able to send a message to SWAPO that we had been arrested by the MPLA in Angola. Luckily the SWAPO soldiers came by while we were still in Kalwecke, and they took us with them. That was a narrow escape.

I left Namibia at the beginning of June and in September I was sent to school in Zambia.[4] I flew to Lusaka and I attended the United Nations Institute for Namibia from 1977 until 1981. From there I went back to Angola for military training. I had to undergo six months of military training. It was not easy at all – the conditions and everything, oh my God! You do all these things, saluting, you have to say yes to everything, 'Yes Chief!' You get used to it. I think I would have preferred to go through military training first and be put in school afterwards. I was trained together with other women and our barracks were separate from the men's. We were very few women, we filled just one or two barracks. We were not completely separated from the men because for security reasons they couldn't put us too far away.

After military training, either you stayed on as an instructor, teaching the new people who are coming from home or from the UN Institute in Lusaka to join the army, or you went to the front, to the battlefield or some other area. They decided that I should stay at that military base to teach the new arrivals. I was trained as a commissar and, after I finished my military training, I was placed in the political section. As a commissar, I was a leader, mobilizing and encouraging soldiers. I had to devote at least one day a week to teaching and training others, telling them what is happening in the country and in the world, why they are fighting, that sort of training.

I did this work for SWAPO at a military base. I stayed for about three months, and then they decided that I had to go to the front. In the military, usually there is no choice. I think this is good because, otherwise, you would end up having nobody who wants to go and fight. We left Namibia because we wanted to fight for our country, but we had no idea what the situation was like. So I went to the front and stayed at the operation command headquarters, the place from which they issued orders to the soldiers, who were deployed at many bases.

On the Frontlines

I was in the army for eight years. I served as a soldier, fighting at the front for four years. I think we were only three or four hundred women. It was not easy at all. When the South African soldiers attacked, there was nothing you could do. When they came, they came armed, so many of them, with many war planes that flew above us. But you just survive, you don't know how, you just survive. It is afterwards when you go back home that you realize, oh my God, I don't believe what I went through! I was strong. The commanders and chiefs came to respect me. They thought they were going to do all those funny things, make love to me and make me pregnant, but I was strong. And now they respect me. It was not easy to stay with all those men, not only to stay among them, but when the situation got bad, when those Boers came and attacked, I thought, oh my God, I'd better get pregnant and go back. But the next day when the situation got better, I'd say, I'm not going back. And then they'd attack again, oh my God!

Most of the fighting took place in Angola and in northern Namibia. Our soldiers used to go on attack inside Namibia, but the South African army didn't wait for us, they came to look for us, for our bases, in Angola. Most of the bases were near the border. And they were near the villages, near Angolan civilians. Those people suffered when the South African army came and bombed our bases. Some villagers were really understanding, especially as Angola became independent only in 1975; they thought we were right to fight for the independence of our country. But there were others who just couldn't understand why they had to hide in the bush during the raids, why they had to suffer, why they were being killed by the South African army. They wanted us to go back home and make peace, they thought that fighting isn't the only solution, that we should sit down and talk and get our independence by peaceful means.

On the other hand, SWAPO soldiers were also defending those civilians against UNITA, because UNITA really used to harass them.[5] UNITA was scared of SWAPO soldiers so, whenever we were there, we protected them. That made relations between the civilian population and our Namibian troops easier. Our situation was unlike other wars of liberation. In Zimbabwe, for example, the guerrillas asked parents to send their daughters to the camps to help soldiers with housekeeping, laundry and preparing food. That didn't happen in Angola; SWAPO men did the cooking. To this day I don't know how to cook.

When it came to sex, I think the only people who used to have sex were the chiefs and the commanders because they were the only ones who used to get hold of women. You rarely found ordinary soldiers with women.

Where would they find them, except the three or four women who used to come to the camps? They were not allowed to go to the villages to find women. There were strict rules. I think it was part of the agreement between SWAPO and the Angolan government. The soldiers were not even allowed to go into a house unless ordered to. If you were seen in the village, you could be suspected of giving information or of trying to escape. The only time they could have sex was when they were sent to the civilian areas which were full of women with only a few soldiers guarding them.

There were few women at the front, perhaps two hundred. At the beginning, they were sending hundreds of women but later they decided not to send so many because the situation at the front was really bad. The conditions worsened when the South Africans attacked our bases. I was at the front when South African soldiers came and bombed all the bases. They used to attack during the dry season when there was no water. When you had to move from base to base, you travelled without any drop of water. Sometimes people were so thirsty they drank contaminated water and they died. Once we stayed seven days without food, there was no food at all. But among those who died were only men, not a single woman. Women are really very strong. It is surprising, but men are cowards when it comes to hunger, they really are. The front was dangerous, and it was not a good idea to send women because South African soldiers used to fire certain guns, I forget the name of the guns, but once they fire them, even if you just finished your menstruation, you start menstruating again automatically.

My responsibilities were to check that all the women were okay, that they had sanitary pads and soap. I used to travel from one base to another, and I also had to go back and forth to Luanda, to look for all those necessary supplies. I was a member of the SWAPO Women's Council, which was responsible for all women abroad, both at the front and in the civilian camps.

They used to send me for refresher courses, sometimes for as long as a year. For example, once they sent me to Bulgaria for a year of leadership training – really it was brainwashing in communism. They would send people to Bulgaria or Russia or East Germany, the communist countries. SWAPO was a socialist party.

Another of my responsibilities was to teach family planning. Many women became pregnant. Some became pregnant because the situation at the front was terrible, the conditions were so bad they couldn't stand it, no one could. If you got pregnant, they sent you to the rear. Some women used pregnancy as an excuse to leave the front. I had to tell these women to use family planning. The men were against family planning and they mocked me. They said, 'How can you listen to that woman, can't you see how old she is and she doesn't have a baby? Because she used family planning, she won't give birth anymore. You listen to her and use that family planning and you will never give birth either.'

We had pills. Only pills. I was surprised that they didn't supply condoms. I didn't see condoms until very late in the war. It was difficult for women to hold onto their supply of pills. Sometimes there were surprise attacks and you had to leave everything right there, and the next day you wouldn't have any pills. Many of the women got pregnant. There were no hormonal injections. SWAPO was very against Depo-Provera, because when people came from home, they told us that women were being forced to take Depo-Provera.[6] There was a rumour that something was killing the black babies. Some said the government paid a special amount of money for every black baby killed after birth. We thought there was an organized campaign to kill all the black kids, so that there would be fewer black people.

I didn't really see rape cases as such, but you know, sometimes, when you are coming from home, you are new, and they train you in the army to say yes. Whenever someone in charge calls you, you shouldn't refuse, you don't say no, you have to go. You feel scared of saying no, you cannot talk directly to a commander. Sometimes the chiefs would call out these poor young girls fresh from home. The chiefs made love to them, and the women became pregnant without knowing the person who impregnated them, sometimes they didn't even know his name. Some commanders had fifteen or eighteen kids. It is not really rape in a direct way as such but just the way the chiefs were. I didn't hear of any case where someone was raped. Maybe it happened in the civilian camps, or maybe women didn't come forward because they felt ashamed about reporting to people what had happened. I haven't really known a case where a woman went and reported that she had been raped.

One problem was that ongoing relationships were not possible. Once they found out that you were pregnant, you had to be sent to the rear. Few soldiers dared to ask for permission to go and see their kids. So it was very rare that a father would see them or that a woman would ask for special permission to go and see the chief, even if she knew who was the father of her child. After a woman gave birth, she was sent to school or she stayed in the camps and attended classes that were held under the trees. We also had kindergartens for the children. Mothers were not sent back to the battlefield, they were not separated from their children. The only way they might be separated was when the child turned six and was sent somewhere else for primary school. In this case, the mother and child would be separated and, in some instances, the mother might be sent again to the front.

Few women found a husband or settled somewhere when they had children. The problem with war is terrible, you cannot even say, okay, now I have my husband or boyfriend, because you will stay with that person maybe for three or four months, then he will be sent to the front and you won't even hear about him anymore. Then you find another man and then again he will be sent away. So, some women ended up having four or five kids with different fathers. You didn't even know if the fathers were still alive or if they were dead, because they wouldn't tell you even if they knew. You wouldn't even know.

But at the time, the women didn't feel that it was bad to have these children. You didn't feel it until you got back home. That is when you realized this was bad. But when you are in that situation, you don't feel it, you experience it as normal, it was just how it was in the war. They realized when they got back. Like now, when they are not able to take care of their children, now is when they realize that this was bad. During the war, SWAPO was taking care of all the kids. The women received clothing, food, everything was there. No matter how much we soldiers were starving at the front, those kids were having a lot of food. So, during the war, the women didn't really feel the absence of husbands because they had no responsibilities, they didn't have to provide anything for the kids. It is now that they feel it because it is so difficult to maintain those kids.

There was no stigma attached to children who weren't with their fathers. These single mothers were not alone, there were three or four women in the same situation at any one time, and they encouraged one another. At the same time, there was a sort of pride, they were proud to have the commander's kid. You were somebody big, somebody special with the commander's kid, with the chief's kid, they really felt proud of it.

Of course there was rape when the South African soldiers captured Namibian women. In 1978 the South Africans attacked two civilian camps, which were full of women and children. Many people were killed in the Kassinga massacre, I think around four hundred, and others were captured alive.[7] There was another camp called Vietnam, in which some people were killed and others were captured alive, among them also were women who were sent somewhere in South Africa and some were sent to camps in Namibia where they were tortured and some were trained as spies. Some of these people were sent back to Angola, they came back to join SWAPO. Who knew that they were sent to spy on SWAPO? They stayed and were trained, but some escaped. I don't know how they managed to escape. By now it was difficult to trust those people. They came and stayed, they were asked some questions, but it was difficult, those people didn't talk. They wouldn't tell you anything. Whatever happened to them, I don't know, I really don't know what the South Africans used to do to those people. You asked them and they wouldn't talk at all. They came back, they just looked at you, and they wouldn't say anything. All the humiliations they went through. And they were brainwashed.

The South Africans also captured SWAPO soldiers during attacks and asked them where our bases were. Whenever someone was captured, we had to move because we knew this person was going to talk. We didn't blame him because he was tortured and made to give the information. If you don't talk, they will kill you and sometimes even if you talked, they killed you anyway. It is not an easy life. If there could be a means of avoiding war....

Real rape occurred inside Namibia, rather than in the battle zones. Women in the villages were raped by the black forces. Those who were not raped were killed or beaten and afterwards their crops were destroyed and they abandoned their houses. Not only were South African soldiers responsible, but also our own brothers who joined the South West African Territorial Force (SWATF), which was different from the South African army. SWATF was an all-black army of Namibians.[8] Those people were really notorious for raping women. During the years of struggle, our lives were organized in such a way that we had to do things against one another, brothers and sisters against brothers and sisters. The hatred was so intense. The South Africans really knew how to divide and rule. They made sure it was black troops who raped. What they did to the black people, changing them into spies and sending them back to Angola to spy on SWAPO, those things were nasty.

Racism in my country was such that I don't think you could find a case where a white man raped a black woman. I don't think that happened. I think that if it did, a white man would kill himself rather than admit it. I don't think that they have sex even with black prostitutes, only white prostitutes.

To fight for your own country is really good. But in this war, you kept whatever politics you were given from the beginning. Our brothers in the South African army [SWATF] were told that SWAPO fighters were terrorists, that if SWAPO took over, they would bring in a communist government and that you have to share everything in a communist society, even your wife. And they really believed this. If I hadn't left the country, I might have joined SWATF, and I am sure I would have believed whatever they told me. I do not blame my brothers and sisters who joined SWATF. The army was the only highly paid job at that time. If you were not a soldier, you starved, and anyway they would have come and killed you or forced you to join SWATF. That is why most young people left the country, or they left the north and went to the south because it was more peaceful in the south. In the north, roads were destroyed, houses were abandoned, and civilians really suffered, especially women and children.[9]

The Return to Namibia

The worst time for me was the first of April 1989, when the ceasefire was supposed to be implemented.[10] The South African soldiers were supposed to be confined to their bases so that the SWAPO soldiers who were already inside the country would be secure. Something went wrong somewhere, we don't know what, maybe the agreement wasn't properly understood. But the South African soldiers started to fight the SWAPO soldiers who were already inside the country. It was a real massacre, a real betrayal. Oh my God, it was awful. People were not supposed to die at that time. We were preparing to go back home in June. This was a real betrayal and it was so bad, really unbelievable. All of this happened in the north of Namibia, where the war mostly took place, and the people really suffered.

It was at this time that I had to return. I was put in the first group to be repatriated from Angola to Namibia. I was the leader of that group, so I had to be the first person to descend from the plane. And all the time I was thinking of April first, and they are sending me to the north of Namibia. There were four flights, one was going to the north and three to the south. The south was safe, there was no war in the south, the worst of the war was in the north where we were going and we were very scared because the massacre had just happened. We landed at Ondangwa airport. Ondangwa was a military base, a military airport. Oh! I had to get out now, I was carrying the picture of President Nujoma, another woman was carrying the SWAPO flag. I cannot describe my feelings.

I had to dress as a civilian, who even knew that I was a soldier? Nobody knew. If they had known, they would have killed me. The South Africans are stubborn, and they would have killed you if they knew that you were a soldier. They were probably thinking that SWAPO would send civilians first and the real soldiers would come later. Nobody knew that we were guerrillas. I had problems putting on a skirt for the first time in years. I was feeling awful. You could see the difference in skin color between my arms and legs, because I used to wear trousers all the time.

And so we returned. We found Boers and some UN soldiers, but I was scared, I was really scared. So many people came to meet us, so many that it took an hour to reach the fence, which was just a few metres from the landing strip. We didn't know what to say. I was crying because I was so happy. I couldn't believe that I was finally home after eight years.

They took us to the UNHCR (UN High Commission for Refugees) resettlement camps. We couldn't go straight to our homes, we didn't know where to go. We stayed in the camps while we sent our names to churches to tell our parents to come and pick us up. When you are in exile, you have no communication with your family. If you write them even once, they will be beaten up by Boers. Letters were intercepted. We didn't know whether our parents were alive and our parents didn't know if we were alive. When I left, my mother was already dead, but my father was still alive.

It was so scary when we returned because so many stories, so many rumours, were circulating. Many people heard that I had been killed. Even my brothers got a letter when they were in Angola saying that I was dead. My brothers were also in exile, one was in the army and one was studying.

It was very difficult to reunite certain families because some had children who had served on both sides. The SWATF and SWAPO soldiers had been enemies. Those who served in SWATF didn't want to feel defeated, and the ones who served in SWAPO thought their brothers had betrayed them. It was brother fighting against brother and sister against sister. It was really difficult to unite these two groups, not only with each other but also with their parents who didn't know what to make of all this. All the children are their flesh and blood, what to do? Parents who supported the South African army didn't want to hear about their own kids in SWAPO, they called them terrorists.

Some parents didn't want their kids to come home and the kids felt bad. It was not an easy situation at all. It took a long time for us to adjust and for our parents to adjust to us. They were told we used to eat grass, that we are bad people, we are killers. Even after we arrived we were not sure of our reception, we were scared of them and they were also scared of us. So it wasn't easy.

I waited and waited for someone from my village to come and pick me up but nobody came. Apparently my father had died and nobody wanted to tell me the truth. One day I decided to go home and check for myself. I went and I found my stepmother. When she saw me, she started to cry and I realized that something was wrong. I learned that my father had died in 1980 or 1981. To this day, we are not positive that he is dead. Perhaps he is still alive somewhere? People at home hoped that he had crossed the border into Angola. When we were in Angola, we thought our father was still at home. We do not know where he is because his body has never been found. We hope that he is dead, because SWATF troops came and took him away. The South African soldiers used to go from house to house. Sometimes, someone would inform them that SWAPO soldiers had come to one of the houses to ask for food. They also punished parents who had kids abroad. My father was looking after his cattle, so they took him and they took the cattle, too. Really, the civilians suffered in this war, especially those in the north.

The civilians really suffered, particularly women and children, but after the war, no one mentioned the contributions women made during the liberation struggle. That's true all over the world. You never find an appreciation of what women did. Men appreciate women who cook for them, and they respect women who fought in the war with them, but after independence, they didn't really consider women as part of the liberation movement.

The UN decided that I should stay at the resettlement camp and take care of other returnees. So I stayed and did that for a year. I distributed provisions like food, soap, blankets, whatever we were giving out. Even after people had gone back to their families, we still had to provide food. There had been a drought in the country for many years, and those who were coming back were bringing six or seven kids with them. It was not an easy time. The food distribution was really helpful, because most people couldn't find jobs right away. And there were no benefits for those who served in the army, not like in Zimbabwe, where soldiers were given money.

I was lucky because I was hired immediately by UNHCR. Then from there I joined UNICEF in 1990. After that the Ministry of Local Government and Housing wanted me to join the government so I left UNICEF and joined the government. Later UNICEF wanted me back, so I went to work for them again. Now I am working for the Desert Research Foundation, a non-governmental organization combating desertification.

I don't want to be separated from my country anymore. I just want to stay home. The war was such a difficult time. Now I respect all those people like Clotilde, who have had a war in their country. I know how it feels. It is not easy. You have to be strong. People committed suicide because they were in such difficult situations. There you are, you don't know when you are going to get your independence, you don't know whether you will die during the war and you will never go back to your country. We couldn't believe it when we were told we had to pack our things, we were going back home. We thought it was a dream.

Notes

1 Cleaver and Wallace 1990:6.
2 The government imposed a dawn-to-dusk curfew in the war zone. (Editors' note.)
3 The MPLA (People's Movement for the Liberation of Angola) is the party that led Angola to independence from Portugal in 1975. (Editors' note.)
4 As a 16-year-old, Teckla would not have been allowed to go and fight; only women between the ages of 19 and 30 were sent to the front (Cleaver and Wallace 1990:15). (Editors' note.)
5 UNITA (National Union for the Total Independence of Angola) is the party that

contested the MPLA's electoral victory with backing from South Africa and the United States. (Editors' note.)

6 For accounts of government use of Depo-Provera, an injectable hormonal contraceptive, see Lindsay 1991 and Cleaver and Wallace 1990:52. (Editors' note.)

7 On 4 May 1978 South African troops destroyed a large refugee camp at Kassinga, killing some 750 Namibians, mostly noncombatants, a majority of them children and students. About 270 were taken captive back to Namibia; after interrogation, frequently accompanied by torture, fewer than 160 were released. The remaining 112 were detained in a concentration camp at the Tenegab military base near Marienthal. (Editors' note.)

8 SWATF was formed in 1978 as part of a policy of 'Namibianizing' the war. It was composed of black troops recruited on a tribal basis, mainly in the southern part of the country. From 1981 conscription was compulsory in the south and voluntary in the north (Cleaver and Wallace 1990:9). There were eight 'ethnic' battalions in October 1988, with a total of 21,900 men. The units came under the command of professional white South African Defence Force (SADF) brigade commanders. The SADF forces also had black infantrymen. The most notorious black units were the 'Koevoet', a highly mobile counter-insurgency unit that perpetrated massacres, sometimes disguised as SWAPO soldiers. (Editors' note.)

9 The northern war zone, where martial law was imposed, encompassed Ovambo, Kavango, Caprivi and Kaoko. (Editors' note.)

10 The UN Plan, to which SWAPO was not a party, assumed that all PLAN forces were in Zambia and Angola; no provision was made for PLAN forces inside Namibia. Angola and Cuba were to ensure that PLAN forces in Angola withdrew north of the 16th parallel following the withdrawal of South African troops from Angola. Hostilities in Namibia would cease. But there were SWAPO forces inside Namibia and others entered on the eve of the ceasefire, and they were attacked by SADF, SWATF, and Koevoet (counter-insurgency) forces. (Editors' note.)

10 The Militarization of Africa

DANIEL VOLMAN

Ever since African countries began to gain their independence from colonial rule in the late 1950s, the lives and security of Africans have been deeply affected by the military activities of the former colonial powers, the global superpowers, other extra-continental states, international and regional organizations, the governments of other African countries, and a wide variety of non-state actors. This external military involvement – particularly the transfer of massive quantities of arms by the superpowers and their allies – was responsible for much of the warfare and other forms of violence that Africans suffered during the Cold War era. And since the end of the Cold War, the legacy of this involvement and the continuing flow of immense amounts of weaponry into Africa are causing even greater violence and devastation throughout the continent. Indeed, Africa today is literally awash in arms, particularly guns and other light weaponry of the sort that have much more impact on the security and daily lives of civilians, especially women, than tanks and combat aircraft.

This chapter will describe and analyse the militarization of the African continent, specifically the role of extra-continental and African actors in the diffusion of weapons and in promoting the violence and insecurity that now pervade many African societies. This analysis is intended to provide a context in which to examine and understand the impact of conflict on African women. The first section will examine the militarization of Africa during the Cold War era. This section will focus on arms sales and other military assistance programmes, foreign military bases and base-access agreements, and direct military intervention in African conflicts. The following sections will be devoted to developments since the end of the Cold War. These sections will examine and analyse recent military activity on the continent, the reasons for recent changes in the weapons trade, the nature of these changes, and their consequences.

Patterns of Militarization in the Cold War Era

The extensive militarization that Africa experienced during the period of the Cold War was the result of numerous factors. The former colonial powers established military relationships with their former colonial possessions and with other African countries to protect and extend their political, economic and cultural influence; to promote their arms industries; and to bolster their status as major powers. The two superpowers and China established military relationships with African countries as part of their global rivalry, in which the African continent was treated as a battlefield that was important strategically but not so vital that competition was likely to lead to dangerous consequences for them. And other countries, both in Africa and in other parts of the Third World, became involved in order to gain political power or economic benefits.

Throughout the Cold War era, the Soviet Union and other members of the Warsaw Pact Organization were some of the most important sources of arms, training, technical assistance and other military support obtained by African governments, insurgents, and other armed groups. From the late 1950s to the late 1980s, they sold or gave approximately $21 billion worth of military equipment to sub-Saharan Africa (and another $25 billion worth to Libya and Algeria).[1] The Soviet Union and its allies also provided training and technical assistance to African military forces. The largest sums were received by the armed forces and insurgent groups in Egypt, Libya, Algeria, Somalia, Ethiopia, Angola and Mozambique. In addition, significant military aid was supplied to armed groups in Congo (Kinshasa), the Zimbabwe African People' s Union in Southern Rhodesia (now Zimbabwe) and the African National Congress in South Africa.

The United States was another important source of military assistance for African governments and insurgent groups. During the Cold War era, Washington sold or gave some $1.5 billion worth of weapons and other military hardware to sub-Saharan Africa through the foreign military sales programme, the military assistance programme and the commercial sales programme (and more than $1.5 billion worth to Morocco, Algeria, and Tunisia).[2] Like the Soviet bloc, the United States also provided training and technical assistance to African military forces. Egypt, Morocco, Tunisia, Sudan, Somalia, Ethiopia, Nigeria, Liberia, Kenya, Congo (Kinshasa) and

Chad received the largest sums. In addition, American military aid was provided covertly to UNITA and FNLA in Angola by the Central Intelligence Agency. And the United States also developed a military and intelligence-sharing relationship with the apartheid regime in South Africa – continuing and expanding a relationship with South Africa that began during the Second World War – although this relationship was inhibited over time by the UN arms embargo, domestic political constraints, and Congressional legislation.

A third important source of military equipment for Africa was France. During this period, France sold or gave more than $5 billion worth of military assistance to sub-Saharan African governments, primarily – but not exclusively – in francophone countries, along with military training and technical assistance (and more than $2 billion worth to Morocco, Algeria, Libya and Tunisia).[3] France gave the largest amounts to Egypt, Libya, Morocco, Tunisia, Cameroon, Gabon, Nigeria, Côte d'Ivoire, Sudan, Angola, Congo (Kinshasa) and South Africa. In addition, France provided major assistance to South Africa to help the National Party government develop its own arms industry, particularly by licensing the South African arms industry to produce French-designed armoured vehicles and other weapons systems.

African governments and insurgents also obtained substantial quantities of weaponry, training, technical assistance and other military support from other industrial countries. Much of this support came from countries in Western Europe, including the United Kingdom, West Germany, Italy, Belgium, Switzerland, Austria and Spain. Other sources included China, Yugoslavia, Brazil, and Israel (which supplied arms and other military assistance to Congo (Kinshasa), Ethiopia and rebel forces in Sudan, and which developed a close military relationship with South Africa that involved both arms sales and cooperation in the development and production of military equipment).

Along with supplying military assistance, foreign powers established their own military bases and gained access to the military facilities of African countries throughout the continent. France maintained military bases in Gabon, Côte d'Ivoire, Djibouti, Senegal, the Central African Republic and Mauritius, and on Réunion Island. The French government stationed up to 16,000 of its troops at these bases and used them frequently to intervene both within these nations and in other African countries; one of the most notable examples of French military intervention was in Chad where thousands of French troops were deployed almost continuously to defend the government against Libyan-backed rebels. The United States negotiated agreements with Ethiopia, Morocco, Tunisia, Egypt, Sudan, Somalia, Kenya and Liberia; these agreements granted American troops access to local bases and Washington deployed its forces to a number of these facilities on several occasions, including the abortive attempt to rescue American hostages in Iran in 1980, the Persian Gulf War, and the humanitarian and military intervention in Somalia from 1992 to 1994. And the Soviet Union had access at various times to local bases in Guinea, Somalia, Ethiopia, Egypt, Libya, Congo, Angola and Mozambique.

Finally, foreign powers dispatched troops to defend friendly governments and intervene directly in African conflicts. A variety of forces intervened in Congo (Kinshasa) during the 1960s, including those of France, Belgium, the United States, the Soviet Union, and the contingents deployed under the mandate of the United Nations Security Council. Troops from France, Belgium, the United States and Morocco intervened in Congo (Kinshasa) in 1977 and 1978 to suppress insurgents in Shaba Province. Soviet, Cuban, Congolese (Kinshasa) and South African troops intervened during various stages of the civil war in Angola. Soviet and Cuban troops intervened in Ethiopia after Somali troops invaded in 1977 and remained in the country to fight against several insurgent groups. And the United States launched air raids against Libya in 1986 in an attempt to kill Colonel Qadaffi and destabilize his government.

In addition to the military activities of non-African states, a number of African states and non-state actors also played a significant role in the militarization of the continent during the Cold War era. The most important role was undoubtedly that played by the apartheid regime in South Africa, both internally and in other African countries. Internally, this included the expansion of the South African Defence Force, the South African Police, and specialized security agencies; the establishment of a major arms industry capable of producing a wide variety of weapons systems and other military equipment; and the transfer of arms to the Inkatha Freedom Party and the armed forces of the 'independent' homeland territories. Externally, this included the expansion of the armed forces of the South African-controlled administration in South West Africa (Namibia); operations conducted by South African military units in Angola, Southern Rhodesia (Zimbabwe), Mozambique, Zambia and other countries in the region; operations conducted by South African security personnel throughout Africa and in other parts of the world against anti-apartheid activists and organizations; military support for UNITA in Angola and RENAMO in Mozambique; and the sale of arms to other African countries, particularly to the Hutu-extremist government in Rwanda prior to the 1994 genocide.[4]

Private arms dealers (usually operating illegally), mercenaries and private noncommercial organizations, including political and religious groups, also played an important role in the militarization of Africa during this period. One of the most notable examples of this was in Mozambique, where extremely conservative political and religious groups and individuals in the United States and other countries provided financial and material support to RENAMO.

The Evolution of Militarization Since the End of the Cold War

Since the end of the Cold War, there have been significant changes in the African arms trade and in the nature of African conflicts. A number of external and internal factors have shaped the evolution of the militarization of Africa. On one hand, this evolution has been due partly to the reduced interest of the former superpowers in Africa as a result of the end of their global rivalry and Africa's declining importance in the new international order. As a consequence of this, the United States and the former republics of the Soviet Union – and, to a lesser extent, France as well – have sharply curtailed or eliminated programmes that provide arms to Africa for free or at concessionary rates.

Because most African governments and other recipients do not have the money to buy most types of military hardware at free market prices, most of them are no longer able to obtain substantial quantities of heavy weaponry (such as tanks and combat aircraft) from their traditional sources. There are, however, some important exceptions to this generalization: Iranian financing makes it possible for Sudan to pay for heavy weapons and other equipment obtained from China; revenues from the sale of oil, diamonds and other valuable resources permit the military forces in Angola (both the government's and UNITA's), Nigeria, Botswana and Zimbabwe to make major arms purchases; and French military credits allow Senegal and Chad to procure heavy weapons systems from France. Its relatively developed economy gives South Africa the money to buy expensive military hardware on the international market. Other African countries, however, are still able to acquire substantial quantities of small arms and other light weapons from their previous suppliers, since these are considerably less expensive.

Furthermore, with the exception of France under certain circumstances (for example, in Rwanda following the 1994 genocide and in the 1996 conflict in the Central African Republic), non-African military powers have been extremely reluctant to use their own troops to intervene in African conflicts because of domestic political and financial constraints. Thus, most African governments and other groups no longer have access to the types and levels of external military support that they once enjoyed. And, as a result, they are far more susceptible to challenges from insurgents, private armies, mercenaries, commercial security firms, criminal gangs and other armed groups. This has contributed significantly to the escalation and spread of internal warfare throughout the continent. This violence has had a particularly grievous impact upon women, who now find themselves under constant threat from a proliferating number of armed groups that operate with few restraints and that increasingly rely upon terror and extortion to control civilians and obtain resources.

On the other hand, debt repayment and structural adjustment programmes have weakened African states to such an extent that truncated governments are no longer able to control their citizenry, as internal disorder rises over increasingly scarce resources. This has led to the breakdown in the capacity of African governments to manage the distribution of material resources in the face of declining supplies, increasing demands, environmental degradation, polarization along ideological and sectarian religious lines, ethnic divisions and growing political stresses. The failure of many African governments to resolve conflicts over the control and allocation of resources by peaceful means has meant that military force has increasingly become the determining factor in struggles for political and economic power. These struggles have become more and more desperate as the stakes, which are often the literal survival of individuals and groups, have risen. As a result, it has become increasingly easy for opportunistic leaders and organizations to mobilize popular support for the use of violence and terror as a means to acquire and control political power and/or economic resources. This has also had a disproportionate impact on women, since they play such a vital role in maintaining their families, farming, trade and other activities that keep their societies functioning; thus they are particularly affected by escalating levels of violence and social chaos.

And while it has become more difficult for Africans, particularly African governments, to obtain expensive heavy weaponry, it has actually become easier for governments and other armed groups to get light weapons (such as handguns, rifles, machine guns, land mines and light artillery). Armed groups of all kinds are able to use violence and terror simply to gain control over labour, food, diamonds, gold and other material resources which, in turn, they use to purchase more light arms which, in turn, are used to maintain and extend control over these resources. In many cases, warfare simply becomes a means to get control of territory with enough resources to make it possible to continue fighting, rather than a means to seize political power on the national level or to achieve any other clear political objective.

The evolution of the African arms trade since the end of the Cold War has been characterized by three basic trends: a diversification of sources, a shift toward small arms and light weaponry, and a growing link with non-state actors, including criminal organizations. Thus, arms transfers from traditional producers and suppliers – the United States, Russia and other former Soviet republics, France, Britain, other European producers, China, Israel and Brazil – to African governments and armed groups have fallen sharply, although they still account for a substantial proportion of the weaponry delivered to African recipients. Between 1988 and 1993, arms sales agreements with countries on the African continent for all types of weapons fell from $5.2 billion to $500 million.[5] This is far less than in the past, but it still amounts to a great deal of military hardware. Again, most of these arms go to countries that receive military funding from foreign patrons or possess valuable natural resources.

At the same time, important new sources of supply and financing have emerged. There has been a major increase in the flow of recycled weaponry, specifically arms left over from earlier conflicts – as in the case of the arms that are now flowing out of Ethiopia, Angola, and Mozambique – and surplus equipment from the arsenals of the NATO and Warsaw Pact countries, substantial quantities of which are now being sold or given away to Africans. Two new African arms producers – Egypt and South Africa – have sold arms to other African countries. Both of these countries, for example, sold light weaponry to the Hutu-extremist military and paramilitary forces in Rwanda for use in the genocide of Tutsis and moderate Hutus in 1994.[6]

Several other African countries have also developed, or are currently seeking to develop, the capability to produce certain kinds of light weapons, ammunition, and other military equipment for the domestic market and, possibly, for export as well. For example, Nigeria is reportedly producing Belgian FN FAL 7.62 mm rifles and Italian Beretta BM-59 7.62 mm rifles and M-95 1.9 mm pistols and ammunition under licence.[7] And in 1996, it was revealed that Fabrique Nationale de Herstal (the Belgian subsidiary of the French GIAT Industries Group) has been constructing an ammunition factory in Eldoret, Kenya, since 1989. Upon completion, the factory will be capable of an annual production of 20 million rounds of 7.62 mm ammunition (used in the American M-14 rifle and many others). This is clearly far in excess of the needs of the Kenyan armed forces, strongly suggesting that the Kenyan government intends to sell most of the ammunition to governments and/or armed groups in other African countries. Opposition from parliamentarians and the public in both Kenya and Belgium compelled Belgian Foreign Trade and Finance Minister Philippe Maystadt to announce in February 1997 that construction work would be halted until the Kenyan government gave formal guarantees that it would not export bullets to countries in the Great Lakes region (for example, Congo (Kinshasa), Rwanda and Burundi).[8]

New suppliers and middlemen have also become involved in the arms trade in pursuit of political objectives or profits. African governments have provided arms to private armies and other domestic paramilitary forces for use against political opponents and dissidents. The Kenyan government, for example, armed Kalenjin forces involved in fighting with other ethnic groups in the Rift Valley, and the Hutu-extremist government in Rwanda armed Hutu paramilitary units and civilians for their role in the genocide of 1994. African governments and insurgent groups have also given arms to allies and proxy forces in neighbouring countries. Sudan has equipped the insurgent forces of the Lord's Resistance Army and the West Nile Bank Front in Uganda; the Eritrean Jihad organization in Eritrea; and Islamic extremist groups in Somalia, Egypt, Tunisia and Algeria. Uganda has supplied weapons to the forces of the Sudan People's Liberation Army operating in southern Sudan. Burkina Faso, Guinea, Côte d'Ivoire, Nigeria and other West African countries provided arms, or allowed them to be passed through their territory, to Charles Taylor's National Patriotic Front of Liberia (NPFL) and other ethnic militias in Liberia. The NPFL, in turn, helped create and arm the Revolutionary United Front in Sierra Leone. Congo (Kinshasa) has helped provide arms to the remnants of the Rwandan Army and Hutu-extremist militias that operated out of bases and refugee camps in eastern Congo and to UNITA forces in Angola. And Algeria gave arms to the forces of the Saharawi nationalist movement, the Polisario Front, fighting against Morocco's occupation of the Western Sahara.

Private illegal arms dealers, drug traffickers, ivory and diamond smugglers have also played an increasingly important role in the arms trade. Primarily through Congo (Kinshasa), they have sold weaponry to UNITA forces in Angola and to Hutu-extremist militias operating in both Rwanda and Burundi; they have also sold their goods to militia forces in Somalia, ethnic factions in Liberia, insurgent groups in Chad, Tuareg insurgents fighting for greater autonomy in Niger and Mali, the Casamance separatists operating in southern Senegal and a variety of other groups in other parts of the continent. A growing number of professional mercenaries and private security companies have also entered the market; mercenaries employed by a South African firm, Executive Outcomes, have trained government forces in Sierra Leone and Angola and have played a major role in combat operations in both countries.

Former combatants have also played a major role in the light weapons trade, particularly in southern Africa. Although arms were supposed to be decommissioned under the terms of the peace agreements in Angola and Mozambique, government troops and insurgents in both countries have sold large quantities of light weapons to buy food and other goods. This weaponry has been acquired by arms dealers and local criminal gangs and has flowed into neighbouring countries, particularly into Kenya and South Africa, where it has exacerbated crime, political violence and violence against women. Another increasingly important source in the African arms trade is the light weapons stolen from military and police arsenals for sale to insurgents and criminals.

Multinational corporations, too, have become involved in the light weapons trade. In 1994 and 1995, for example, the Shell Petroleum Development Company of Nigeria negotiated with the Nigerian government on a plan to import more than half a million dollars worth of pistols, shotguns, rifles and sub-machine guns to equip police officers guarding its installations. The plan was approved, but Shell Nigeria decided to abandon the deal (at least temporarily) because of international criticism of the Nigerian government's human rights record.[9]

The massive flow of guns and other light weaponry through all these channels has clearly had a devastating impact on the lives of African women. It has created pervasive insecurity and has ignited an escalating level of violence throughout the continent, much of which is specifically directed against women. It has created famine and mass starvation, which has had a disproportionate impact upon women and children; and it has transformed a large proportion of the population, again predominately composed of women, into refugees or displaced persons.

Through these channels, Africans now have access to arms and other military equipment from a far greater number of sources than ever before. With some important exceptions, however, these arms producers and suppliers are no longer willing, as they once were, to provide conventional arms and other military assistance to African recipients at little or no cost through military aid programmes. As a result, few African governments have access to expensive heavy weaponry and they have become increasingly dependent upon the use of small arms and other light weaponry to equip their security forces and repress challenges to their authority. Both African governments and their opponents, however, can obtain light weaponry at relatively cheap prices from many more sources than heavy weaponry, and it is relatively easy for them to maintain and operate this equipment without external assistance. Insurgents and other armed groups, which were formerly at a distinct military disadvantage compared with the armed forces of the governments they were fighting, now confront security forces that are often little better armed than themselves.

In order to pay for this light weaponry, African forces, especially non-state forces, have developed a wide variety of new sources of financing for their arms purchases, many of which involve crime. These range from drug trafficking and the trade in ivory and other products from endangered species to diamond smuggling, kidnapping, extortion, fraud, corruption and other criminal activities. With the proceeds from this criminal activity, African criminal gangs, political factions, and governments are now able to buy large quantities of light weaponry even though revenues from legitimate economic activity are declining in many African countries. Moreover, as a result of the decline of legitimate economic activity due to internal conflict and changes in the international economy, warfare has become increasingly important as a way to establish or retain control over food and other means of sustenance, particularly as other sectors of the economy are being destroyed in violent conflicts. In a very real sense, therefore, warfare has become the dominant mode of production or a significant sector of the economy in such countries as Liberia, Somalia and Angola.[10]

Consequences of the Changed Arms Trade

These trends in the pattern of African arms transfers have had a decisive impact on the stability of countries throughout the continent. The ease with which virtually any group can obtain light weaponry has encouraged political dissidents, ethnic groups, and sectarian movements to abandon non-violent political activity and to resort to the use of force to advance their interests. Moreover, it has promoted the proliferation of armed groups by encouraging internal factionalization and fragmentation. This proliferation process has been most evident in Somalia and Liberia, where it has produced what have come to be known as 'failed' or 'collapsed' states, but it is a general process that can now be seen in many other countries, including Congo (Kinshasa), Sudan, Kenya, Nigeria, Algeria and Egypt.

At the same time, political weakness frequently has led many African governments to resist domestic demands for civil rights and multiparty democracy and to rely on the use of force to stay in power. This reliance on force has resulted in the increased militarization of the state, often through the creation of new security forces either by the state itself or by private organizations allied to the government, and an escalating level of state and state-sponsored violence. Militarization has blocked or distorted the democratization process in a number of African countries, including Rwanda, Burundi, Congo (Kinshasa), Kenya, Nigeria, Chad, Congo (Brazzaville), Sudan, Ethiopia and Algeria.

The spread of violent conflict, crime and corruption, in addition to promoting the flow of light weapons throughout the continent, has also had a disastrous impact on the economies of many African countries. It has killed, wounded or displaced workers, business people and professionals; destroyed infrastructure and other facilities; and blocked or impeded trade. It has also disrupted or halted the functioning of governmental institutions and private firms; and it has deterred or impeded the efforts of international financial institutions, public agencies and banks and other corporations to invest in Africa or conduct other activities that promote economic development. Violence directed specifically against women has had particularly grave consequences, since women play such a central role in the economies of African countries.

These trends have also led to the spread of violence and conflict throughout the continent as arms and combatants move from one country to another and as criminals become more deeply involved in the arms trade. This spreading violence has led to the emergence of what might be called conflict clusters or spill-over zones where weapons and armed groups move freely across national boundaries. One such zone is northern Africa where civil wars in Algeria and Egypt have been sustained by the Iranian and Sudanese governments and a variety of armed Islamic extremist groups. These actors have created an arms-trading network that has also exacerbated violence in Morocco, Tunisia and Libya, and ignited a campaign of terrorism in France.

A second cluster has emerged in West Africa as a byproduct of the civil war in Liberia. A number of countries in the region have been involved in the transfer of weaponry to different Liberian factions or in the effort mounted by the members of the Economic Community of West African States to resolve the conflict militarily by deploying a regional peacekeeping force (ECOMOG). This regional involvement has led to armed conflict and violence in several other neighbouring countries, particularly in Sierra Leone, where rebel forces have been armed by one of the Liberian factions in retaliation for the government's support of ECOMOG. Regional involvement has also sparked a crime wave in Côte d'Ivoire, which has served as one of the main conduits for the supply of arms to Liberian factions, as weapons and former combatants moved into the country.

A third cluster has emerged in the Horn of Africa where a number of governments have supplied weaponry to favoured clients in strife-torn countries and where criminals and other private arms dealers have moved to meet the growing demand for arms in the region. Thus, governments and private businessmen in Egypt, Saudi Arabia, Iran, Sudan and Kenya have given military assistance to different factions in Somalia, while Sudan has also provided arms to Islamic extremists in Eritrea and to Christian extremists in Uganda, and Uganda has countered by supplying arms to insurgent forces in southern Sudan.

A fourth cluster has emerged in Central Africa, where armed conflicts in Rwanda, Burundi, and Congo (Kinshasa) have led to the involvement of neighbouring governments, arms producers such as France, South Africa and Egypt, and private arms dealers in several networks that supply arms to military and paramilitary forces throughout the region.

Finally, a fifth cluster has emerged in southern Africa as a consequence of conflicts in Angola and Mozambique. Arms procured by both sides in the civil war in Mozambique and smuggled across the border into South Africa have fuelled both crime and political violence for years, particularly in the KwaZulu/Natal region. More recently, the disarmament and demobilization of former combatants in both Mozambique and Angola as part of the implementation of UN peace plans has led many ex-soldiers to become involved in banditry and other criminal activity. It has also resulted in the appearance of a new phenomenon: the movement of well-armed illegal migrants into adjacent countries.

In conclusion, the militarization of Africa, through arms transfers and other activities, has played a major role in promoting and prolonging conflicts, increasing their intensity and destructiveness, and making them more intractable and more difficult to resolve. This, in turn, has created a pervasive situation of violence and insecurity in many parts of the continent, which, as the other chapters in this book show, has a particularly grave impact on women, as well as on children and the elderly. Moreover, the consequences of the growth and spread of conflict and crime in Africa are not confined to the African continent alone. They have produced a growing demand for humanitarian assistance from the international community, ignited massive refugee migrations, facilitated the flow of drugs and other illegal products around the globe, prompted acts of terrorism, complicated efforts to monitor and control the spread of disease, and accelerated environmental degradation. The continuing militarization of Africa, therefore, is not just an African concern, but a process that affects the entire world and that demands the concerted attention of, and action by, the international community. For without such attention and action, the violence will escalate and spread, and none of us will be unaffected by the consequences.

Notes

1 ACDA 1975:79; ACDA 1980:161; ACDA 1987:102, 143, 149; ACDA 1991:131.
2 See note 1.
3 *Ibid.*
4 For more information see, for example, Seegers 1996.
5 ACDA 1995:152.
6 Human Rights Watch Arms Project 1994, especially pp. 18–21.
7 Keegan 1983:433; Hogg 1991:125, 521.
8 *Reuters News Service*, 27 March 1996; 'Concern Expressed Over Eldoret

Ammunition Factory', *East African*, 20 May 1996, p. 1; 'New Issues Raised on Eldoret Ammo Factory', *East African*, 10 June 1996, p. 1; 'Opposition Alarmed Over New Belgian-Sponsored Arms Factory', *De Standaard*, 25 June 1996, p. 1; ' "Secret" Arms Factory Sparks Fear in Kenya', *Weekly Mail and Guardian*, 28 June 1996; F. Misser, 'Secret Arms Factory', *New African*, July/August, 1996, p. 20; R. Onim, 'Row Over Munitions Factory,' *New African*, October 1996, p. 32; 'Belgium Halts Construction of Kenya Bullets Plant', *Reuters News Service*, 27 February 1997.

 9 Ghazi and Duodu 1996:A14; and Media Relations, Shell International Limited, *News Release*, 9 February 1996.

10 For more information regarding Liberia and its neighbours, see for example Reno 1995; Reno 1996; 'Statement of Dr William Reno Before the House Committee on International Relations, Subcommittee on Africa, 6 June 1996', pp. 1–12; and Reno 1996a.

Bibliography

Aberg, M.-B. Jansson and I.E. Andersson (1994) 'Care and Rehabilitation of Women Suffering Sexual Violence from the War in the Republics of the Former Yugoslavia', paper presented to the Nordic Conference on The Health Aspects of Refugee Families in Nordic Countries. Linkoping, November.

ACDA (1975) *World Military Expenditures and Arms Transfers 1966–1975,* US Arms Control and Disarmament Agency, Washington, DC.

— (1980) *World Military Expenditures and Arms Transfers 1969–1978,* US Arms Control and Disarmament Agency, Washington, DC.

— (1987) *World Military Expenditures and Arms Transfers 1986,* US Arms Control and Disarmament Agency, Washington, DC.

— (1991) *World Military Expenditures and Arms Transfers 1991,* US Arms Control and Disarmament Agency, Washington, DC.

— (1995) *World Military Expenditures and Arms Transfers 1993–1994,* US Arms Control and Disarmament Agency, Washington, DC.

Africa Watch (1993) 'Traditional Dictatorship: One Party State in KwaZulu Homeland Threatens Transition to Democracy', *News from Africa Watch,* Vol. 5, No. 12, Human Rights Watch, New York.

Agger, I. (1989) 'Sexual Torture of Political Prisoners: An Overview', *Journal of Traumatic Stress* Vol. 2, No. 3, pp. 305–18.

Allodi, F. and S. Stiasny (1990) 'Women as Torture Victims', *Canadian Journal of Psychiatry,* Vol. 35, pp. 144–8.

American Assembly (1997) 'Africa and U.S. National Interests', Report of the Ninetieth American Assembly, 13–16 March, Columbia University, New York.

Amnesty International (1996) 'Rwanda and Burundi. The Return Home: Rumours and Realities', AI Index: AFR 02/0196, International Secretariat, London.

— (1996a) *Chad: Cases for Appeal,* AI Index: AFR 20/05/96, 18 September, London.

— (1996b) *Chad: a country under the arbitrary rule of the security forces with the tacit consent of other countries*, AI Index: AFR 20/11/96, 10 October, London.

— (1995) 'Rwanda crying out for justice', AI Index: AFR 47/05/95, International Secretariat, London.

— (1991) *Women in the Front Line: An Amnesty International Report*, Amnesty International Publications, New York.

An'Naim, A.A. (1990) *Toward an Islamic Reformation: Civil Liberties Human Rights and International Law*, Syracuse University Press, N.Y.

Anonymous (1989) 'Detention', *Agenda*, Vol. 4, pp. 23–9.

Anti-Slavery International (1993) 'Trafficking and Slavery of Mozambican Refugees in S. Africa', unpublished briefing to United Nations Economic and Social Council, Commission on Human Rights, May.

Austin, K. and W. Minter (1994) *Invisible Crimes: U.S. Private Intervention in the War in Mozambique*, Africa Policy Information Center, Washington, DC.

Baroum, J. (1996) 'Les ingérences étrangères: la main de la France', in *Tchad 'conflit Nord-Sud': mythe ou réalité?*, pp. 1–4, Centre Culturel Al-Mouna, Diffusion Sépia, N'Djaména.

Barrett, L. (1994) 'Liberian Women Get Tough', *West Africa*, No. 4019, 10–16 October, pp. 1743–4.

Barry, K., C. Bunch and S. Castley, eds (1984) *International Feminism: Networking Against Female Sexual Slavery*, International Women's Tribune Center, New York.

Beall, J. *et al.* (1987) 'African Women in the Durban Struggle, 1985–1986: Towards a Transformation of Roles?', *South African Review*, Vol. 4.

Berkeley, B. (1996/7) 'The "New" South Africa: Violence Works', *World Policy Journal*, Winter, pp. 73–80.

Bell, A.N. and R.D.A. Mackie (1985) *Detention and Security Legislation in South Africa*, Centre for Adult Education, University of Natal, Durban.

Bernstein, H. (1985) *For Their Triumphs and for Their Tears: Women in Apartheid South Africa*, International Defence and Aid for Southern Africa, London.

Bonner, R. (1995) 'Defining and Proving Rights Abuses: Debate Splits Amnesty International', *New York Times*, 26 July.

Boyd, R.E. (1989) 'Empowerment of Women in Uganda: Real or Symbolic', *ROAPE* No. 45/46, pp. 106–17.

Brand, R. (1996) 'Tales of a Society without Morality', *The Star*, 13 May, p. 9.

Brunet, A. and S. Rousseau (1996) 'Acknowledging Violations, Struggling Against Impunity: Women's Rights as Human Rights', working paper presented at the Consultation and Planning Meeting for the Campaign Against Impunity in Africa, Ouagadougou, Burkina Faso, 22–23 March.

Bunch, C. and N. Reilly (1994) *Demanding Accountability: The Global Campaign and Vienna Tribunal for Women's Human Rights*, UNIFEM, New York.

Charlton, R. and R. May (1989) 'Warlords and Militarism in Chad', *ROAPE* No. 45/46, pp. 12–25.

Chossudovsky, M. (1996) 'Economic Genocide in Rwanda', *Economic and Political Weekly*, 13 April, p. 22.

Cleaver, M. and T. Wallace (1990) *Namibia: Women in War*, Zed Books, London.

Clement, M. (1995) 'Report from the Peace Train and the Beijing Conference', Women's International League for Peace and Freedom, New York.

CNP/DNE, Demography Department (1994) 'Annual Projections of Population by Province: 1990–2000', Maputo.

Cock, J. (1989) *War and Society: the Militarisation of South Africa* David Philip, Cape Town.

— (1989a) 'Keeping the Homes Fires Burning: Militarisation and the Politics of Gender in South Africa', *ROAPE* 45/46, pp. 50–64.

— (1991) *Colonels and Cadres: War and Gender in South Africa,* Oxford University Press, Cape Town.

Connell, B. (1985) 'Masculinity, Violence and War', *Intervention,* Sydney, Australia.

Cooper, C. and L. Ensor (1980) *The African Woman's Handbook on the Law,* South African Institute of Race Relations, Johannesburg.

Copelon, R. (1995) 'Gendered War Crimes: Reconceptualizing Rape in Time of War', in *Women's Rights, Human Rights: International Feminist Perspectives,* edited by J. Peter and A. Wolper, Routledge, New York.

Copson, R. W. (1990) 'Africa's Internal Wars: Thoughts on a Stronger Regime for Protecting Civilians', paper prepared for the 33rd meeting of the African Studies Association, Baltimore, MD, 2 November.

Crary, D. (1995) 'Generation of Rape Is Born in Rwanda', *The Guardian,* 11 February.

Crossette, B. (1996) 'U.N. Investigating Rwanda War Crimes Tribunal Officials', *New York Times,* 30 October, p. A3.

Daley, S. (1997) 'In Mozambique, Guns for Plowshares and Bicycles', *New York Times,* 2 March, p. A3.

Damu, J. and D. Bacon (1996) ' Oil Rules Nigeria', *The Black Scholar,* Vol. 26, No. 1, Winter, pp. 51–4.

Deng, F. M. (1993) *Protecting the Dispossessed: A Challenge for the International Community,* Brookings Institution, Washington, DC.

Desjarlais, R. *et al.* (1995) *World Mental Health: Problems and Priorities in Low-Income Countries,* Oxford University Press, New York.

Desouter, S. and F. Reyntjens (1995) 'Rwanda: les violations des droits de l'homme par le FPR/APR', *Institut de Politique et de Gestion du Développement,* Université d'Anvers, Antwerp, unpublished working paper.

De Waal, A. and M. Duffield (1992) 'Can Africa Conquer Famine?' *Dissent,* Summer, pp. 390–6.

Dieu De, T. Thi (1989) 'Vietnamese women and sexual violence', unpublished report, Refugee Health Care Centre, Rijswijk, March.

Einhorn, B. (1996) 'Links Across Difference: Gender, Ethnicity, and Nationalism', *Women's Studies International Forum,* Vol. 19, Nos 1–2, pp. 1–3.

El-Bushra, J. and C. Mukarubuga (1995) 'Women, War and Transition', *Gender and Development,* Vol. 3, No. 3, pp. 16–22.

Enloe, C. (1983) *Does Khaki Become You? The Militarization of Women's Lives,* South End Press, Boston.

Etienne, M. (1995) 'Addressing Gender-based Violence in an International Context',

Harvard Women's Law Journal, Vol. 18, pp. 139–70.

Farah, N. (1986) *Maps*, Pantheon, New York.

FEDTRAW (1987) *A Woman's Place is in the Struggle, Not Behind Bars!*, Federation of Transvaal Women, Johannesburg.

First, R. (1988) *117 Days: an Account of Confinement and Interrogation under the South African Ninety-day Detention Law*, Bloomsbury, London.

Fitzpatrick, J. (1994) 'The Use of International Human Rights Norms to Combat Violence Against Women', in *Human Rights of Women: National and International Perspectives*, edited by R.J. Cook, University of Pennsylvania Press, Philadelphia.

Foster, D. (1987) *Detention and Torture in South Africa: Psychological Legal and Historical Studies*, David Philip, Cape Town.

Francke, L.B. (1997) *Ground Zero: The Gender Wars in the Military*, Simon and Schuster, New York.

Franco, J. (1992) 'Gender, Death and Resistance: Facing the Ethical Vacuum', in *Fear at the Edge: State Terror and Resistance in Latin America*, edited by J.E. Corradi *et al*, University of California Press, Berkeley, pp. 104–18.

French, H.W. (1997) 'In Liberia, 2 Africans Vie for Votes', *New York Times*, 17 June, p. A11.

— (1997a) 'Liberian Militias Lay Down Arms and Raise Hopes', *New York Times*, 27 January, p. A8.

Friends of Liberia (1996) 'Liberia: Opportunities and Obstacles for Peace, A Report on the Abuja II Peace Process', December, unpublished report.

Gender Policy Group, Durban (1991) 'State, Gender and Restructuring in South Africa in the 1980s', paper presented to the Conference on Women and Gender in Southern Africa, Durban.

Gerhart, G.M. (1978) *Black Power in South Africa: the Evolution of an Ideology*, University of California Press, Berkeley.

Ghazi, P. and C. Duodu (1996) 'Shell Sought Arms for Nigerian Police', *The London Observer*, reprinted in *The Washington Times*, 22 February, p. A14.

Goldblatt B. and S. Meintjes (1996) 'South Africa's Truth and Reconciliation Commission: Bringing Gender into Focus', Centre for Applied Legal Studies, University of the Witwatersrand, Johannesburg.

Gourevitch, P. (1997) 'The Vanishing: How the Congo became Zaire, and Zaire became the Congo', *New Yorker*, 2 June, pp. 50–3.

— (1997a). 'Kabila's March: Zaire's Rebels Confront the West's Legacy', *New Yorker*, 19 May, pp. 7–8.

Govender, P. (ed.) (1995) *Beijing Conference Report: 1994, Country Report on the Status of South African Women*, Government Printer, Pretoria.

Graycar, R. and J. Morgan (1990) *The Hidden Gender of Law*, The Federation Press, Sydney.

Hanlon, J. (1991) *Mozambique: Who Calls the Shots?*, James Currey, London.

— (1996) *Peace Without Profit: How the IMF Blocks Rebuilding in Mozambique*, James Currey, Oxford.

Harris, B. L. (1995) 'Rape and the Liberian Conflict', Unpublished ms.

Harsch, E. (1993) 'Mozambique: Out of the Ruins of War', *Africa Recovery Briefing*

Paper, No. 8, May.

Hassim, S. *et al.* (1987) 'A Bit on the Side? Gender Struggles in the Politics of Transformation in South Africa', *Transformation,* Vol. 5, pp. 3–32.

Hayner, P.B. (1994) 'Fifteen Truth Commissions – 1974 to 1994: A Comparative Study', *Human Rights Quarterly,* Vol. 16, pp. 597–655.

Heise, L. *et al.* (1994) 'Violence against Women: A Neglected Public Health Issue in Less Developed Countries', *Social Science Medicine,* Vol. 39, No. 9, pp. 1165–79.

Hicks, G. (1995) *The Comfort Women: Japan's Brutal Regime of Enforced Prostitution in the Second World War,* W. W. Norton, New York.

Hilsum, L. (1995) 'Rwanda's Time of Rape Returns to Haunt Thousands', *The Observer,* 26 January.

Hogg, I. V. (ed.) (1991) *Jane's Infantry Weapons, 1991–1992,* Jane's Information Group, Coulsdon, UK and Alexandria, VA.

Howard, K. (ed) (1995) *True Stories of the Korean Comfort Women,* Cassell, London.

Human Rights Watch (1995) 'Rearming With Impunity: International Support for the Perpetrators of the Rwandan Genocide', Human Rights Watch, New York.

— (1996) *Behind the Red Line: Political Repression in the Sudan,* Human Rights Watch, New York.

— (1996a) *Shattered Lives: Sexual Violence during the Genocide and its Aftermath,* Human Rights Watch, New York.

— (1997) 'Sudan's Secret Military Trials and Illegal Arrests Show Human Rights Deterioration', letter to the Sudanese government, 19 February, Human Rights Watch, New York.

Human Rights Watch/Africa (1994) 'South Africa: Impunity for Human Rights Abuses in Two Homelands; Reports on KwaZulu and Bophuthatswana', Vol. 6, No. 2, Human Rights Watch, New York.

— (1995) 'South Africa: Threats to a New Democracy; Continuing Violence in KwaZulu-Natal', Vol.7, No.3, Human Rights Watch, New York.

Human Rights Watch Arms Project (1994) *Arming Rwanda: The Arms Trade and Human Rights Abuses in the Rwandan War,* Human Rights Watch, New York.

Human Rights Watch Women's Rights Project (1995) *The Human Rights Watch Global Report on Women's Human Rights,* Human Rights Watch, New York.

Hyslop, J. (1988) 'School Student Movements and State Education Policy: 1972–87', in *Popular Struggles in South Africa* edited by W. Cobbett and R. Cohen, James Currey, London.

IDAF (1981) *To Honour Women's Day: Profiles of Leading Women in the South African and Namibian Liberation Struggles,* International Defence and Aid Fund, London.

Irish, J. (1993) 'Massacres, Muthi and Misery: Women and Political Violence', *Agenda,* Vol. 16.

Kaganas, F. and C. Murray (eds) (1994) *Gender and the New South African Legal Order,* Juta, Cape Town.

Kaplan, R.D. (1994) 'The Coming Anarchy: How Scarcity, Crime, Overpopulation, and Disease are Rapidly Destroying the Social Fabric of our Planet', *Atlantic Monthly,* February, pp. 44–76.

Keegan, J. (1983) *World Armies,* Gale Research Company, 2nd edition, Detroit, MI.

Keen, D. (1994) *The Benefits of Famine: A Political Economy of Famine and Relief in Southwestern Sudan 1983–1989,* Princeton University Press, Princeton.

Keller, B. (1994) 'In Mozambique and Other Lands, Children Fight the Wars', *New York Times,* 9 November, p. A14.

Konig, B. (1983) *Namibia: the Ravages of War; South Africa's Onslaught on the Namibian People,* International Defence and Aid Fund, London.

Lamb, B. and E. Pajibo (1993) 'Liberia, Land in Conflict', *Bulletin of the Association of Concerned Africa Scholars,* Nos 40–1.

Layika, F.U. (1996) 'War Crimes against Women in Rwanda', in *Without Reservation: The Beijing Tribunal on Accountability for Women's Human Rights,* edited by N. Reilly, Center for Women's Global Leadership, New Brunswick, NJ.

Lemarchand, R. (1970) *Rwanda and Burundi,* Pall Mall, London.

— (1995) 'Rwanda: the Rationality of Genocide', *Issue: A Journal of Opinion,* Vol. 23, No.2, pp. 8–11.

Lindsay, Jenny (1991) 'The Politics of Population Control in Namibia', in *Women and Health in Africa,* edited by M. Turshen, pp. 143–67, African World Press, Trenton.

Littlewood, R. (1997) 'Military Rape', *Anthropology Today,* Vol. 13, No. 2, pp. 7–16.

Lodge, T. (1983) *Black Politics in South Africa since 1945,* Ravan, Johannesburg.

Loncar, M. (1994) 'Rape as Method of Torture and as War Crime', *RAHAT's Medical Journal,* Vol. 1, No. 3, November.

Lorch, D. (1995) 'Wave of Rape Adds New Horror to Rwanda's Trail of Brutality', *New York Times,* 15 May, pp. A1, A6.

Luckham, R. (1994) 'The Military, Militarization and Democratization in Africa: A Survey of the Literature and Issues', *African Studies Review,* Vol. 37, No. 2, pp. 13–75.

Magnarella, P. J. (1997) 'Judicial Responses to Genocide: The International Criminal Tribunal for Rwanda and the Rwandan Genocide Courts', *African Studies Quarterly,* Vol. 1, No. 1.

Mahmoud, U. and S.A. Baldo (1987) *The Diein Massacre and Slavery in the Sudan,* Khartoum.

Makhoere, C.K. (1988) *No Child's Play: In Prison under Apartheid,* The Women's Press, London.

Malou, M.J. (1997) 'Uprooted Sudanese Women Between Today and Tomorrow', paper prepared for the International Sudanese Studies Conference, Cairo, 11–14 June.

McKinley, J.C. (1996) 'Rural Rwanda Faces Uneasy Balance of Fear as Refugees Return', *The New York Times,* 26 December, pp. A1, A12.

— (1996a) 'Legacy of Rwanda Violence: The Thousands Born of Rape', *New York Times,* 23 September, pp. A1, A9.

McLachlan, F. (1993) 'Life During Wartime: Women and Conflict in Afghanistan', *Focus on Gender,* Vol. 1, No. 2, pp. 13–14.

Manicom, L. (1991) 'Ruling Relations: Rethinking State and Gender in South African History', paper presented to the Conference on Women and Gender in Southern Africa, Durban.

Meijer, M. (1985) 'Some Aspects of Oppression in the Torture of Women', unpublished, Lochem.

Michalon, T. and A. Moyrand (1991) 'Le Tchad malade de l'état-nation', *Le Monde Diplomatique,* January, p.13.

Middleton, S. *et al.* (1991) 'The Hidden Burden: The Impact of Detention on the Women Left Behind', paper presented to the Conference on Women and Gender in Southern Africa, Durban, January.

MINEC (National Preparatory Committee for the Fourth World Conference on Women) (1995) 'National Report on the Situation of Women in Mozambique 1986–1994', Maputo, August.

Moorehead, C. (1995) 'Hostage to a Male Agenda', *Index on Censorship,* Vol. 4, pp. 64–9.

Morris, P. (1981) *A History of Black Housing in South Africa,* South Africa Foundation, Johannesburg.

Moser, C.O.N. (1993) *Gender Planning and Development: Theory, Practice and Training,* Routledge, London.

National Catholic Secretariat, Justice and Peace Commission (1996) 'Briefing Paper on Liberia: Political Situation', 11 September, Monrovia, unpublished report.

Neier, A. (1990) 'What Should Be Done about the Guilty?' *New York Review of Books,* 1 February.

Newbury, C. (1988) *The Cohesion of Oppression: Clientship and Ethnicity in Rwanda: 1850-1960,* Columbia University Press, New York.

— (1995) 'Background to genocide: Rwanda', *Issue: A Journal of Opinion,* Vol. XXIII, No. 2, pp. 12–17.

Newbury, C. and D. Newbury (1995) 'Identity, Genocide, and Reconstruction in Rwanda', paper prepared for the Conference on Les racines de la violence dans la région des Grands-Lacs, Parlement Européen, Brussels, 12–13 January.

Newbury, D. (1995) 'Gender and Genocide', Department of History, University of North Carolina at Chapel Hill, unpublished manuscript.

Newitt, M. (1995) *A History of Mozambique,* Hurst, London.

Niarchos, C.N. (1995) 'Women, War and Rape: Challenges Facing the International Tribunal for the Former Yugoslavia', *Human Rights Quarterly,* Vol. 17, pp. 649–90.

Nordstrom, C. (1991) 'Women and War: Observations from the Field', *Minerva: Quarterly Report on Women and the Military,* Vol. IX, No. 1, pp. 1–15.

— (1992) 'The Backyard Front', in *The Paths to Domination, Resistance, and Terror,* edited by C. Nordstrom and J. Martin, pp. 260–74, University of California Press, Berkeley.

— (1996) 'What John Wayne Never Told Us: Sexual Violence in War and Peace', unpublished manuscript.

Ntezimana, L. (1994) 'De Charybde en Scylla?' *Dialogue,* No. 178, October, pp. 61–8.

NUSAS (1982) Women's Conference Report, Johannesburg, Mimeo.

Osaghae, E.E. (1995) 'The Ogoni Uprising: Oil Politics, Minority Agitation and the Future of the Nigerian State', *African Affairs,* Vol. 95, pp. 325–44.

Oyo, R. (1997) 'Liberia: Elections to Go Ahead as Planned, Says ECOMOG Chief ', InterPress Third World News Agency (IPS), 26 May.

Pienaar, A. (1995) 'The Truth and Reconciliation Commission in South Africa', *ASICL Proc.,* No.7, pp. 453–67.

Platzky, L. and C. Walker (1985) *Surplus People: Forced Removals in South Africa,* Ravan Press, Johannesburg.

Ranger, T. (1992) 'The Invention of Tradition in Colonial Africa', in *The Invention of Tradition,* edited by E. Hobsbawm and T. Ranger, pp. 211–62, Cambridge University Press, Cambridge.

Rayner, R. (1997) 'The Warrior Besieged', *New York Times Magazine,* 22 June.

Reilly, N. (ed.) (1996) *Without Reservation: The Beijing Tribunal on Accountability for Women's Human Rights,* Center for Women's Global Leadership, New Brunswick, NJ.

Reno, W. (1995) 'Reinvention of an African Patrimonial State: Charles Taylor's Liberia', *Third World Quarterly,* Vol. 16, No. 1, pp. 109–20.

— (1996) ' The Business of War in Liberia', *Current History,* May, pp. 211–15.

— (1996a) 'Warlords in the Neighborhood: The Spread of Private War Fighting in West Africa', paper presented at the 39th annual meeting of the African Studies Association, San Francisco, California, 23 November 1996, pp. 1–30.

Report of the Chilean National Commission on Truth and Reconciliation, Vol. 2, Chapter 4.

Reyntjens, F. (1996) 'Rwanda: The Conspiracy of Silence', Posted on Rwandanet@ msstate.edu, 3 September.

— (1995) 'Rwanda: Trois jours qui ont fait basculer l'histoire', *Cahiers Africains,* No. 16.

Richards, P. (1996) *Fighting for the Rain Forest: War Youth and Resources in Sierra Leone,* James Currey, Oxford.

Riley, S. and M. Sesay (1996) 'Liberia: After Abuja', *ROAPE,* No. 69.

Rohter, L. (1997) 'Guatemalan Rights Group Tracing Abuses in War', *New York Times,* 7 April, p. A8.

Romero, M. (1985) 'A Comparison Between Strategies Used on Prisoners of War and Battered Wives', *Sex Roles,* Vol. 13, No. 9/10, pp. 537–47.

Routledge, N.M. (1996) 'An Overview of Women's Struggles and Their Experience of Politically Motivated Violence in Natal', Truth and Reconciliation Commission Women's Hearing, 25 October, Durban.

Royte, E. (1997) 'The Outcasts', *The New York Times Magazine,* 19 January.

Ruay, D.D.A. (1994) *The Politics of Two Sudans: The South and the North 1821–1969,* Nordiska Afrikaninstitutet, Uppsala.

Russell, D.E.H. (1989) *Lives of Courage: Women for a New South Africa,* Basic Books, New York.

Sadou, Z. (1996) 'Algeria: The Martyrdom of Girls Raped by Islamic Armed Guards', in *Without Reservation: The Beijing Tribunal on Accountability for Women's Human Rights,* edited by N. Reilly (1996) pp. 28–3.

Samoura, D.K. (1996) 'African Commission of Health and Human Rights Promoters', *Health and Human Rights,* Vol. 2, No.1, pp. 145–50.

Schadeberg, J. (1994) *Voices from Robben Island,* Ravan Press, Randburg.

Schreiner, B. (ed.) (1992) *A Snake with Ice Water: Prison Writings by South African Women,* Congress of South African Writers, Johannesburg.

Sciolino, E. (1997) 'Courtship Leads to Marriage and Maybe Officer's Ouster', *New York Times,* 3 July, pp. A1, A18.

Seegers, A. (1996) *The Military in the Making of Modern South Africa,* I. B. Tauris, London and New York.

Seifert, R. (1996) 'The Second Front: The Logic of Sexual Violence in Wars', *Women's Studies International Forum,* Vol. 19, No. 1–2, pp. 35–43.

Sikainga, A. (1995) 'Shari'a Courts and the Manumission of Female Slaves in the Sudan, 1898–1939', *The International Journal of African Historical Studies,* Vol. 28, No.1.

Simpson, G. and P. Van Zyl (1994) 'South Africa's Truth and Reconciliation Commission', Centre for the Study of Violence and Reconciliation, Johannesburg.

Smaldone, J.P. (1990) 'Militarization in Africa: Methodology, Measurement and Mystery,' paper presented at the 33rd meeting of the African Studies Association, 1–4 November 1990, Baltimore, MD.

Smith, W. (1992) *American Daughter Gone to War: On the Front Lines with an Army Nurse in Vietnam,* William Morrow and Company, New York.

South African Pressclips (1981) *Women in South Africa: a Presscuttings Supplement.*

Swiss, S. (1991) 'Liberia: Women and Children Gravely Mistreated', Physicians for Human Rights, May, Boston, mimeo.

— (1992) 'Liberia: Anguish in a Divided Land', Physicians for Human Rights, May, Boston, mimeo.

Swiss, S.and J.E. Giller (1993) 'Rape as a Crime of War', *JAMA,* Vol. 270, No. 5, pp. 612–15.

Sy, A.D. (1993) 'Conflict and the Women of Chad,' *Focus on Gender,* Vol. 1, No. 2, pp. 10–12.

Szeftel, M. (1989) 'Editorial: Warlords and Problems of Democracy in Africa', *ROAPE* No. 45/46, pp. 3–11.

— (1994) 'Ethnicity and Democratization in South Africa', *ROAPE,* No. 60, pp. 85–199.

Tarr, S.B. (1993) 'The ECOMOG Initiative in Liberia: A Liberian Perspective', *Issue: A Journal of Opinion,* Vol. 21, Nos 1–2.

Tchad 'conflit Nord-Sud': mythe ou réalité? (1996) Centre Culturel Al-Mouna, Diffusion Sépia, N'Djaména.

Thomas, D.Q. and R.E. Ralph (1994) 'Rape in War: Challenging the Tradition of Impunity', *SAIS Review,* Winter–Spring, pp. 81–99.

Turok, M. (1989) 'Women Political Prisoners', paper presented to the Malibongwe Conference, Amsterdam.

Turshen, M. (1986) 'Health and Human Rights in a South African Bantustan', *Social Science and Medicine,* Vol. 2, No. 9, pp. 887–92.

Ugwu-Oju, D. (1995) *What Will My Mother Say: A Tribal African Girl Comes of Age in America,* Bonus Books, Inc., Chicago.

UNHCR (1995) *Sexual Violence Against Refugees: Guidelines on Prevention and Response,* UN High Commissioner for Refugees, Geneva.

UNICEF (1996) *The State of the World's Children 1996,* Oxford University Press, New York.

United Nations (1990) *Demographic Yearbook,* United Nations, New York.

United Nations (1995) *The World's Women 1995: Trends and Statistics,* United Nations, New York.

US Committee for Refugees (1996) *World Refugee Survey 1996,* Immigration and Refugee Services of America, Washington, DC.

Valentich, M. (1994) 'Rape Revisited: Sexual Violence Against Women in the Former Yugoslavia', *Canadian Journal of Human Sexuality,* Vol. 3, No. 1, Spring, pp. 53–64.

Van Willigen, L.H.M. (1984) 'Women Refugees and Sexual Violence', *Medisch Contact* (Netherlands Medical Joumal), No. 50, December.

Walker, C. (1982) *Women and Resistance in South Africa,* Onyx Press, London.

Welch, G.W., F. Dagnino and A. Sachs (1987) 'Transforming Family Law: New Directions in Mozambique', in *Women and Law in Southern Africa* edited by A. Armstrong, Zimbabwe Publishing House, Harare.

Wren, C. (1990), 'Out of Mozambique's Fire and Into a Frying Pan', *New York Times,* 8 October.

Zwane, P. (1994) 'The Young Lions and the Sexual Face of Violence in the Black Townships: the Inheritance of the Future Govemment', Centre for the Study of Violence and Reconciliation, Johannesburg.

Zur, J. (1993) 'The Psychological Effects of "La Violencia" on Widows of El Quché, Guatemala', *Focus on Gender,* Vol. 1, No. 2, pp. 27–30.

Index

abduction 15, 19-20, 31-2, 47, 51, 60n, 68-9, 74-7, 94, 105, 130-1, 158
abortion 14, 109, 116n, 132
Abreu, Cecilia 82
Abuja II accords 133
Addis Ababa Treaty 85
African Charter on Human and People's Rights 22n, 136n
African National Congress (ANC) 13, 27, 31, 48-51, 63-5, 69-70, 151
African Studies Centre (CEA) 82
Afrikaans language 140
Agger, Inger 38
agriculture 8, 19, 30, 33, 75, 77, 102
aid, 2, 9, 17, 93-4, 134-5
AIDS 11, 19, 21, 109-11, 117n
Akosombo Amendment 133
Algeria 6, 20, 96, 151-2, 157, 159-60
Allah, Khalifah Abd 100n
Almeida, Manuela 78
Amabutho 63
Amin, Idi 23n
Amnesty International 3, 103, 106, 119-21
amnesty 5, 27, 29, 51-8, 70
Amzoer 125
An'Naim 93
Angola 5-7, 14, 138-49, 151-4, 156-7, 159, 161
apartheid 10, 21, 30-4, 42, 45, 48, 62-3, 73, 152-3
Arabic speakers 87, 95
Ariath 94
Armed Forces of Liberia (AFL) 129
Armée nationale Tchadienne en dissidence (ANTD) 122
arms trade 4-7, 19, 23n, 130, 150-62
Arusha accords 101
Association for Rural Advancement 45
Association of Female Lawyers of Liberia (AFELL) 30-3
Association of Women Educators (AMME) 82
Austria 152
Aweil 93

Babanusa 93
Baltimore Sun 95
Barré, Siad 9
Bébedjia 121
Béboto 122
Békaroua 121
Belgium 101-2, 152-3, 156
Bernstein, Hilda 38
Biafra 8, 15
Biko, Steve 27, 41
Black Consciousess Movement 27, 38, 41, 58-9n
Black Sash 10, 66-7, 72n
Boipatong massacre 47
Bomi county 135
Bophuthatswana 62
Bosnia 64, 98
Bosnian Serbs 98
Botswana 154
Brazil 24n, 152, 156
Britain 31, 85, 88, 152, 156
Brownell, Mary 133
Bulgaria 142

Burkina Faso 129, 157
Burundi 6, 14, 101, 111-12, 15, 156, 159-60
Butare prison 103, 106
Buthelezi, Chief Mangosuthu 63
Byumba 108

Cachalia, Amina 43
Cairo 89
Cameroon 119, 122-3, 126, 152
Carter, President Jimmy 133
Casamance 157
Central African Republic 126, 152, 154
Central Hospital, Maputo 78
Central Intelligence Agency (CIA) 152
Centre for Abused Women and Girls 131
Centre for Applied Legal Studies 29
Chad 3, 5-6, 14, 20, 118-28, 152, 154, 157, 159
Chari Baguirmi 123
Cheeks, Christiana 135
Chesterville 67
children 14-17, 19, 21, 23n, 32-6, 40-1, 44-5, 51, 54, 64-6, 70, 74-5, 77, 79, 86, 89, 94-5, 98, 104-6, 108, 110, 119-22, 129, 131-4, 143-4, 147-8
China 151-2, 154, 156
Christianity 85
Ciskei 62
class 10, 28, 30, 38, 45
Cock, Jacklyn 1, 51
Cold War 7, 150-1, 153-5
colonialism 4, 6, 9, 21, 29, 85, 93, 102, 118-19, 129, 138, 150-1
Commission for Gender Equality 71
Congo (Brazzaville) 6, 119, 126, 159
Congo (Kinshasa) 6, 14, 101, 119, 151-3, 156-7, 159-60
Congo Town 135
Congress of South African Trade Unions (COSATU) 56, 63
Convention Against Torture (1984) 3
Convention on the Elimination of All Forms of Discrimination Against Women (CEDAW) 11, 22n, 71, 136n
corruption 4, 62, 113, 129, 135, 158-9
Côte d'Ivoire 126, 129-30, 134, 152, 157, 160
Cradock 51
Cradock Four 36-7
criminal gangs 2, 155-7, 159-60

Cuba 138, 153
Cuito Canavale 138
Cyangugu prefecture 106

Da Silva, Terezinha 20
Danane 130
death squads 2
debt repayment 155
Deby, General Idriss 119, 121
Dénembaye, Agnès 124
Deng, Francis 95
Depo Provera 143
Desert Research Foundation 148
Detainees' Parents Support Committee (DPSC) 36-7, 40
detention 18, 27, 30-2, 34-45, 64, 86, 97, 119
Dia 133
dignity 3, 17, 74, 78-9, 87-9, 91, 94, 133
Dinka people 85-6, 95
Diplae, Joyce 38
disappeared persons 36, 73
disease 4, 17
displacement 14-15, 19-20, 33, 45, 62, 74, 85, 87-91, 101, 108, 129, 131-2, 134-5, 158; see also refugees
Djibouti 6, 152
Doe, Samuel 129-30
drugs trade 157-8
Duarte, Jessie 35, 37, 43, 47-8, 52-3
Durban 63, 65, 67, 69

Eastern Cape 36, 43, 46
Economic Community of West African States (ECOWAS) 129, 135, 160
ECOWAS Monitoring Group (ECOMOG) 129-30, 135, 136n, 160
education 7, 17, 19-20, 30, 45, 57, 62, 69, 73, 75, 79-81, 115, 130, 134, 139
Egypt 85, 151-3, 156-7, 159-60
Eldoret 156
End Conscription Campaign 67
Enloe, Cynthia 1
Equatoria region 96
Eritrea 6, 14, 18, 20, 157, 160
Eritrean Jihad 157
Ethiopia 2, 6-7, 14, 19, 151-3, 156, 159
ethnic conflicts 2, 4, 9, 28, 32, 45, 47, 62-3, 85, 94, 98, 101-4, 111, 114, 118, 129, 155, 157

Europe 19, 156
Executive Outcomes 157
Exxon 120

Fabrique Nationale de Herstal 156
famine 85
Farah, Nuruddin 24n
Farrakhan, Louis 94-5
First World War 101
First, Ruth 31
Flame 50, 100n
Force d'intervention rapide (FIR) 120
Forces armées pour la République fédérale (FARF) 122
Forum Mulher 82
France 6, 31, 118-19, 130, 152-4, 156, 160
Franco, Jean 36-7
FRELIMO 73
Friends of Liberia 134
Front national du Tchad rénové (FNTR) 122
National Liberation Front of Angola (FNLA) 152

Gabon 152
Gafunzo Commune 106
Gaisan 94
Gambia 6
Gauteng Province 35
Gaza Province 77
gender, and African National Congress 48-50; and amnesty 51-8; and apartheid 33-7; and consumer boycotts 46; and crime 87; in division of labour 20; and history 28, 57; and human rights 29; and inequality 20; in Kwa Zulu/Natal conflict 63; in liberation struggle 65; and militarism 5; and race 67; and rape 10; and solidarity 9, 16; in South Africa 71; and torture 37-45; and truth commissions 28-9, 55-8; and violence 10-14, 34-8; war impact on 20, 96-7, 114, 126-7, 160-1
General Women's Union of Sudan 94
Geneva Convention 2-3, 52, 130, 136n
genocide 11, 19-20, 86, 92, 94, 1002-3, 105, 107, 110-13, 153-4, 156-7
German East Africa 101
Germany 27, 101, 138, 152
Ghana 18

Gikongoro 112
Gisees, Father Macrum 95
Gisenyi Technical Schooll 106
Gitarama Prefecture 107
Gitarama Prison 107, 111
Goldstone, Justice 92
Gonadjé 124
Gordon, Charles George 99-100n
Grand Cape Mount County 135
Graves, Robert 1
Guatemala 22n, 25n
Guguletu 36
Guinea 18, 129, 134, 153, 157
Guinea-Bissau 6
Gulf War 153

Habré, President Hissène 5, 118-19
Habyarimana, President Juvénal 101, 115n
Hague Appeal for Peace 21
Hague Convention 2
Harris, Dr B. L. 132
health 7, 17-19, 73, 75, 109-11, 134
Hogan, Barbara 42, 44
homelands 30, 62-3
Horn of Africa 160
hostels 32, 43, 45-8
Human Rights Watch 86, 94, 110, 112-13, 130
Human Rights Watch/Africa 94
human rights 2-3, 9, 27-9, 33-4, 36, 48, 54-7, 71, 82, 92, 96-9, 110, 119-20, 125, 129-31, 133, 135
Hurt, J. 70-1
Hutu 4, 101-17, 153, 156-7

Ilitha Labantu Centre 53
Inanda 45
Independent National Patriotic Front of Liberia (INPFL) 129
Inkatha Freedom Party (IFP) 45, 63-5, 68-70, 153
Interahamwe 104-6, 111, 115n
International Conference on Women (Beijing) 25n, 81, 92, 96, 110, 114
International Court of Justice 138
International Monetary Fund (IMF) 4, 17, 102
International Tribunal for War Crimes in Former Yugoslavia 12, 92, 98
intsinzi 109

Iran 86, 153-4, 160
Iraq 86
Ireland, Northern 18
Islam 85-6, 80, 92-6, 98, 118, 126, 157, 160
Israel 10, 152, 156
Italy 152, 156

Japan 13, 27
Jarrett, Juanita K. 130
Johannesburg 34
Johnson, Prince 129
Johnson-Sirleaf, Ellen 134

Kalenjin 157
Kalwecke 140
Kamara, M. Masa 130, 132
Kanombe Commune 105-6
Kanzenze District 107
Karemera, Dr Joseph 110
Kassinga massacre 144, 149n
Katlehong 47
Katorus 48
Kenya 6, 14, 105, 151-2, 156-60
Khartoum 16, 19, 86-7, 89-90
Khuyzwayo, Khanyisile Doris 68-9
Kibungo Prefecture 107
Kigali 101, 104, 109, 111-12
Kigali Rural Prefecture 107
Kinyamakara Commune 112
Kitchener,Lord 100n
Koevoet Unit 51
Koloni, Placide 107
Kompe, Lydia 31, 33-4, 43
Kulaya 78-80, 82
Kundera, Milan 60
Kurmuk 94
Kururama 78, 81-2
Kwadengezi 67
KwaMakutha massacre 64-5, 72n
KwaZulu/Natal 9, 14, 45-6, 62-72, 161

La ligue Tchadienne des droits de l'homme (LTDH) 119, 121, 123-5, 127n
land mines 7, 17, 129
Langa, Adosinda 15
Latin America 27
law, human rights 2-3, 92, 97-8, 125, 130; humanitarian 2-3, 91, 97-8, 125, 130

League of Nations 101, 138
Lee, Antonio Anchonfok 78
Lelem, Thérèse 121
Lesotho 6
Liberal Party 45
Liberia 3-4, 33-4, 6-7, 18, 22n, 129-36, 151-2, 159-60
Liberian National Conference 133
Liberian National Transitional Government 133
Liberian Women's Initiative 133
Libya 6, 119, 126, 129, 151-3, 160
literacy 75
Logone, Eastern 122-3; Western 120-1, 123
Lord's Resistance Army 157
Lusaka 140
Lutya, Maudline 36
Lutya, Wiseman 36

Madlala, Nozizwe 39
Mahamat, Koubra 125
Mahdi, the 99-100n
Mahdist state 95
Mailao 121
Majozi, Frieda 68
Maker 94
Makhoere, Caesarina Kona 42, 48
Makouyonodji, Martine 124
Malan, General Magnus 65, 71n, 72n
Mali 6, 14, 18, 157
Malu, Victor 135
Mandela, Nelson 63
Mandela, Winnie 39
Manondji, Mrs 121
Maputo 78, 82
Maputo Province 76
Matola-Rio 77
Matsequenha 76
Matusse, Marta 74
Mauritania 6, 14
Mauritius 152
Maystadt, Philippe 156
Mengistu 14
mercenaries 2, 153, 155, 157
Mfaco, Dorothy 57-8
militarization 2, 5-7, 11-12, 19, 22n, 23n, 31, 150-62
Mlangeni, Andrew 35
Mlangeni, Bheki 36
Mlangeni, June 35, 54

Mlangeni, Sepati 36
Mobuto Sese Seko, President 134
Modise, Thandi 50
Mogadishu 86
Mohammed, Elaine 39
Mohapi, Mapethla 41
Mokonyane, Nomvula 37,43-4
Monakali, Mandisa 53
Monrovia 130-1, 133-5
Morocco 6, 151-3, 157, 160
Motsuenyane Commission 27
Moundou 121-2
Mouvement pour la democratie et le
    developpement (MDD) 121-2
Mozambique 2, 6-11, 14, 17-20, 23n, 51,
    63, 73-84, 151, 153, 156-7, 161
MPLA 140, 148n
Mpumalanga 67
Mtintso, Thenjiwe 13, 31, 38-9, 41, 48-50
Mukacyibibi, Savina 107
Mukamazimpaka, Marie 106
Mukantwali, Janvière 111
Mulher (MULEIDE) 77-8, 80-1
multinationals 4, 158
Murekatete, Seraphine 107
Musangamfura, s. 105
Museveni, Yoweri 1, 21

N'Dajamena 121, 123
Nairobi 106
Namibia 6-7, 12-13, 50-1, 138-49, 153
Nation of Islam 94
National Islamic Front 86
National Patriotic Front of Liberia (NPFL)
    129, 131, 157
National Resistance Army (NRA) 1-2, 20-1
National Resistance Movement (NRM) 15,
    20-1
NBC TV 94
Ndzanza, Rita 30
necklacing 10, 43, 46
Népitimbaye, éatrice 124
Niger, 6, 157
Nigeria 6, 8, 15, 23n, 119, 129, 134, 151-
    2, 154, 156-9
Nile 95
Nimieri, Colonel Jaafer 85
Njuba, Gertrude 2
non-governmental organizations (NGOs)
    27, 56-7, 77, 79-82, 112, 131, 134

Nordstrom, Carolyn 38, 52
North Atlantic Treaty Organization (NATO)
    156
Nsimbii, Rachel 14
Nsukka 15
Ntuli, Victor 65
Nujoma, President Sam 146
Nyamabuye-Gitarama 108
Nyarugunga 105
Nyirambibi, Immaculee 107
Nyoni, Israel Hlongwane 70

Ogoni people 23n
Omdurman prison 90
Omdurman, battle of 100n
Ondangwa 146
Organizaçao da Mulher Moçambicana
    (OMM) 73, 82
Oshaha 139
Ouaddai 123
Outapi 139
Oxfam Women's Project 125

Pan African Congress (PAC) 30-1
paramilitary forces 2, 65, 157
patriarchy 5-6, 20, 29-30, 35, 91, 104, 108,
    126
People's Liberation Army of Namibia
    (PLAN) 138-9
Perry, Ruth 133-4
Physicians for Human Rights 130
Pietermaritzburg 67, 70
Pinto, Maria Elisa 82
Polisario Front 157
polygamy 16
Port Sudan 86
Portugal 73, 138, 140
poverty 4, 16, 75, 79-80, 85, 112, 127
pregnancy 11, 13, 116, 37, 69, 109, 117n,
    121, 132, 141-3
private armies 2, 157
prostitution 3, 8, 10-11, 16, 19, 89, 121

Qadaffi, Colonel 153

race 10, 28, 30, 34, 42-3, 45, 66-7, 87, 145
rape, accountability for 3-4; aggression in
    49, 80; anger and 49; children of 94-5,
    104-5, 110, 130; as destabilization
    technique 11, 38, 47-8, 105; in

detention 38-9, 64; displacement and 14-15, 46; as ethnic cleansing 11, 103-5; and extortion 108-9, 121; by familiars 109, 119-20, 131; family forced to watch 14, 46, 51, 68, 76, 132-3; 'favours' demanded 108-9, 140, 143; feminist analysis of 11; gang rape 11, 14, 39, 45, 105; as gendered violence 10, 29, 57, 65, 86, 103; and Geneva Convention 3; genocidal 11, 94, 104; by guerrillas 2, 12-13; guilt felt by victims 13, 17-18, 109-10, 132; and hatred of enemy 11, 145; health consequences of 11, 14, 18, 37, 68, 78-80, 109-11; and 'honour' 90-1, 95, 97, 105; with impunity 120, 123; intelligentsia targeted 103; as intimidation 122; legal redress 3-4, 12, 30, 53-4, 57, 69, 78, 80-2, 110, 113-14; by liberation movements 48-51; male arousal in 12; mass 87; of men 10, 56; and militarization 8, 11-12; as morale boosting 11, 96-7; of older women 131; personal motives in 52, 120; political organizations and 46-7, 52, 64, 68, 104; and power relations 12; as 'private' event 92; as punishment 45, 47, 52, 65; reluctance to speak of 36-8, 55-6, 65-6, 68-9, 91, 95, 113, 147-8; from resentment 47, 49, 103, 105; as revenge 103; as 'reward' 11, 96, 104, 106-7, 109; sex and 12, 46; in Shari'a law 87; stigma of 8, 11, 13, 16-18, 32, 37-8, 48, 50-6, 66, 68, 78-9, 81, 104, 106, 109-11, 113, 132, 144-5; as strategy of war 10-11, 51-2, 94; support structures for victims 14, 17, 53, 74-5, 70-82; and survival 13; as terrorization 11, 51, 105; testifying to 5, 8, 11-13; as torture 11, 31, 37, 55, 64, 71, 87, 91-2, 106, 125, 130; and traumatic stress syndrome 79-80, 110; typology of 11; and war booty 11, 94-5, 108; as war crime 11, 91; and weapon proliferation 7, 74-5, 132, 155, 158
Reef townships 45, 47-51
refugees 14-15, 19, 46-7, 87, 102, 134; *see also* displacement
religious conflicts 4, 155

Remera 109
RENAMO 14, 22n, 23n, 51, 73-4, 83n, 153-4
Reunion Island 152
Revolutionary United Front 129, 157
Richmond 69
Ririma prison 112
Rivonia Trial 35
Robben Island 35
Roman Catholic church 22n, 134-5
Ros-Lehtinen, Ileana 134
Routledge, Nozizwe Madlala 67
Ruhango 107
Rukira District 107
Russell, Diana 39
Rutgers University 139
Rwanda 4, 6, 8-10, 13-14, 16, 18-20, 27, 98, 101-18, 153-4, 156-7, 159-60
Rwanda Patriotic Army (RPA) 103-4, 106-8, 112
Rwanda Patriotic Front (RPF) 101-3, 105-6, 108-9, 112

Saharawi people 157
Saleh, Fatimé
Saudi Arabia 160
Save the Chilfren Fund 23n
Sawyer, Mrs Amos 133
Scandinavia 17
Schreiner, Jenny 31, 38-40, 42
Sebokeng 46
Second World War 27, 96, 152
security companies 157
Sendashonga, Seth 106
Senegal 6, 14, 119, 152, 154, 157
sexism 50
sexual abuse 12, 31-2, 37, 41, 44, 46-51, 74, 119; *see also* rape
sexual relationships 13, 16, 141-4
sexual slavery 11, 32, 43, 51, 95, 131
Shari'a law 85, 89, 92-3, 95, 99n
Sharpeville 30
Shaw, Maureen 133
Shell Oil Company 23n 158
Sierra Leone 6-7, 14, 18, 129, 134, 157, 160
Sisulu, Albertina 30, 37, 39-40, 43
Sisulu, Walter 40-1
Sitoe, António 74
Skweyiya Commission 27

slavery 19, 21, 86, 90-6, 98
Somalia 4, 6, 9, 14-15, 18, 151-3, 157, 159-60
Somers, Trevor Gordon 133
Sotho people 47
South Africa 7, 8, 10, 14, 17-118, 27-73, 76, 138-9, 141, 144, 146, 151-4, 156-8, 160-1
South African Communist Party (SACP) 31
South African Defence Force (SADF) 51, 138, 149n, 153
South African Police 153
South African Rapists Association (SARA) 46-7
South African Students Organization (SASO) 31
South West Africa People's Organization (SWAPO) 12-13, 16, 50-1, 138-49; Women's Council 139, 142
South West African Territorial Force (SWATF) 145, 147, 149n
Soviet Union 19, 151, 153-4, 156
Spain 152
Sri Lanka 9
structural adjustment programmes 4, 17, 155
Sudan 6-8, 14, 16, 19-20, 85-100, 118-19, 151-2, 154, 157, 159-60
Sudanese News Agency (SUNA) 94
Sudanese People's Liberation Army (SPLA) 85, 96-7, 157
Sudanese People's Liberation Movement (SPLM) 85
Swaziland 76
Sweden 86
Swen, Annie W. 130
Swiss, Shana 131-3
Switzerland 152
Sy, Achta Djibrine 125

Taba Commune 107, 111
Tanzania 6, 101, 107
Taylor, Charles 129-30, 134, 157
Third World 151
third force 47, 60n
Tilo 122
Torit 88
torture 3, 5, 11, 13, 17-18, 22n, 29-32, 34, 37-45, 50, 55-6, 64, 66, 71, 86, 91, 97, 119, 125, 130, 145

Transkei 62
tribalism, *see* ethnic conflicts
Truth and Reconciliation Commission (TRC) 28-9, 36, 48, 52-7, 65, 67-70
truth commissions 5, 27; *see also* TRC
Tuareg 157
Tunisia 151-2, 157, 160
Tutsi 4, 101-17, 156

Uganda 1, 6-8, 11, 14-15, 20, 23n, 27, 97, 101, 108, 157, 160
Umbumbulu 45
Umkhonto we Sizwe (MK) 13, 31, 50
Umutoniwase, Marie-Claire 107
UNITA 1411. 148-9n. 152-4, 157
United Democratic Front (UDF) 45, 63-5, 70
United Liberation Movement for Democracy in Liberia (ULIMO) 129
United Nations (UN) 27, 94, 102, 129, 133-4, 138, 140, 146, 148, 152, 161
United Nations Commission on Human Rights 94
United Nations Convention on the Elimination of All Forms of Discrimination Against Women (CEDAW) 10-11, 22n, 71, 136n
United Nations Convention on the Rights of the Child 22n, 136n
United Nations General Assembly 11
United Nations High Commissioner for Refugees (UNHCR) 88, 146, 148
United Nations Institute for Namibia 140
United Nations International Children's Emergency Fund (UNICEF) 148
United Nations Security Council 113, 129, 153
United Nations Special Rapporteur 90, 98
United Nations Special Representative for Internally Displaced People 95
United States (US) 4-5, 12-13, 19, 23n, 31, 62, 95, 129-31, 133-4, 151-4, 156
United States Committee for Refugees 130
Universal Declaration of Human Rights 74
Universidado Eduardo Mondlane 20, 78, 82
University Hospital, Butare 110
Unwamahoro, Carine 107

Venda people 62

Verulam 69
Vietnam 13
Vietnam camp 144
vigilantes 2, 45, 63
violence, apartheid founded on 30, 33-4;
    black on black 64; culture of 8, 17;
    domestic 32, 50, 76, 81; entrenchment
    of 6-10; fallacies about 4; gendered 10-
    14, 34-8, 45, 103; internal 33-4; low-
    intensity 63-4; militarized societies and
    7-8; as military value 5; privatization of
    1-2; public acknowledgement of 28, 55;
    social violence caused by war 79, 83;
    South African sites of 45-51; state 45;
    theatre of 7, 132; 'third force' 47;
    women perpetrators of 19

warlords 3, 118-19, 134
Warsaw Pact 151, 156
Wau 93-4
Wedweil 93
Weinberg, Sheila 43
West Nile Bank Front 157
Western Sahara 6, 14, 157
women, under apartheid 33-7; as
    breadwinners 20, 90; as combatants 1,
    31, 96-7, 138-49; as heads of house-
    holds 16, 75, 83, 114, 126; as mothers
    36; in Mozambique 755-6, 78; as
    participants 1-2, 5-6, 19-21, 29, 31, 36-
    7, 57, 66-7, 69, 81, 88, 114, 126-7,

133-4, 138-49; and peacemaking 133-
    4; as perpetrators of violence 10, 43-5;
    roles changed by war 19-20, 90, 966-7,
    114, 126-7; stories suppressed 36-8,
    55-6, 65-6, 68-9, 91, 95, 113, 147-8; as
    survivors 66-7, 88, 125-7; and truth
    commissions 28; as victims 1, 5, 11, 29,
    31, 34-7, 54-5, 57, 64, 66-7, 78-82, 87-
    8, 155; and warlordism 118; and
    widowhood 16, 35-6, 75, 102, 107,
    114, 130; as workers 75; see also gender
Women in Black 10
Women's Commission for Refugee Women
    and Children 131
Women's International League for Peace
    and Freedom (WILPF) 114
World Bank 4, 17, 102
World Conference on Human Rights 28

Yondiguissiel, Damaris 124
Yugoslavia 10, 20, 24n, 27, 92, 98, 152

Zaire 4, 102, 106-7, 111, 134
Zambezia Province 76-7
Zambia 138, 140, 153
Zimbabwe 6, 11, 20, 50, 73, 141, 148, 151,
    153-4
Zimbabwe African People's Union (ZAPU)
    151
Zulu 47, 65
Zwane, Pule 46